HAMLYN
# Junior
# Encyclopedia

*Cattle in the snow in New Zealand.*

*Sowing wheat on land where the eucalyptus trees
have been cleared, in New South Wales,
Australia.*

First published in 1985 as the *New Junior Encyclopedia*.
This edition published 1989 by
The Octopus Publishing Group Limited
Michelin House, 81 Fulham Road, London SW3 6RB, England
Reprinted 1990, 1992

ISBN 0 600 56427 4

Produced by Mandarin Offset, printed in Hong Kong

# HAMLYN
# Junior
# Encyclopedia

Consultant Editors: C J Tunney and Diane James

Authors: Robert Burton, M C Canning, Ken More,
George Steiner, Kirsten Stephenson

# HAMLYN

# Acknowledgements

DOUG ALLAN, UNDERWATER IMAGES/B.A.S., Dunfermline, 57 top, 112 top; ED BARBER, London, 142 left; C. BLACKIE, London, 15 top, 15 bottom, 50–51, 58 top, 64 bottom, 70, 155, 158, 172, 188; BRENARD PHOTO SERVICES, Hounslow, 207; BBC – BLUE PETER, London, 223; BRITISH HOVERCRAFT CORPORATION, East Cowes, 204; BRITISH STEEL CORPORATION, London, 168–9; BRITISH TELECOM, London, 214; CADBURY SCHWEPPES LTD, Bournville, 186, 187; CAPITAL RADIO, London, 221; BRUCE COLEMAN, Uxbridge, 112 bottom; BRUCE COLEMAN, Uxbridge – Jen & Des Bartlett 92, Jane Burton 5 and 79, 85 top, 85 bottom left, Alain Compost 126, Jeff Foot 128 bottom left, W W F/H Jungins 128 top, Allan Power 85 bottom right; COLOURSPORT, London, 248 top; COMPIX, London, 42, 43, 54, 58 bottom, 154 right, 161, 167, 184–185; COURTAULDS LTD, London, 164–165; CRAFTS COUNCIL, London, 236, 237; DANISH TOURIST BOARD, London, 56; FREW FRANCES PUBLICITY SERVICES, London, 170; HAMLYN GROUP PICTURE LIBRARY, 128 bottom right, 6, 80, 113, 117, 130, 133 top, 134–135, 197, 230, 233, 234 right, 235 left, 235 right, 239 left, 239 right, 247 left, 247 top right; BRIAN HAWKES, Sittingbourne, 23, 25, 39, 47 bottom, 5 and 53, 71, 73, 78, 94, 96, 98, 108, 118, 119 top, 119 bottom, 127 bottom, 131, 4 and 142–143, 159; IBM UNITED KINGDOM, Portsmouth, 219; ICI PETROCHEMICALS AND PLASTICS DIVISION, Welwyn Garden City, 171; ICI PLANT PROTECTION DIVISION, Fernhurst, 121; JAPAN INFORMATION CENTRE, London, 240; BRIAN LESSWARE ABIPP/SOUTH WEST WATER, Exeter, 160; THE MALAYSIAN RUBBER PRODUCERS' RESEARCH ASSOCIATION, Brickendonbury, 77; LUIZ CLAUDIO MARIGO, Rio de Janeiro, Brazil, 61, 133 bottom, 192; METEOR CRATER OFFICE, Winslow, Arizona, 10; NASA, Washington DC, 16, 29, 193, 208, 209, 210, 7 and 210; NATIONAL COAL BOARD, London, 144–145; NATIONAL MARITIME MUSEUM, London, 202; OVERSEAS CONTAINERS LTD., London, 183; PHOTOFEATURES, London, 229; THE PHOTOGRAPHERS' LIBRARY, London, 46, 58 centre, 124 left, 129, 225, 7 and 246 left, 246 right, 247 bottom right; THE POST OFFICE, London, 213, 214; JOSEPHINE POWELL, Rome, 62; RIDA, London – Linda Parry, 89; G R ROBERTS, Nelson, New Zealand, 9; BRYAN L SAGE, Potters Bar, 20; SAVE THE CHILDREN FUND, London – Mike Wells, 175 right; SCALA, ANTELLA, 234; SHELL, London, 146–147; SPECTRUM COLOUR LIBRARY, London, 34, 60, 65, 75, 107 bottom, 110, 151, 164, 198–199; W M THOMPSON, Loughborough, 47 top; JUDY TODD, London, 38, 40; TWYCROSS ZOO – EAST MIDLAND ZOOLOGICAL SOCIETY, 6; UNITED AFRICA COMPANY, London, 154 left; WELLCOME RESEARCH LABORATORIES, Beckenham, 66; ZEFA, London, 55, 103, 244–245; ZEFA, London – R Bond 63 top left, W Braun 63 top right, H Buchner 156, Eric Carle 64 top, R Halin 127 top, G R Heilman 107 top, A Hurbrich 140, D Maney 35, Puck-Kornetzki 21, Dr Seeberg 124 right, Ung Werbeshidio 177 left, UWS. 6 and 175 left, 176, 248, W H Müller 177 right, G Viollon 62–63;

© SPADEM, Paris, 1983, p. 235 right

*Front and back cover illustrations:*
Photographs supplied by Zefa Picture Library U.K. Ltd. – D. Bruin, K. Goebel, P. Steel.
Artwork – The Hamlyn Publishing Group Limited.

*The illustrations on page 199 are reproduced with the permission of the Controller of Her Majesty's Stationery Office.*

*Illustrated by*
John Green
The Maltings Partnership
(Groom and Pickerill)

# Contents

## The Universe and the World we live in

## Plants and Animals

# Contents

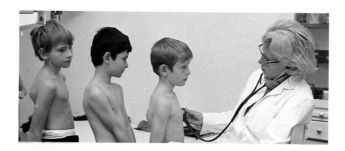

# How we live

# Transport and Communications

# Arts and Entertainment

# Introduction

When writing books or television script outlines, I sit in a room surrounded by books, and there's another like it next door. Books on shelves, tables and piled on the floor; books of all shapes and sizes, mainly packed with detailed information concerning plants, animals, places and people. A wealth of knowledge ready to hand and yet hardly a session passes when I don't get stuck for a bit of basic information: How long is the River Nile? What date did Captain Cook land in Australia? How heavy was a Brachiosaurus? Then I rush upstairs to find one of my children's reference books, the most dog-eared of which bear the Hamlyn logo.

With four bedrooms all overflowing with books, and five children all overflowing with different interests to choose from, it is often no easy task. However, once the book is located it is a simple matter to find the facts I want. If you are saying, 'Why doesn't he buy some of his own?', I do, and they always borrow them.

Books of reference! even the thought sounds very dry and dusty. The word Encyclopedia has a much grander ring, but the image is all too often of something to be looked at on the shelves rather than taken down to be opened and read. Of course, once you have taken the plunge, they are not like that at all, they are the most fascinating things to read, again and again.

This Encyclopedia is going to help a lot of youngsters to take that plunge, they will not only be able to look in, but actually will own their own encyclopedia.

It's bursting with fantastic information in full colour, images to excite, compelling them to read the clear, always concise text. Most important of all, it is to the point, for it is about the complex world we all live in. It is just as important to know about banks and banking, exports and imports, how a large store or hospital works, as to understand the Solar System and fossil fuels.

It really is a super book. There is only one problem I can see, and that is that it will finally blow away the dusty image of the reference library. Librarians, get ready for the invasion of those sacrosanct shelves.

DAVID BELLAMY

*Bedburn, 1984*

8

# The Universe and the World we live in

*Eglington River in New Zealand, photographed from the air.*

# The Solar System

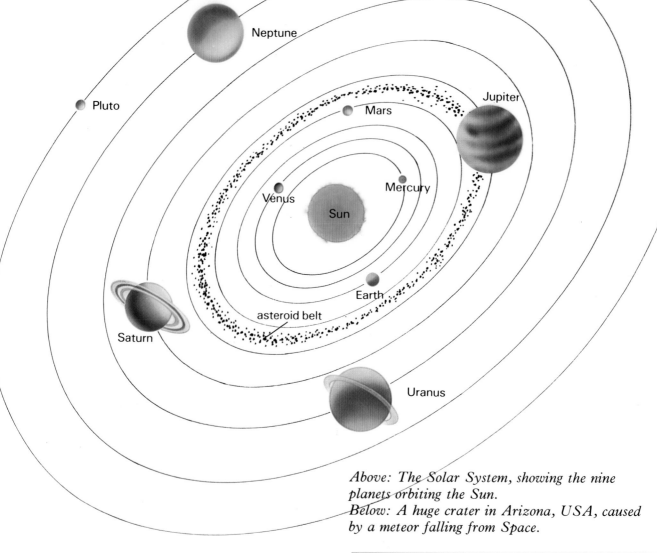

Neptune

Pluto

Mars

Jupiter

Venus

Sun

Mercury

Earth

asteroid belt

Saturn

Uranus

*Above: The Solar System, showing the nine planets orbiting the Sun.*
*Below: A huge crater in Arizona, USA, caused by a meteor falling from Space.*

The Earth on which we live is one of nine worlds called *planets* that move round and round the Sun. The Sun holds its 'family' of planets near it by the pull of *gravity*. Gravity is the force that attracts objects and makes things fall to the ground when you drop them. The Sun, Earth and other planets (and the Moon) all have their own gravity attracting with different strengths. The gravitational pull on the planets by each other, and by the Sun, keeps them all where they are.

The Sun and its planets are called the Solar System. The word solar means belonging to the Sun. We could not live without the heat and light that the Sun gives us.

# Parts of the Solar System

The Sun, which is the centre of the Solar System, is a *star*. Stars are different from planets, because stars make their own heat and light. The planets have no heat and light except what the Sun gives them. As well as the Sun and the planets, the Solar System contains more than 30 moons, and thousands of asteroids, meteors, and comets.

**The planets** The nine planets are Mercury, Venus, Earth, Mars, Jupiter, Saturn, Uranus, Neptune, and Pluto. Some, including Earth and Mars, are solid. Others, including Jupiter and Saturn, seem to be great balls of liquid and gas. As far as we know Earth is the only planet that has living things.

The planets do not bump into each other because they are millions of kilometres apart, and millions of kilometres from the Sun. Their paths around the Sun are called *orbits*. Each planet has an *elliptical* (oval) orbit.

The time that a planet takes to complete one orbit round the Sun is called its *year*. The Earth's year is just over 365 days long. Every fourth year, *Leap year*, we have an extra day in February to make up for the extra time. Mercury's year is only 88 Earth days but Pluto has a year of more than 90 000 days.

While the planets are moving round the Sun, they are also spinning around on their own in the way that a top spins. The time that a planet takes to spin around once is called its *day*. Earth's day lasts 24 hours.

**Moons** Some of the planets have moons that move round them just as the planets themselves move round the Sun. Earth has one moon, which we call *the Moon*. But other planets also have moons. The giant planet Jupiter has at least 16 moons, and Saturn has at least 20. Uranus has five, Neptune and Mars have two and Pluto has one.

## Where are we in Space?

The Solar System seems too huge to think about. But it is only a tiny speck compared with the Universe. The *Universe* means everything that exists, from our Earth to the most distant stars. Nobody knows just how big the Universe is.

The Universe includes millions of *galaxies*. Each galaxy is made up of millions of stars. The galaxy in which we live is called the *Milky Way*. The Sun is only one of millions of stars in the Milky Way.

Earth

Solar System

Milky Way

**Asteroids and meteors** Thousands of large, rough pieces of rock also move round the Sun. They are called *asteroids*. The largest of them, Ceres, is about 1000 kilometres across. Millions of other smaller pieces of rock or metal come near the Earth every day. They are called *meteors* or *meteoroids*. They can be seen flashing across the sky as 'shooting stars'.

# The Planets, Sun and Moon

The bodies that make up the Solar System (Sun, planets, and moons) are very different from each other. Some are burning hot; some are icy cold. Some are blindingly bright; others are almost hidden in darkness. Some are made of solid rock and metals; others are balls of gas.

## The Sun

The Sun, the centre of the Solar System, is too bright for us to look at directly. Its diameter is over 100 times wider than the Earth's diameter, and its surface is 60 times as hot as boiling water. To people on Earth, the Sun is the largest and most important object in the sky. It gives us energy, light, and warmth; without it, we could not live. But the Sun is really only a very small star. Millions of other stars are much bigger than the Sun. They are so far away, however, that we can hardly see them.

## The Moon

The Moon is Earth's nearest neighbour. It is the only body in space that astronauts (space travellers from Earth) have yet reached. The Moon is about one-quarter the size of the Earth. It is tiny compared with the Sun. It appears to be almost as big as the Sun because the Sun is 400 times farther away from us. The Moon shines brightly in the sky, but it has no light of its own. Moonlight is only light reflected from the Sun.

The Moon travels around the Earth once in about every 28 days. At the same time, it turns around slowly, completing a full turn once in every 28 days. For this reason, the same side of the Moon always faces the Earth. Nobody knew what the far side of the Moon looked like until 1959. In that year, a Russian space probe photographed it.

The planets of the Solar System, showing their sizes in relation to each other and the Sun.

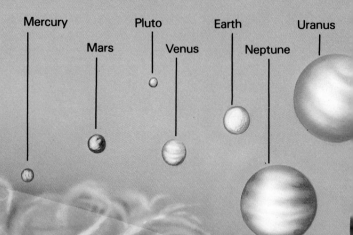

Mercury  Mars  Pluto  Venus  Earth  Neptune  Uranus

Sun

# The planets

On a clear night, you can see Mercury, Venus, Mars, Jupiter, Saturn and sometimes Uranus. To see Neptune and Pluto, you have to use a *telescope*. You can tell which of the lights in the sky are stars and which are planets because the stars seem to twinkle. The planets have a steady light. They also appear to move.

**Mercury** The smallest planet, it seems to have a surface like that of the Moon. It is the nearest planet to the Sun and is very hot. It has no air or water, like the Moon.

**Venus** This is the nearest planet to the Earth. It is usually the brightest light in the sky, apart from the Sun and Moon. Its surface is hidden under thick clouds.

**Earth** Life seems to exist only on this planet. It is at just the right distance from the Sun to get the light and warmth that living things need.

**Mars** People call this planet the Red Planet because its surface is covered with red, sandy deserts. It also has mountains.

**Jupiter** This is the biggest planet, and is a swirling mixture of liquids and gases. A large red spot can be seen on its surface. This is a rotating mass of cloud.

**Saturn** Like Jupiter, this planet is made of liquids and gases. Beautiful, shimmering rings circle it. They are made up of little pieces of rock covered with frozen gas.

**Uranus** and **Neptune** These planets are so far away that nobody can tell for certain what they are made of. They are probably made of liquids and gases.

**Pluto** Nearly 6000 million kilometres from the Sun, this planet must be very cold and dark.

Saturn

Jupiter

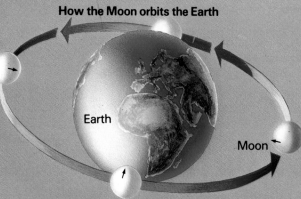

How the Moon orbits the Earth

Earth

Moon

# Effects of the Sun and Moon

The Moon moves round and round the Earth without stopping, and the Earth moves round and round the Sun. At the same time, our whole Solar System travels swiftly through the Milky Way. All this movement brings changes that affect us every day.

## Day and night

The word *day* has two meanings. Sometimes it means the hours of daylight. At other times, it means the *solar day*. This is a period of 24 hours that includes daylight and darkness (night).

**Why is it dark at night?** The Earth spins round on its axis once in every 24 hours or solar day. As it spins, some places face the Sun and get light. In these places it is day-time. The places that are not facing the Sun are dark. In these places, it is night. Because the Earth never stops spinning, the change from day to night and back again to day goes on and on.

**Sunrise and sunset** The Earth spins towards the east. As a result, the Sun seems to rise in the east and sink in the west.

## The seasons

The Earth moves round the Sun once every year. As it moves, the seasons change on Earth. There are four seasons: summer, autumn, winter, and spring. The different seasons bring changes in weather, and affect animal and plant life.

**Why do the seasons change?** The Earth does not stand upright as it goes round the Sun. It *tilts* (leans) slightly to one side. This tilt causes the seasons. In June, the Earth's North Pole is tilted towards the Sun and so there is summer in the northern hemisphere

**The Seasons**

A **March** – it is spring in the northern hemisphere and autumn in the southern hemisphere

B **June** – the North Pole is tilted towards the Sun and it is summer in the northern hemisphere, winter in the southern hemisphere

C **September** – it is autumn in the northern hemisphere and spring in the southern hemisphere

D **December** – the South Pole is tilted towards the Sun and it is summer in the southern hemisphere and winter in the northern hemisphere

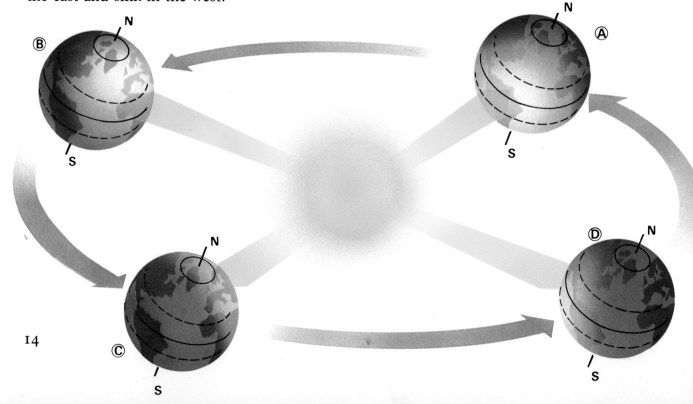

and winter in the southern hemisphere. Six months later, in December, the South Pole is tilted towards the Sun, causing summer in the southern hemisphere. The in-between seasons are autumn and spring.

People living near the equator are near the Sun all year. In these places it is always hot.

*Top: A snowy scene in winter.*
*Above: Flowers blooming in summer.*

**What are the seasons like?** Each of the seasons is different from the others.

*Summer* is usually hot and sunny. There are lots of flowers. Some animals lose their thick winter coats.

*Autumn* is the season when some trees lose their leaves. The weather gets cooler and rain showers fall.

*Winter* is the cold season. Sometimes there is snow. Many animals *hibernate* (go to sleep for the whole season).

*Spring* brings the warm weather back again. Animals wake from their winter sleep and plants begin to grow again.

## The tides

The Moon's gravity pulls the Earth's oceans towards it as it moves round the Earth. Then it lets them go again. These movements of the oceans are the *tides*. The Sun also affects the tides.

At the seaside you can see that sometimes the sea covers the beach completely. This is called *high tide*. At other times, the water goes back, leaving the shore uncovered. This is called *low tide*. Most seaside places have two high tides each day and two low tides.

**The effect of the Sun and Moon on tides**

Moon orbiting the Earth

Earth

Moon's gravity pulls the Earth's oceans

Earth    Moon

Sun

Sun and Moon's gravity pulls the Earth's oceans

spring low tide    neap low tide

low tides

average low tide

average high tide

neap high tide

spring high tide

high tides

Twice a month, the Sun, Moon and Earth are in a straight line, so the Sun's gravity and the Moon's gravity pull on the Earth's oceans. Then there are extra high and low tides called spring tides. In between, twice a month, the Sun and Moon form a right angle with the Earth and act against each other. Then the tides only move a short way called neap tides.

# The Structure of the Earth

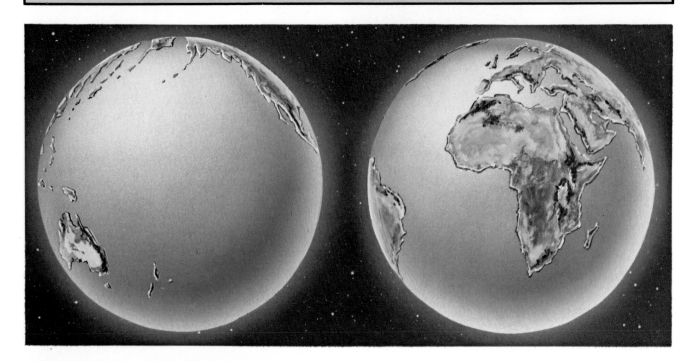

## Parts of the Earth

The Earth is made up of gases (the *atmosphere*), solids (the *lithosphere*), and liquids (the *hydrosphere*).

**The atmosphere** This is the covering of air that forms the outer part of the Earth. We could not live without it because it contains the oxygen that we breathe. It also protects us from the burning rays of the Sun.

**The hydrosphere** This part of the Earth is the part which is water. Water covers more than seven-tenths of the Earth's surface. It includes all the oceans, seas, lakes, and rivers. The water of the hydrosphere lies in the hollows on the uneven surfaces of the lithosphere. It also lies below the surface of the land. Sometimes this underground water rises to the surface as a *spring*. Much of it comes from rain.

**The lithosphere** This is the solid, land part of the Earth, which is made up chiefly of rocks and metals.

*Top: These pictures of opposite sides of the Earth show how much of the Earth is covered by water. Above: A picture of part of Earth taken from Space. It shows the Nile delta and some of the Middle East.*

Many scientists believe that the Earth was formed about 4500 million years ago. Gas and dust that were floating around the Sun came together to make the Earth. Heavy materials became the Earth's *core* (centre). Lighter materials became the *crust* (outer surface).

# Inside the Earth

The lithosphere (the solid part of the Earth) is made up of several different layers, from its centre to its outside surface. These layers merge gradually into each other. Working outwards from the centre, they are the *inner core*, the *outer core*, the *mantle*, and the *crust*.

**The inner core** Nobody has ever reached this because it is 5000 kilometres beneath the surface of the Earth. Scientists think that it is solid and heavy, and is probably made of the metals iron and nickel.

**The outer core** About 2200 kilometres thick, this part of the core is probably hot and liquid.

**The mantle** This lies round the outer core and is about 900 kilometres thick. It is made of heavy rocks.

**The crust** The outer surface of the Earth, this is the part we live on. It is very thin, compared with the size of the Earth. In some places, it is only 6 kilometres deep. In some other places, it is 60 kilometres deep.

The crust has two layers. The outside layer is called the *continental layer*. It is made mostly of a rock called *granite*, and forms the main part of the continents (such as Asia and Australia). The lower *subcontinental layer* is made mostly of a rock called *basalt*. It forms the bottom of the oceans. It also lies underneath the continents.

The Earth's crust is broken up into huge pieces called *plates*. The Earth's continents and oceans rest on these plates. The plates are separated by wide cracks. They keep moving slowly. The movements are so small that we do not notice them. Most earthquakes happen in places near the edges of the plates, and volcanoes too are common here.

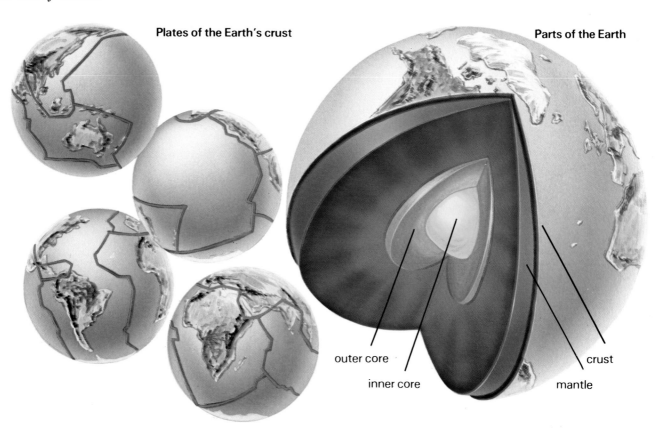

Plates of the Earth's crust

Parts of the Earth

outer core

inner core

crust

mantle

# Earth and its Atmosphere

The air around us is just as much part of the Earth as the ground under our feet. It is called the Earth's *atmosphere*. As the Earth moves through Space, its atmosphere moves with it.

Animals and plants could not live without the atmosphere, because it contains *oxygen* that they breathe. The amount of oxygen gets less, higher and higher in the atmosphere.

## The air around us

Air cannot be seen or smelt or tasted. We know that it is there because of its effect on other things. For example, when the wind blows, it makes leaves move on the trees and makes the clouds move across the sky.

**What is air?** Air is a mixture of gases. Nearly four-fifths of it is nitrogen. Most of the rest of it is oxygen. It also has small amounts of argon, neon, hydrogen, ozone, and other gases. Air also contains some substances that are not part of it. Most air has some water in it. And it usually has some dust.

**Has air weight?** It is possible to prove that air has weight. First, weigh an empty rubber balloon. Then blow the balloon up, and weigh it again. You will see that it now weighs more. The extra weight is the weight of the air inside the balloon.

The weight of the air pressing down on the land or the sea is called *air pressure*. It changes a little from day to day. A change in air pressure is one of the reasons for a change in the weather. Air pressure becomes less higher up, because there is less air above and therefore less weight of air.

The amounts of different gases in the air

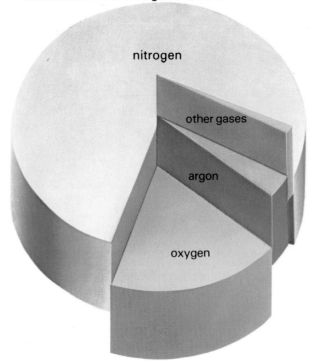

nitrogen

other gases

argon

oxygen

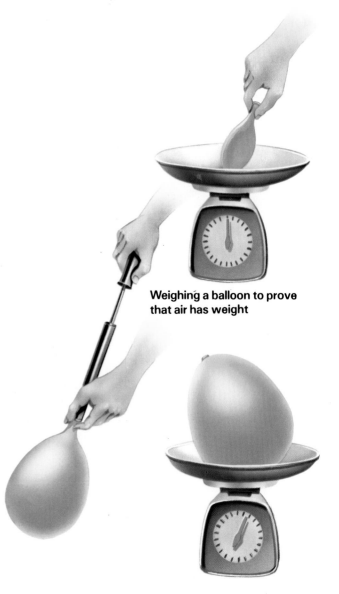

Weighing a balloon to prove that air has weight

18

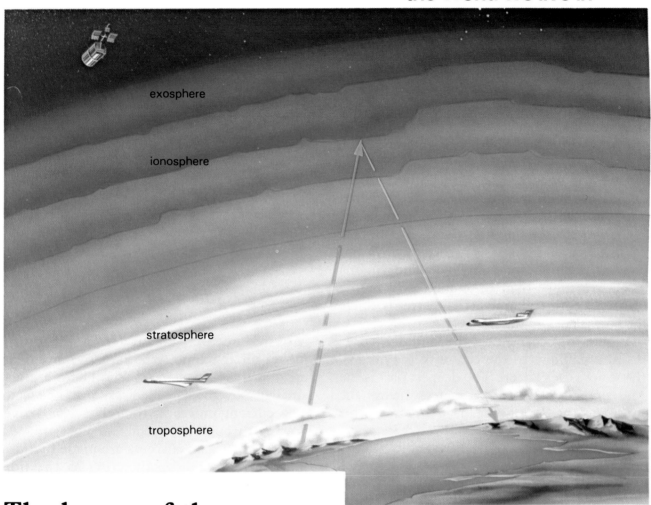

exosphere

ionosphere

stratosphere

troposphere

# The layers of the atmosphere

Scientists think of the atmosphere as having four layers. From the lowest layer upwards, they are the *troposphere*, the *stratosphere*, the *ionosphere*, and the *exosphere*.

**The troposphere** This layer extends upwards from the ground for about 7 kilometres at the North Pole and the South Pole, and about 17 kilometres at the equator. Weather and clouds are usually inside this layer of the atmosphere.

The higher in the troposphere, the lower the temperature is. That is why people climbing mountains or travelling in aeroplanes get colder and colder the higher they go.

**The stratosphere** The next layer extends from the troposphere to about 80 kilometres above the ground. Aeroplanes often fly in the stratosphere to avoid bad weather. The upper part of the stratosphere, however, can be very windy. One current of air, the *jet stream*, can reach speeds of 500 kilometres an hour.

**The ionosphere** This layer goes from the stratosphere up to about 500 kilometres above the ground. It is useful for long-distance radio communications. Radio signals can be bounced off the ionosphere from one part of the Earth to another.

**The exosphere** The outside layer of the atmosphere has very little air.

# Water on the Earth

## Oceans

Earth is sometimes called the Blue Planet because seven-tenths of it is covered by the sea, which looks blue. The sea is divided into five huge oceans. They are the Pacific, Atlantic, Indian, Arctic, and Southern (Antarctic).

**Under the oceans** The *floor* (bottom) of the oceans has high mountains and deep valleys like those on land. Some ocean mountains are higher than the highest land mountains. Mauna Loa, in Hawaii, is higher than Mount Everest, the highest mountain on land. Mauna Loa rises more than 9150 metres from the ocean floor, though only 4170 metres is above the surface of the water.

Where the oceans meet the land, the water is quite shallow. In the centre of the oceans, the water is very deep. The deepest part is the Mariana Trench, 11033 metres below the surface of the Pacific Ocean.

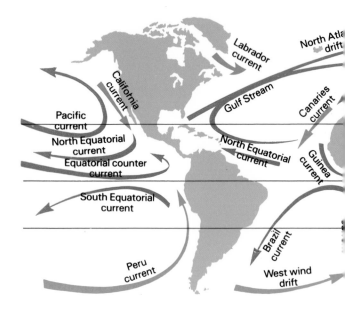

**Moving oceans** The water in the oceans moves all the time. The largest movements are the tides. (See page 15.) There are also smaller movements called *currents*. The water in a current moves as though it was a river flowing through the ocean.

Near the coast, currents are made by tides. The currents change direction as the tides come in and out. These currents can be very dangerous to swimmers because they are very strong. Farther out in the ocean, currents are made by the wind. In these places, the wind nearly always blows in the same direction. Large ships use currents to go faster.

## The oceans' treasures

Many important things come from the oceans. Oil and natural gas come from the oceans' floor. Most of the fish we eat are caught in the oceans.

oil and natural gas

fish

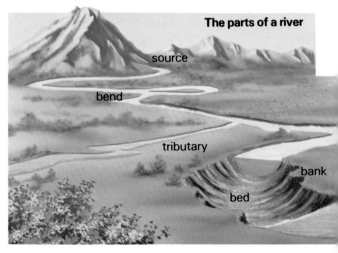

**The parts of a river**

source

bend

tributary

bank

bed

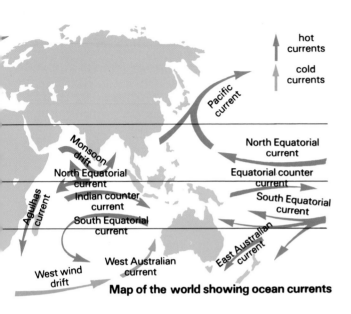

hot currents

cold currents

**Map of the world showing ocean currents**

# Rivers

Most rivers start as tiny trickles of water high in the mountains. They always flow downhill. From their small beginnings, many streams grow into wide rivers of water flowing for hundreds or thousands of kilometres. They end in the sea or in a lake.

**The parts of a river** The beginning of a river is called its *source*. The source may be rainwater which has collected underground and comes out again as a *spring*. It may be a lake or pond, or may flow from a melting glacier.

The bottom of a river is called its *bed*. Its sides are called *banks*. Smaller rivers that join the main river are called *tributaries*.

silt

delta

**From beginning to end** From its source in the mountains, a river flows very fast. It quickly cuts a deep channel in the soil and rocks over which it passes. Lots of soil and rocks, called *silt*, are swept along in the water. At this stage, the river has few bends.

The river slows down when it leaves the mountains and flows across flat land. It becomes wider and some of the silt sinks to its bed. The river makes wide bends as it finds the easiest way to go.

The river slows down even more as it reaches the sea. It drops any silt that it is still carrying. Sometimes, there is so much silt that the river makes a marshy patch of land called a *delta*. The river divides into smaller streams and flows across the delta to the sea.

**How we use rivers** Rivers help us in many ways. Most of the water we drink comes from rivers. It is cleaned before we drink it.

We also use rivers for making electricity. (See page 150.) Farmers *irrigate* (give water to) their crops with river water. River boats transport passengers and *freight* (goods).

*Below: the Mosel river in West Germany. A barge on the river is transporting goods.*

# Earth Movements

The ground beneath us seems very firm and still. It is hard to believe that it is really moving all the time. Sometimes the movements, deep in the Earth, are very small. At other times, they are very strong. Strong Earth movements can push up mountains, make volcanoes *erupt* (explode) and cause earthquakes.

*Above: Mt McKinley in Alaska, the highest mountain in North America.*

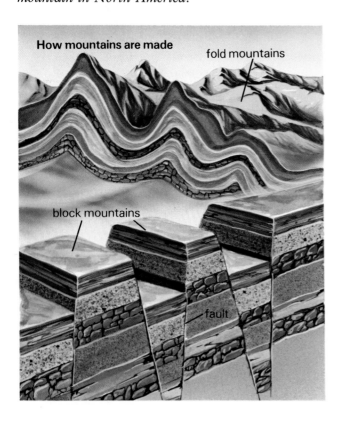

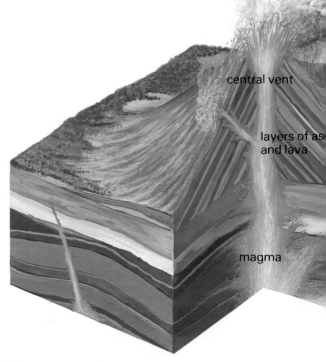

central vent

layers of ash and lava

magma

## Mountains

Most mountains were made millions of years ago. They were higher and smoother then. Over the years, they have been *eroded* (worn away) by the weather, by rivers, and by *glaciers*, large masses of ice which move very slowly down valleys. Now the mountains look rough and jagged. Most mountains are made by movements in the Earth's crust.

**Fold mountains** Sometimes Earth movements push layers of rock up from the sea bed. The force is so great that the rock is pushed in a hump high above the level of the water. It forms mountains called fold mountains.

**Block mountains** Mountains are also made by movements of land between *faults* in the Earth's crust. Faults are breaks or weaknesses in the rock. Sometimes the land between two faults is pushed upwards. The land that has been pushed up forms block mountains.

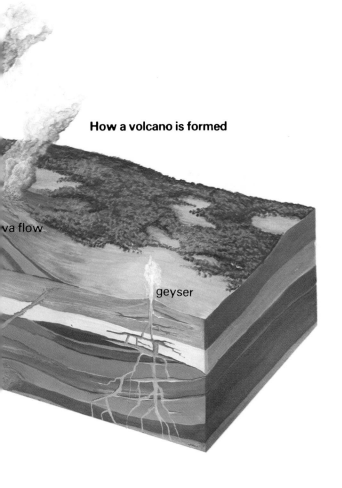

**How a volcano is formed**

va flow

geyser

*Below: A road in Hawaii, damaged by an earthquake.*

# Volcanoes

Volcanoes are another type of mountain. They are formed in an exciting and sometimes dangerous way. They are made when hot, melted rock from deep inside the Earth forces its way through the Earth's crust. The hot rock, called *magma*, sometimes breaks through slowly. At other times, it is mixed with gases and erupts violently.

The tunnel that is made by the magma as it pushes upwards is called a *vent*. As the magma bursts through to the surface and cools, it changes to a thick, flowing stream of *lava*. The lava pours down the side of the volcano, burning everything in its path.

**Types of volcanoes** Some volcanoes erupt once or twice but never again. Those that will not erupt again are said to be *extinct*. Other volcanoes go on erupting from time to time.

There are more than 500 volcanoes in the world. Some of them are under the sea. The biggest volcanic eruption happened in 1883 on the island of Krakatoa in Indonesia, in south-east Asia. Nearly 200 villages were destroyed. People 5000 kilometres away heard the explosion.

# Earthquakes

Sometimes we can feel the movements in the Earth. They may just be a slight tremble, or they may be so strong that buildings collapse and great cracks appear in the land. Sometimes, whole cities are destroyed. These dangerous movements are called earthquakes. Most of them happen near the edges of the huge plates that make up the Earth's crust.

Earthquakes happen when a section of rock in the crust of the Earth slips. This often happens when there is a fault in the crust.

About a million earthquakes happen every year. A machine called a *seismograph* can measure the strength of an earthquake.

# The Land

## Rocks and minerals

Everything in the world is either an animal, a plant, or a mineral. Animals and plants have life, but minerals have no life. All minerals are solid except for water and mercury, which are both normally liquid.

Some minerals are single chemical *elements*. Examples of such minerals are sulphur and gold. Others are made up of two or more elements. Quartz, for example, is made up of silicon and oxygen. Many minerals are metals.

People often refer to coal and petroleum as minerals or mineral fuels because they are products of the mining industry. They are not really minerals, but are formed from materials that were once living.

All rocks are made of minerals. Some rocks, such as limestone and marble, consist of only one mineral. Most rocks, however, contain two or more minerals. Granite, one of the commonest rocks in the Earth's crust, is made up of the minerals quartz, feldspar, and mica. If you look at a piece of granite through a microscope, you can see that it has crystals of these minerals mixed up and pressed together.

**The cycle that rocks go through**

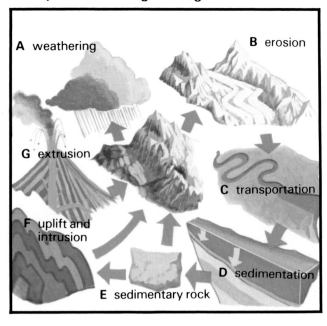

A weathering

B erosion

G extrusion

F uplift and intrusion

C transportation

D sedimentation

E sedimentary rock

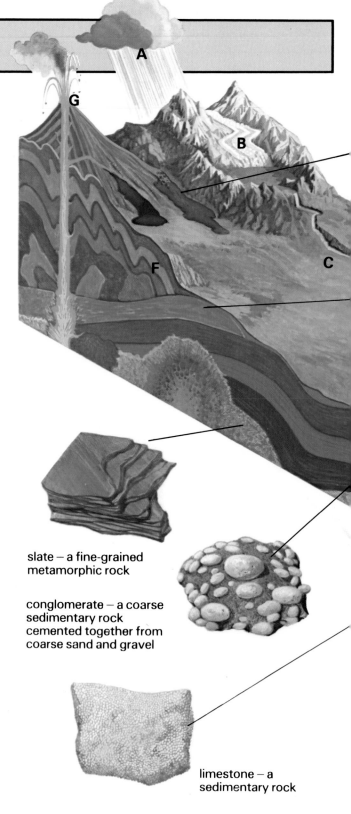

slate – a fine-grained metamorphic rock

conglomerate – a coarse sedimentary rock cemented together from coarse sand and gravel

limestone – a sedimentary rock

*Above and left: Rocks are formed and changed in many different ways. They are eroded, transported, deposited, dragged back into the Earth, remelted and then uplifted again.*

basalt – a dark extrusive igneous rock

granite – a hard light-coloured intrusive igneous rock

D

E

**Rock formation and change**

# Types of rocks

The Earth's crust is made up of three main types of rocks: *igneous*, *sedimentary* and *metamorphic* rocks.

**Igneous rocks** These are made from magma, which is hot melted material deep within the Earth. When magma cools, it solidifies and becomes rock. Sometimes it is *extrusive*, and bursts up in an eruption from a volcano as a stream of lava. Then it solidifies on the surface. Sometimes it is *intrusive*, and cools and solidifies under the surface. This rock is then exposed when rocks above are eroded. Common igneous rocks include granite, basalt and pumice.

**Sedimentary rocks** These are made from tiny pieces of older rocks that decayed and crumbled over millions of years. The tiny pieces of rock were swept away by rivers, and spread over the floors of lakes and oceans as *sediments*. Layers of sediments were pressed together to form new rocks called sedimentary rocks.

Sometimes the lake or ocean floors later rose, and the sedimentary rocks became land again. Sedimentary rocks include limestone, shale, sandstone, and dolomite.

**Metamorphic rocks** These are igneous or sedimentary rocks that have been changed by terrific heat and pressure. The action of liquids and gases from magma also causes changes. The word *metamorphosis* means change. Metamorphic rocks include marble (formed from limestone) and slate (formed from shale).

## Erosion

The surface of the Earth is generally eroded (worn away) by natural forces. These forces include wind, rain, ice, rivers, the waters of the sea, and changes of temperature. During thousands of years, even the hardest rocks are worn away or broken up.

*The Grand Canyon in Arizona, USA.*

# Fossils

Millions of years ago, long before there were any people on Earth, the world was already full of animals and plants. No human being ever saw them while they were living. Yet we know exactly what they looked like, because the remains of some of them still exist. These remains are called *fossils*. The oldest fossils are those of bacteria and simple algae, found in rocks over 3200 million years old.

*Above: Woolly mammoths, huge animals that lived millions of years ago.*

## Where fossils are found

Most of the animals and plants that have become fossils are found in sedimentary rocks. Over millions of years, more and more layers of sand and mud covered the animals or plants. Gradually, the layers hardened and became rock. Fossils can be seen in places where wind and water have worn away the rock.

**A variety of fossils**

ant in amber

fossil fern

fossil nest
of dinosaur eggs

trilobite

dinosaur footprint

fossil fish

ammonite

## Telling the age of fossils

Scientists can tell the age of fossils in several ways. They can sometimes tell the age of rocks, and the fossils in them, by measuring any changes to the rocks that have taken place. They can also discover the age of some fossils by seeing how much they contain of certain chemicals.

Fossils tell us a lot about changes in the Earth. For example, when remains of sea animals are found on land, we know that the land was once under the sea.

# Kinds of fossils

Fossils have been found in other materials as well as in rock. Many fossils are found in ice, tar, and amber.

**Whole animals** Sometimes, a whole animal has been preserved. A few woolly rhinoceroses and woolly mammoths, animals that lived millions of years ago, were 'deep frozen' when they fell into holes in snow and ice. Insects have been preserved for millions of years in amber.

**Parts of animals** Usually, only the hard parts of animals' bodies have been preserved, such as teeth, bones, and shells. Sometimes, an animal's flesh has dried out until only a film of carbon is left. The carbon shows the outline of the animal's body.

**Petrified fossils** Often, a fossil has been *petrified* (turned to stone). Water in the soil or rock has slowly dissolved away the animal or plant. Then minerals carried by the water have built up in the space left, and have formed a piece of rock that looks just like the animal or plant.

**Moulds** When water dissolves away the body of a buried animal, an empty space may be left in the rock exactly the shape of the animal. This is called a *mould*. If scientists fill the mould with plaster, they get a *cast* that looks like the animal.

**Tracks** Among the most interesting fossils are *tracks* (footprints) left by animals when they walked across mud. The mud hardened to rock, preserving the footprints.

# Weather and Climate

One of the first things most people do in the morning is to see what the weather is like. The weather affects our lives in all kinds of ways. When there is rain, we usually try to stay indoors. Ice and snow make roads dangerous. Storms and long periods of bad weather destroy farmers' crops. Warm weather often makes people feel cheerful.

Weather is not the same as climate. Weather includes daily conditions such as hot or cold, windy or still, raining or dry. Climate refers to the typical weather of a place over a long period, such as a tropical or Mediterranean climate.

## Weather conditions

Weather changes all the time. It depends on temperature, moisture, wind, and air pressure.

**Temperature** The Earth's heat comes from the Sun. Heat is trapped and held by the Earth's atmosphere. Most places always have some heat, even at night when the Sun is on the far side of the Earth. The amount of heat depends on the season, the part of the world, the wind, and the amount of moisture that is held in the air.

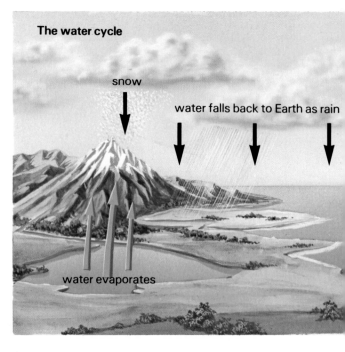

The water cycle
snow
water falls back to Earth as rain
water evaporates

**Moisture** The heat of the Sun changes some water from lakes, rivers, and the sea into *vapour* (gas). This process is called *evaporation*. Much of the water vapour is held in the atmosphere. If it *condenses* (turns to liquid) it forms clouds. Often it then falls as rain. This movement of water is called the *water cycle*. Hail is frozen rain, and snow is frozen water vapour. Moisture also causes fog.

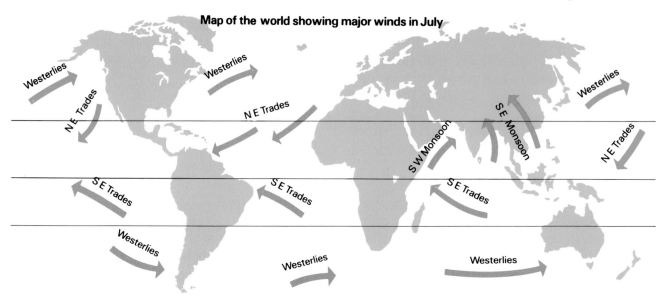

Map of the world showing major winds in July

Westerlies    Westerlies    Westerlies
N E Trades    N E Trades    S E Monsoon    N E Trades
S W Monsoon
S E Trades    S E Trades    S E Trades
Westerlies    Westerlies    Westerlies

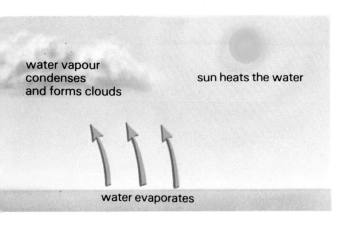

water vapour
condenses
and forms clouds

sun heats the water

water evaporates

**Wind** The weather is affected by the wind in many ways. Winds may be fierce typhoons or hurricanes which can kill people and destroy houses. They may be pleasant, cooling breezes.

**Air pressure** This is the weight of the atmosphere pressing on the Earth's surface. The pressure keeps changing, from place to place. When the pressure is low it is called a *depression* or *cyclone*. It usually causes cloudy or stormy weather. When the pressure is high it is called an *anticyclone*. This usually causes good weather.

# Why does the weather change?

Regions near the equator receive more heat from the Sun than regions near the North Pole and the South Pole. (See page 14.) This unequal heating of the Earth's surface causes movements of air. These movements are the winds.

As the Earth spins, the winds are formed into patterns. The patterns are broken up by the continents and oceans, and by changes in air pressure. As a result, huge masses of air drift around the Earth. They rise and fall, bump into each other, carry rain, and carry heat or coldness. It is these masses of air that cause most changes of weather.

## Weather forecasting

Weather forecasters, called meteorologists, study information collected from weather stations, aircraft and also artificial satellites. Weather charts are drawn, and from these, forecasters can try to work out what future weather will be like. A weather chart has lines called *isobars* on it which represent lines of equal pressure. Spikey or bumpy lines represent *fronts* or boundaries between different air masses. At a front, there is an abrupt change in the weather. At a warm front, there is a belt of rain followed by a wide band of cloud. At a cold front it is often showery with thunderstorms developing along the front.

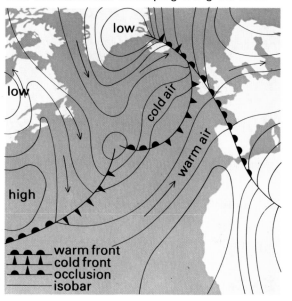

*Above: A weather chart.*
*Below: A cyclone photographed from space.*

# Our World

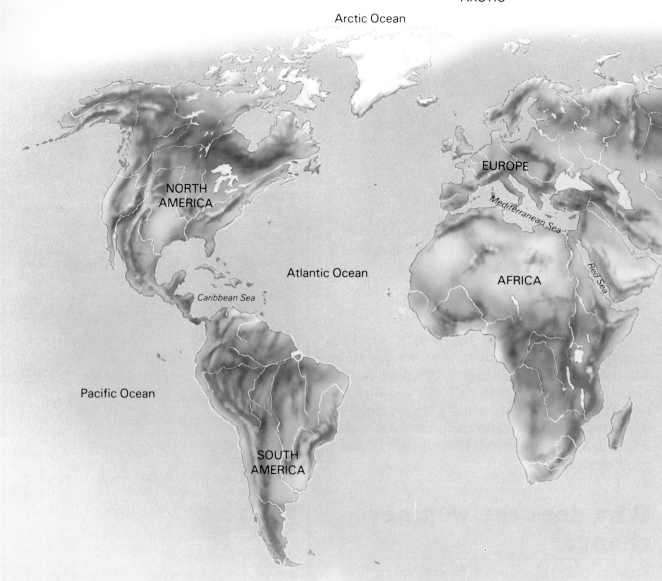

ARCTIC

Arctic Ocean

EUROPE

Mediterranean Sea

NORTH
AMERICA

Atlantic Ocean

AFRICA

Red Sea

Caribbean Sea

Pacific Ocean

SOUTH
AMERICA

Southern Ocean

ANTARCTIC

| Some facts about our world | | |
|---|---|---|
| Largest continent | Asia | 42 700 000 sq km |
| Highest mountain | Everest (Nepal/Tibet) | 8848 m |
| Largest ocean | Pacific | 181 000 000 sq km |
| Greatest ocean depth | Mariana Trench (Pacific) | 11 033 m |
| Largest lake | Caspian Sea (USSR/Iran) | 440 300 sq km |
| Deepest lake | Baikal (Siberia, USSR) | 1519 m |
| Longest river | Nile (Africa) | 6679 km |
| Highest waterfall | Angel Falls (Venezuela) | 979 m |

# Land and sea

The Earth's surface has seven main land areas or continents. Its five oceans are really all parts of one huge ocean.

**The continents** Land makes up less than three-tenths of the Earth's surface. It is divided up into the seven continents: North America, South America, Africa, Asia, Europe, Australasia and Antarctica.

Within the continents, there are three main kinds of places: low plains and valleys, high plains called *plateaux*, and mountains. The low plains are often the best places for people to live. Travel and food production are easy there. Some of the world's first civilizations grew up in low-lying river valleys.

In hot countries, many people prefer to live on high plains, which are cooler than the lowlands. Few people live in mountainous regions, except in the valleys between the hills. Life in mountainous regions is usually hard.

**The oceans** These cover seven-tenths of the Earth's surface, consisting of three large oceans (the Pacific, Atlantic, and Indian Oceans) and two smaller ones (the Arctic and Southern Oceans).

Several smaller bodies of water are connected to the oceans. They include the Mediterranean Sea, which separates Europe from Africa, the Caribbean Sea, which is really part of the Atlantic, and the Red Sea, an arm of the Indian Ocean. The Red Sea is the saltiest part of the world's oceans. The oceans and seas all contain a large amount of dissolved substances taken originally from the land. The main one is common salt. The Red Sea is surrounded by land and is therefore more salty. Some inland seas have even more salt. The Dead Sea (between Israel and Jordan) and the Great Salt Lake (in Utah, in the United States) are both nearly five times as salty as the Red Sea.

ASIA

Pacific Ocean

Indian Ocean

AUSTRALASIA

Our world, the Earth, is more varied and has more different features than any of the other worlds (the stars and the planets) that we know about. We usually think of our world as being mainly land, but its surface is really a great ocean broken up by large pieces of land. We call these *continents*. We think that there are cities and villages scattered all over all the land regions of the world. But most regions have very few inhabitants or no inhabitants at all.

# North America

North America is the third largest of the seven continents. Only Asia and Africa are bigger. North America stretches from the frozen regions of the Arctic in the north to the warm, tropical lands around the Caribbean Sea in the south.

The continent includes the world's richest country, the United States of America, and the world's second largest country, Canada, and the world's largest island, Greenland. The West Indies are islands in the Caribbean Sea.

The most southerly part of North America is often called Central America. It is a neck of land joining North America to South America.

## Mountains and plains

North America still has vast regions of land that are almost empty. It has some of the world's greatest mountain ranges, and some of its largest plains.

*A grizzly bear in the Rocky Mountains.*

**The western mountains** Great chains of mountains stretch for more than 6000 kilometres along the western side of the continent, from Alaska in the north-west to Central America in the south. Their largest range is formed by the Rocky Mountains, often called the Rockies. More than 50 of its snow-capped peaks rise to heights of 4000 metres or more. To the south, the Rockies continue through Mexico as the Sierra Madre Oriental.

Among the mammals of the mountain regions are grizzly bears, moose and Rocky Mountain goats. Eagles soar in the sky.

West of the Rockies there are other ranges of mountains along the Pacific coast. Between them and the Rockies is a lower region that includes several famous places. One of them is the area of the Yukon River, the scene of the great Gold Rush of the 1890s. Another is the Grand Canyon in Colorado. It is a steep-sided gorge over 1·5 kilometres deep in some places, and 450 kilometres long.

**The south-eastern mountains** The Appalachian Mountains rise near the Atlantic coast. Some of the poorest groups of people in the United States live in the Appalachians.

**The interior plain** This is a vast lowland between the mountains of west and east. It is the heart of North America, and includes some of the best farming land in the world. Its higher western part is called the Great Plains. The Great Plains have thousands of square kilometres of wheat and other cereals. The animals of the plains include beavers, coyotes, and snakes. Bison used to roam here in their millions but only live in parks and preserves now.

**The Canadian Shield** This is another lowland region, which lies north of the interior plain. It includes half of Canada, and also some parts of the United States. In most places, its soil does not produce good crops.

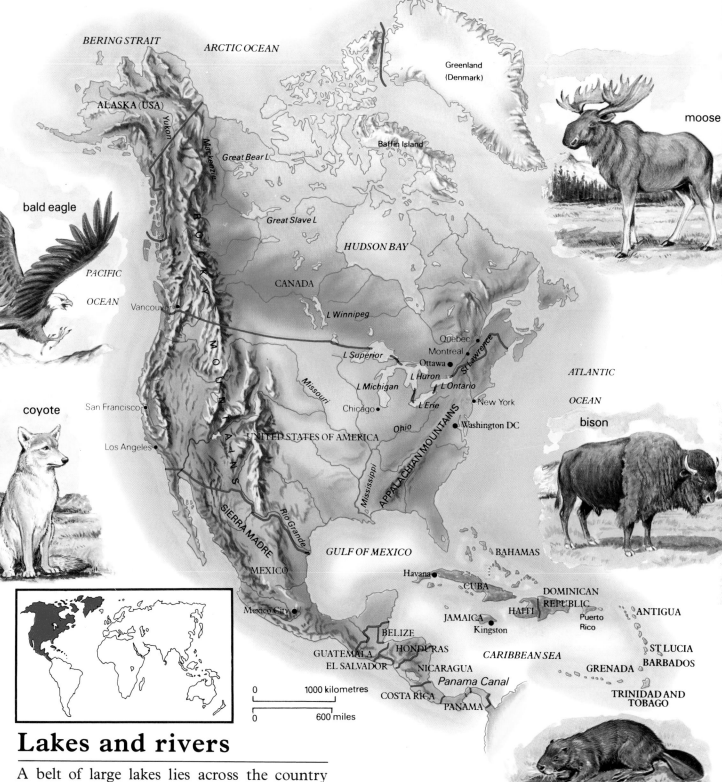

BERING STRAIT

ARCTIC OCEAN

Greenland
(Denmark)

ALASKA (USA)

Yukon

Mackenzie

Great Bear L

Baffin Island

moose

bald eagle

PACIFIC

OCEAN

ROCKY

Great Slave L

HUDSON BAY

CANADA

Vancouver

L Winnipeg

Québec
Montreal
Ottawa
St Lawrence

ATLANTIC

OCEAN

coyote

San Francisco

MOUNTAINS

Missouri

L Superior

L Huron

L Michigan

L Ontario

L Erie

New York

Chicago

Ohio

Washington DC

bison

Los Angeles

UNITED STATES OF AMERICA

APPALACHIAN MOUNTAINS

Mississippi

SIERRA MADRE

Rio Grande

GULF OF MEXICO

BAHAMAS

MEXICO

Havana

CUBA

DOMINICAN
REPUBLIC

ANTIGUA

Mexico City

JAMAICA
Kingston

HAITI

Puerto
Rico

ST LUCIA
BARBADOS

BELIZE

HONDURAS

CARIBBEAN SEA

GRENADA

GUATEMALA
EL SALVADOR

NICARAGUA

TRINIDAD AND
TOBAGO

0        1000 kilometres

COSTA RICA

Panama Canal

PANAMA

0        600 miles

# Lakes and rivers

A belt of large lakes lies across the country
from north-west to east. This includes the
Great Lakes between Canada and the United
States. One of the Great Lakes, Lake Superior,
is the largest body of fresh water in the world.

The continent has many long rivers. They
include the Mackenzie in the north, the St
Lawrence in the north-east, and the Mississippi in the south-east.

beaver

# Climate

The north is cold and icy. Evergreen trees
grow in some places. The centre of the continent can be very hot in summer, and very
cold in winter. The south is usually warm all
the year round.

33

Above: Navajo women making traditional crafts.
Below: People of every race and colour now live in the cities of North America.

Iroquois

Apache    Sioux

**Some different North American Indians**

# The people of North America

The living standards of the people of the United States and Canada are among the highest in the world. Few families are without good homes, cars, television sets, washing machines, and refrigerators. In the south of the continent, life is very different. Many of the people of Mexico, Central America, and the Caribbean islands do not have enough food and are without proper houses.

North America's population of more than 360 million is very unevenly spread through the continent. Most people live in cities, and in the south-east and south.

**American Indians** These were the first people to live in North America. Their ancestors probably crossed into North America from Asia. They created two great civilizations: the *Aztec* in what is now Mexico, and the *Mayan* in parts of Mexico and Central America. In northern regions, the Indians lived in tribes, such as the Sioux, the Blackfoot, and the Cree.

Today, most Indians in the United States and Canada live in crowded reservations, the only areas left to them.

**Eskimos** These people live in the far north of Canada and in Greenland. They also came from Asia, but came later than the Indians.

**Europeans** White people started to arrive in North America in the 1500s. They settled wherever there was good farming land for crops or for cattle, and where there were natural resources, such as iron, coal, or petroleum, to bring wealth to the country. They turned the United States into the richest country in the world.

**Africans** European slave traders took Africans to North America by force. They made them work as *slaves* (people 'owned' by other people) on *plantations* (large farms). Today, black and white people live as equal citizens in America.

# Languages

In the United States and Canada, most people speak English. In some parts of Canada, people speak French, as the first settlers in Canada were French. Mexicans and most of the people of Central America and the Caribbean islands speak Spanish. These regions belong to an area called Latin America, where most countries were once ruled by Spain or Portugal.

# Ways of life

North America is the most productive region in the world. Its factories and farms supply most of the things its people need.

**Agriculture** The United States and Canada have huge areas of good farming land. Farmers use the most efficient methods and the latest machinery. They produce huge crops of wheat, fruit, and vegetables. In Mexico and the other countries of the south, farming is inefficient and the farmers do not use modern methods.

**Industry** North America has rich natural resources, including petroleum, iron, coal, lead, and copper. Factories in the United States produce large amounts of goods of all kinds. Many of its industries, such as the making of cars, are the biggest in the world.

# History

The civilization of the Aztecs and the Mayas were destroyed by the first European invaders, the Spanish *conquistadores* (conquerors). The northern regions were settled by the French and the British. In 1776, 13 British colonies (districts in which British people had settled) declared themselves independent or separated from Britain. Led by George Washington, they created the United States. Later, hundreds of thousands of people from all parts of Europe settled in the continent.

*Above: A cattle drive. Rearing cattle is an important part of farming in North America.
Below: The Aztecs built a city called Tenochtitlan in Mexico in 1364.*

# South America

toucan

turtle

PACIFIC
OCEAN

L. Maracaibo
Caracas
Orinoco
VENEZUELA
GUYANA
Georgetown
SURINAME
Paramaribo
FRENCH GUIANA
Cayenne
Bogotá
COLOMBIA
Quito
ECUADOR
PERU
Manaus
Amazon
Amazon
A
N
D
E
S
Lima
BOLIVIA
Titicaca
La Paz
Paraguay
BRAZIL
Recife
Salvador
Brasilia
BRAZILIAN HIGHLANDS
Sao Francisco
Rio de Janeiro
PARAGUAY
Asunción
Salado
Parana
ATLANTIC
OCEAN
URUGUAY
Santiago
Buenos Aires
Montevideo
ARGENTINA
Mar del Plata
CHILE
Colorado
Falkland
Islands
(UK)
TIERRA DEL
FUEGO
CAPE HORN

0          1000 kilometres
0          600 miles

dolphin

vicuña

The continent of South America is joined to
North America by a narrow neck of land which
is often called Central America. About half of
South America is made up of great mountain
ranges, thick forests, and wide plains where
hardly anybody lives. There are probably still
places that no human being has ever seen.

puma

Andean condor

# The wild continent

The equator crosses the northern part of the continent. Because of its position here, much of South America is hot all the year round. Many places are also very wet.

**The Andes Mountains** The high, jagged Andes Mountains stretch all the way along the Pacific coast. They are the longest mountain range in the world. Their total length is nearly 6500 kilometres. The Andes extend into seven countries, from Venezuela in the north to Argentina in the south.

The highest peak in the Andes is Mount Aconcagua (6960 metres high) in Argentina. More than 50 other peaks rise to more than 6000 metres. Some of the mountains are volcanoes. The Andes region is also sometimes shaken by earthquakes.

Many of the high peaks of the Andes have caps of snow. The mountain sides are forested. Some valleys have huge *glaciers* (rivers of ice) moving slowly towards the sea. Altogether, there are hundreds of valleys between the mountains, and many *plateaux* (high plains).

People living in the Andes keep animals called llamas to carry loads. They also keep alpacas and vicunas for their wool. All three animals are related to camels. Other animals in the Andes include pumas and a kind of vulture called a condor.

**The Amazon River** The Amazon is the second longest river in the world. It flows for 6516 kilometres. Only the Nile in Africa is longer. The Amazon's *basin*, the region drained by the river, is almost as big as the whole of Australia. It includes parts of six countries. Hundreds of smaller rivers are *tributaries* of the Amazon, that is, they flow into it, and become part of it.

Much of the Amazon region is covered by thick tropical rain forests called *selvas*. Plants in the forest grow so fast that a newly-cut path may disappear in a few weeks.

More than 700 different kinds of fish live in the Amazon. They include piranhas, small fish with sharp teeth, which eat other fish and sometimes large animals. Caimans, turtles and dolphins also live in the river. Hundreds of different mammals, snakes, and beautiful birds live in the forests.

**Other regions** Much of the eastern part of the continent has mountain ranges called the Brazilian Highlands. They are lower than the Andes. The low-lying region between them and the Andes includes the Gran Chaco and the pampas. The Gran Chaco is rough and has some forests. The pampas is a huge plain in Argentina where millions of cattle and sheep graze.

# Lakes and waterfalls

South America's lakes include the huge Lake Titicaca on the border of Bolivia and Peru. Steamships travel on it, although it is nearly 4000 metres up in the Andes Mountains. An even larger lake is Lake Maracaibo in Venezuela which covers 8446 square kilometres. Most of the continent's rivers have waterfalls. The Angel Falls on a small river in Venezuela is the highest waterfall in the world. The water drops about 980 metres. One of the most spectacular falls is the Iguacu Falls on the border of Brazil and Argentina.

# The people of South America

About 240 million people live in South America. Two-thirds of them are farmers or farm workers in *rural* (country) areas. They are poor, and their small houses are often made of *adobe*, a mixture of dry clay and straw. A small number of rich people own large ranches or plantations called *haciendas* or, in Brazil, *fazendas*.

South America has many fine cities, such as Rio de Janeiro in Brazil and Buenos Aires in Argentina, but most cities have large slum areas where poor people live. In the slums, many houses are just shacks made of wood, corrugated iron, or even cardboard.

The people of South America are descended from American Indians, Europeans, and Africans. People in most countries'speak Spanish, because Spain ruled large areas of South America for hundreds of years. The people of Brazil speak Portuguese, because Portugal once ruled Brazil. Many Indians speak their own languages. The most common Indian language is Quechuan, and in Paraguay, the Guarani Indians' language is the official language as well as Spanish.

*Christopher Columbus landing in South America.*

*South American Indians of today in Peru.*

**Indians** The first people in South America were the Indians. They are related to the Indians of North America. They have nothing to do with India. (See page 44.) The explorer Christopher Columbus called them Indians when his ships reached the Americas in 1492, because he thought he had reached India.

Europeans went to South America from the 1500s onwards as conquerors and settlers. The first Spanish invaders were called *conquistadores*, a Spanish word meaning conquerors. They were brave but cruel, and they made themselves the rulers of South America. Later, many other Europeans from Spain, Portugal, Italy, and other countries settled in South America.

**Africans** Europeans brought Africans to South America as slaves. They worked as unpaid labourers on the plantations.

**Mestizos and mulattos** Many people in South America today are of mixed Indian, European, and African ancestry. *Mestizos* are people with European and Indian ancestors. *Mulattos* are people with European and African ancestors.

# Ways of life

South America is very rich in natural resources, such as petroleum, copper, iron, tin, lead, tungsten, silver, gold, and nickel.

**Agriculture** Half of South America's people live by growing crops or keeping cattle, sheep, or other animals. Most farmers grow just enough beans, cassava (a plant whose roots are used as food), or maize for their families to live on.

South America also has large plantations where coffee, sugar cane, wheat and other valuable crops are grown. Large herds of cattle and sheep graze on huge ranches.

**Industry** South America has little industry compared with North America, but its industries are growing. Factories make goods from materials found in the continent. Textiles (cloth) are made from wool; meat and other food products are tinned; and chemicals are made from petroleum and minerals.

*Right: The Incas built fine cities.*
*Below: A hacienda in Ecuador.*

# History

In the 1400s and 1500s, the Inca Indians had fine cities in the countries that are now Peru, Ecuador, and Bolivia. The first Spaniards in the continent were searching for gold, silver, and jewels. Until the 1700s and 1800s, Portugal ruled Brazil and Spain ruled most of the rest of South America. Then the people of the continent made themselves independent. A man called Simon Bolívar played a leading part in bringing freedom to several countries. In modern times, the countries of South America have had many wars and revolutions.

# Africa

Africa is the second largest of the continents. Only Asia is bigger. Africa has the world's largest desert, the Sahara. It also has the world's longest river, the Nile. The equator crosses the centre of Africa, and nearly everywhere is hot and sunny for much of the year.

## A continent of varied places

From the north to the south of Africa, there are many different kinds of places.

**The Sahara** In the north is the huge, sandy, rocky desert that stretches right across northern Africa. Its name, Sahara, means desert.

Only a few people, animals and plants live in the desert, because there is hardly any water. When rain falls, it quickly sinks into the sand or dries up. Here and there, trees and other plants grow in small areas called *oases*. An oasis has water from underground springs.

**Savannah** South of the desert is rough grassland called *savannah*. Many wild animals live on the savannah. They eat grass and also the *foliage* (leaves) of scattered trees and bushes. The trees and bushes shade the animals from the sun.

*Below: Hippopotamuses by the Tsavo River in Kenya, in West Africa.*

**Forests** In regions near the equator, forests grow thick and green. They are called *tropical rain forests*. In some places, the rain falls almost every day. The trees and other plants grow strong and tall, and are crowded together. They give shelter to many animals, including some beautiful birds.

**Savannah and game parks** South of the forests there are more grasslands and lands with bushy vegetation. In this part of Africa, some areas have been made *game parks*. Lions, elephants, giraffes and other wild animals can live safely in the parks as people are not allowed to hunt them.

**The Kalahari Desert** This desert is in southern Africa. It is a dry, bush-covered plateau.

**Farming lands** In southern Africa there are rich farming lands, especially in the south and east coastal regions.

*Below: Some elephants and a cheetah in the savannah near Mt Kilimanjaro, Tanzania.*

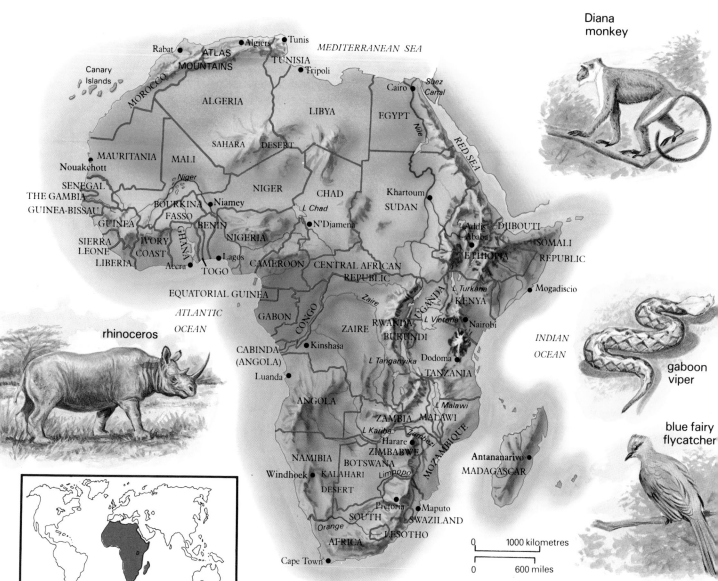

Diana monkey

MEDITERRANEAN SEA

rhinoceros

gaboon viper

blue fairy flycatcher

0    1000 kilometres

0    600 miles

# Mountains, rivers and lakes

Africa has high mountains, long rivers, and large lakes.

**Mountains** The highest mountain in Africa is Mount Kilimanjaro in Tanzania (5895 metres high). It stands near the equator, where the climate is very hot. Kilimanjaro is so high that its *summit* (top) is cold and is covered in snow. Africa also has high mountains in the north-west called the Atlas Mountains, and near the south-eastern coast, called the Drakensberg or Dragon Mountains reaching about 3500 metres.

**Rivers** The Nile flows northwards for 6679 kilometres from central Africa to the Mediterranean Sea. It cuts through the Sahara. From an aeroplane, the Nile valley looks like a ribbon of rich green trees and fields lying across the bare, brown desert. Other long rivers in Africa are the Zaire, the Niger, and the Zambezi. Most African rivers have many waterfalls and *rapids* (dangerous, fast-flowing stretches). The Victoria Falls on the Zambezi River is 108 metres high.

**Lakes** Lake Tanganyika is 676 kilometres long, and is the longest freshwater lake in the world. It lies in the Great Rift Valley, a huge valley that runs through eastern Africa. Lake Victoria is bigger in area (69485 square kilometres), but is not as long. This lake lies between two arms of the rift valley.

41

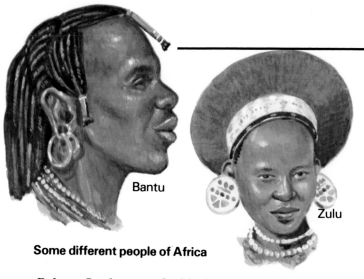

Bantu

Zulu

**Some different people of Africa**

Tuareg

Masai

*Below: Students at the National University, Nairobi, Kenya.*

# The people of Africa

One of the world's earliest civilizations, the civilization of Ancient Egypt, was in Africa. Then, for thousands of years, life in Africa did not improve, while other continents became strong and rich. Today, many Africans are very poor and cannot read or write. The governments of African countries are trying to give their people a better life. They show farmers how to grow more food, and they are building factories, houses, schools, hospitals, and roads.

About 458 million people live in Africa. Some parts of the continent, the deserts and the tropical rain forests, have almost no people at all. Other places have many people because there is good farm land. The people are mainly *negroid* or *caucasoid*. (See page 58.)

**Negroid people** The black Africans are the largest group living in the continent. The Negroid group is made up of many smaller groups, such as Zulu, Masai, Yoruba, Matabele, Bushman, and Negrillo. These groups look different from each other, and have different ways of life.

Black Africans speak hundreds of different languages. Their languages are grouped into two main 'families' of languages. The *Bantu* family is made up of about 250 languages spoken by people in parts of central and southern Africa. The *Sudanic* family has about 200 languages spoken in parts of central and western Africa.

**Caucasoid people** These people live in northern Africa. Most of them live north of the Sahara. A small number live in the Sahara, either in the oases or as *nomads* (wanderers, with herds of sheep and goats). Some also live in eastern Africa. They had the same ancestors, thousands of years ago, as the peoples of Europe and northern India. Nearly all of them speak Arabic.

Caucasoids of European origin live mainly in the Republic of South Africa. Many of them are descended from Dutch people who settled in Africa more than 200 years ago. They speak *Afrikaans*, a language based on Dutch. Some others are descended from British settlers. They speak English.

# Ways of life

Africa has rich natural resources, including coal, iron, copper, gold, diamonds, uranium, petroleum, and valuable wood, such as ebony and mahogany. It also has fast rivers that can be used for making *hydro-electricity*. (See page 150.) These resources can be used to give its people better lives.

**Agriculture** Most Africans are farmers. They grow crops or keep cattle. Many of them are *subsistence farmers*. They produce just enough food to feed their families. In some countries, *cash crops* are grown on plantations. Cash crops are crops that can be sold. They include cacao (for cocoa), palm oil, coffee, sisal (for making sacks, ropes, and carpets), cotton, tea, tobacco, and fruits.

**Industry** Compared with other continents, Africa has little industry. The only major industrial country is the Republic of South Africa. Zimbabwe, Nigeria, and the countries of northern Africa also have some industries.

*Right: Ancient Egyptians.*
*Below: Oranges being washed in Swaziland.*

# History

The great civilization of Ancient Egypt lasted for 3000 years. South of the Sahara there were also civilizations. These included the Ghana, Mali, and Songhai empires, from the 700s to the 1500s, and the Yoruba kingdoms of Oyo and Benin, which lasted until the 1800s. In the 1400s, slave traders from Europe began capturing Africans and sending them as slaves to the Americas. Later, Europeans settled in Africa. By the 1900s, all of Africa was ruled by European countries, except for Ethiopia, then called Abyssinia, and Liberia. But after the Second World War (1939–45) the African countries became independent, one by one. (The Republic of South Africa, although independent, is still governed by white people descended from the European settlers.)

# Asia

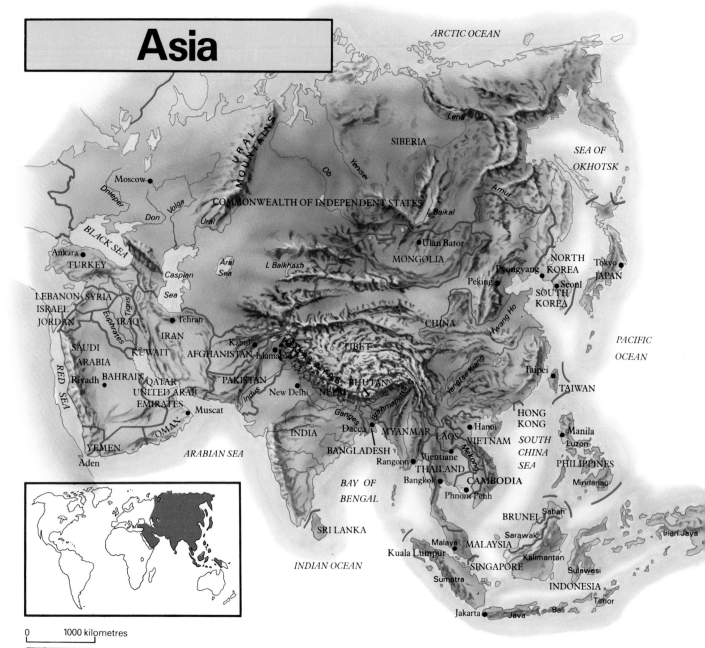

ARCTIC OCEAN

SIBERIA

SEA OF OKHOTSK

Lena

Ob

Yenisei

Amur

COMMONWEALTH OF INDEPENDENT STATES

L. Baikal

Moscow

Dnieper

Don

Volga

Ural

MOUNTAINS

URAL

BLACK SEA

Ankara

TURKEY

Aral Sea

Caspian Sea

L Balkhash

Ulan Bator

MONGOLIA

NORTH KOREA

Tokyo

JAPAN

Pyongyang

Peking

Seoul

SOUTH KOREA

PACIFIC OCEAN

LEBANON SYRIA

ISRAEL

JORDAN

Tigris

Euphrates

IRAQ

Tehran

IRAN

CHINA

Hwang Ho

SAUDI ARABIA

KUWAIT

Kabul

AFGHANISTAN

Islamabad

TIBET

HIMALAYAS

BHUTAN

Taipei

TAIWAN

Riyadh

BAHRAIN

QATAR

UNITED ARAB EMIRATES

Muscat

PAKISTAN

Indus

New Delhi

NEPAL

Brahmaputra

Yangtse Kiang

HONG KONG

RED SEA

OMAN

Ganges

INDIA

Dacca

MYANMAR

LAOS

Hanoi

VIETNAM

Manila

Luzon

SOUTH CHINA SEA

PHILIPPINES

YEMEN

Aden

ARABIAN SEA

BANGLADESH

Rangoon

Vientiane

THAILAND

Bangkok

Mekong

CAMBODIA

Phnom Penh

Mindanao

BAY OF BENGAL

SRI LANKA

INDIAN OCEAN

BRUNEI

Sabah

Sarawak

Irian Jaya

Malaya

MALAYSIA

Kuala Lumpur

Kalimantan

SINGAPORE

Sumatra

Sulawesi

INDONESIA

Timor

Jakarta

Java

Bali

0    1000 kilometres

0    600 miles

## The varied lands of Asia

Asia is the biggest of the seven continents. It has almost a third of the world's total land and more than half of its people. Vast areas of northern Asia are in the frozen wastes of the Arctic. The equator crosses southern Asia, and some parts of the continent have burning deserts or hot, wet, tropical rain forests.

Asia has the highest mountain on Earth, Mount Everest, which is about 8840 metres high. It also has the lowest land region, the deep valley of the Dead Sea, between Jordan and Israel.

Asia is part of the same mass of land as Europe, but the Ural mountains and the Caspian Sea form the boundary between the two continents. The former USSR (now called the CIS – Commonwealth of Independent States since December 1991), and Turkey are both partly in Asia and partly in Europe. Asia is linked to Africa by the Isthmus of Suez. Mountain ranges divide it into six main regions.

**Northern Asia** Here is the cold region of the CIS called Siberia. It is a land of swampy, treeless plains. The frozen ground, called *permafrost*, thaws briefly in summer.

Some animals of Asia

**Central Asia** Deserts and high, bare plains are fringed by mountains. The region includes Tibet, Mongolia, and western China.

**Eastern Asia** Known as the Far East, this is a region of hills, deep valleys, and plains. It includes most of China, the islands that make up Japan, and also the island of Taiwan.

**South-Eastern Asia** Myanmar, the Indochina Peninsula, Malaysia, and the islands that make up Indonesia and the Philippines are included here. The mainland has wooded mountains in the north, and river plains in the south.

**Southern Asia** Sometimes called the Indian Sub-Continent, this region lies south of the Himalayas. The Himalayas are the world's highest mountain range. Southern Asia includes India, Pakistan and Sri Lanka.

**South-Western Asia** This region is often called the Middle East or the Near East. It is a hot region, with much desert land. It includes 12 Arab states, Iran, Israel, Cyprus, and most of Turkey.

# Lakes and rivers

The Caspian Sea, a saltwater lake, is partly in Asia and partly in Europe. It is the largest lake in the world covering 440300 square kilometres. Other large lakes include the Aral Sea and Lake Baikal in the CIS.

Asia has many great rivers. In Siberia, the Ob, Yenisei and Lena flow northwards to the Arctic Ocean. They are frozen for half the year. In the east, the Amur, Hwang Ho and Yangtze Kiang flow to the Pacific. The Mekong also reaches the Pacific. It flows southwards through South-Eastern Asia.

The chief rivers of Southern Asia are the Brahmaputra, the Ganges, and the Indus. The Tigris and Euphrates in South-Western Asia join together before flowing to the Persian Gulf.

# Climate

Asia's climate varies greatly. The north is cold and damp. The south is hot and wet. Monsoon winds from the Indian Ocean bring summer rain to much of southern Asia.

# Plants and animals

In the cold north there are forests of fir and pine. The hot, wet south has tropical rain forests. Much of the continent has grasslands, and some areas are desert. The varied vegetation includes bamboo, palms, and nutmeg and mango trees.

Brown bears and wolves live in Siberia. Yaks (wild oxen) live in Tibet. Giant pandas also live in Tibet, as well as in China. In the southern regions there are elephants, tigers, leopards, monkeys, and many snakes. Some animals are used for work. They include yaks, camels, elephants, and buffaloes. They are used for transport, for pulling ploughs and carts, and elephants especially are used for lifting heavy things such as large logs.

# The people of Asia

The world's oldest civilizations came into being in Asia. Most of the world's great religions started in Asia, including Hinduism, Buddhism, Judaism, Christianity, and Islam. (See page 62.) Asian artists have made some of the world's most beautiful things.

Asia has about 3000 million people. This is four times as many as Europe, the next most highly-populated continent. Most people in the CIS live west of the Ural Mountains, in Europe. The population of Asia is very unevenly spread. Vast areas of Northern, Central and South-Western Asia have hardly any people at all. The cities of India and China, however, are among the most crowded places in the world.

**Mongoloid people** These people live in Eastern Asia and many regions of Central Asia. They include the Chinese and Japanese and many of the people of Siberia. Some people of Mongoloid race have gone to live in countries of South-eastern Asia, including Malaysia and Singapore.

*Below: A camel convoy in Delhi, India. The camels are being used to pull the carts.*

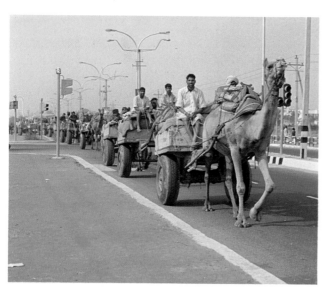

**Caucasoid people** Related to the people of Europe, these people live in South-Western Asia and in Pakistan and northern India.

**Negroid people** These people are related to the Negroid people of Africa. They live in the islands of South-Eastern Asia. Some also live in the Malay Peninsula.

# Languages

The people of Asia speak hundreds of different languages. Most Asian languages belong to one of four language groups. The first group includes the languages of most people in Iran, the CIS, Pakistan, and India. The second group includes the languages of China and of Tibet.

Most of the people of South-Western Asia speak languages in the third group. One of these languages is Arabic. The fourth group is made up of languages spoken in parts of Siberia and Central Asia.

**Some different people of Asia**

Chinese

Japanese

Malayan

Siberian

Indian

**Industry** South-Western Asia has much of the world's petroleum. The most advanced industrial country is Japan. It is famous for its cars, ships, cameras and radio and television equipment. The CIS is also an important manufacturing country. Other countries with many factories include India, Malaysia, Singapore and China.

# History

In its long history, Asia has had many great civilizations and empires. They include the Persian, Chinese, Mongol and Japanese empires, and also the many empires in India. In the 1500s and 1600s, Europeans began to settle in Asia. By the 1800s, they ruled much of the continent. After the Second World War (1939–45) the colonial countries became independent.

*Above left: Winnowing rice in India.*
*Left: Picking tea in Sri Lanka.*
*Below: Even the Great Wall of China could not stop the Mongols invading China in the early 13th century.*

# Ways of life

Asia's population is increasing rapidly. Millions of people live at subsistence level. That is, they have just enough food to eat to stay alive. When farmers can grow only small crops of food because of bad weather or floods, thousands of people die of starvation. Each year, as the population increases, the problem gets worse.

**Agriculture** Most of Asia's people live by growing crops. The best farming lands are in Southern and South-Eastern Asia, China, and the south-western areas of Siberia. The chief food crops are rice and wheat.

Some crops are grown for selling to other countries. Sri Lanka, India, and China grow tea. Malaysia and Indonesia grow rubber. Many of the islands grow spices. Other crops grown for selling are tobacco, cotton, and jute.

# Europe

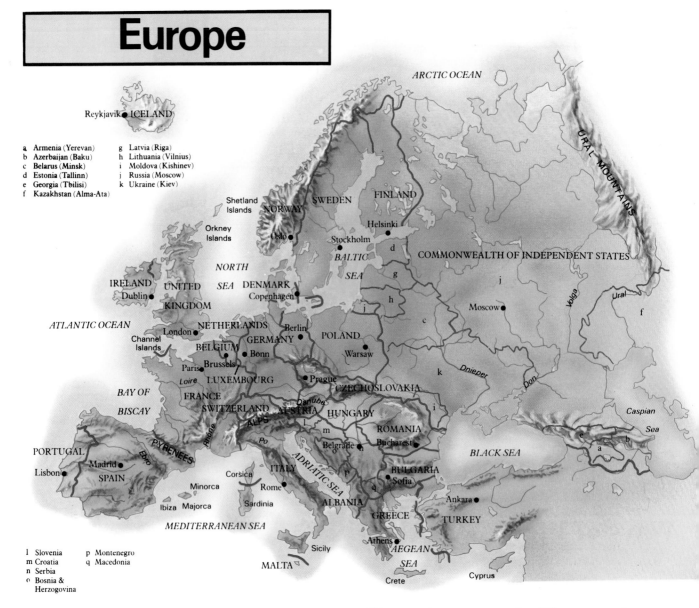

Reykjavik● ICELAND

a Armenia (Yerevan)
b Azerbaijan (Baku)
c Belarus (Minsk)
d Estonia (Tallinn)
e Georgia (Tbilisi)
f Kazakhstan (Alma-Ata)

g Latvia (Riga)
h Lithuania (Vilnius)
i Moldova (Kishinev)
j Russia (Moscow)
k Ukraine (Kiev)

ARCTIC OCEAN

URAL MOUNTAINS

Shetland Islands
Orkney Islands
NORWAY
SWEDEN
FINLAND
Helsinki
Oslo
Stockholm
BALTIC SEA
COMMONWEALTH OF INDEPENDENT STATES
Moscow
Volga
Ural
NORTH SEA
IRELAND
Dublin
UNITED KINGDOM
DENMARK
Copenhagen
ATLANTIC OCEAN
London
Channel Islands
NETHERLANDS
Berlin
GERMANY
POLAND
Warsaw
BELGIUM
Bonn
Paris
Brussels
LUXEMBOURG
Prague
CZECHOSLOVAKIA
Dnieper
Don
Loire
BAY OF BISCAY
FRANCE
SWITZERLAND
AUSTRIA
HUNGARY
Danube
ALPS
ROMANIA
Bucharest
Caspian Sea
Rhône
Po
Belgrade
BLACK SEA
PORTUGAL
Lisbon
Madrid
SPAIN
PYRENEES
Ebro
ITALY
Rome
ADRIATIC SEA
BULGARIA
Sofia
Minorca
Corsica
Sardinia
ALBANIA
Ankara
TURKEY
Ibiza
Majorca
GREECE
MEDITERRANEAN SEA
Athens
Sicily
AEGEAN SEA
Cyprus
MALTA
Crete

l Slovenia
m Croatia
n Serbia
o Bosnia & Herzogovina

p Montenegro
q Macedonia

Europe is the second smallest of the continents, but for hundreds of years it has had a greater influence on the world than any of the others. It belongs to the same mass of land as Asia, but it is always treated as a separate continent. The Ural Mountains and the Caspian Sea mark the boundary between Europe and Asia. At the Strait of Gibraltar, in the south-west, Europe and Africa are only 14 kilometres apart.

## Land regions

Europe has a more uneven shape than any other continent. It has three main regions.

**The northern mountains** These stretch across the north of the British Isles and into Norway and Sweden. In the east of Europe, they bend southwards to form the Ural Mountains in the CIS. On the coast of Norway, they are cut by beautiful *fiords*, bays and inlets of the sea, with steep rocky sides.

**The central plains** These make up most of the continent. They extend from Ireland in the west to the CIS in the east.

Once, they were covered by thick forests, but now, few forests are left except in the north and centre. Some of the world's best farming land is in this region together with most of Europe's town and villages.

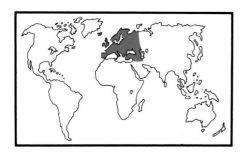

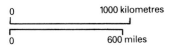

## Climate

Westerly winds from the Atlantic Ocean warm much of the continent in winter and cool it in summer. The countries on the Mediterranean Sea in the south, have hot dry summers. Some northern and eastern parts of the continent also have warm summers, but the winters are cold. The extreme north is within the icy Arctic.

## Plants and animals

Most of Europe's remaining forests consist of coniferous trees, but other trees grow, too. Olives and palms grow in many Mediterranean areas.

Few large mammals are left in the continent. Animal life has been greatly reduced by the destruction of animals' natural homes and by hunting. However, some bears, wolves, wild boars, and deer still remain. There are many small mammals, such as squirrels, badgers and rabbits, and the plentiful bird life includes many varieties of song birds, birds of prey and game birds.

**The southern mountains** These include several great mountain ranges. The Pyrenees in the west rise between Spain and France. The Alps stretch in a huge curve from southeast France, across Switzerland, Austria and northern Italy into Yugoslavia. Their highest peak is Mont Blanc on the border between France and Italy. It rises to 4810 metres. The higher slopes of the Alps are always covered in snow.

In the east, in the CIS are the Caucasus Mountains. They stand between the Black Sea and the Caspian Sea. Mount Elbrus, 5633 metres high, in the Caucasus is the highest mountain in Europe.

## Lakes and rivers

The Caspian Sea in the south-east is really a lake, because it is completely surrounded by land. It is the largest lake in the world. Its water is salt. There are thousands of lakes in northern Europe.

Boats carry *freight* (goods) and passengers, on many of the continent's large rivers. The longest river is the Volga, which flows southwards for 3742 kilometres through the CIS to the Caspian Sea. Other important rivers are the Danube, which flows eastwards through central Europe to the Black Sea, and the Rhine, which flows northwards to the North Sea.

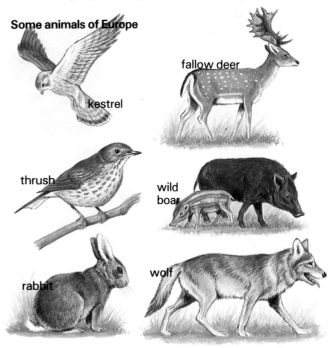

Some animals of Europe

kestrel

fallow deer

thrush

wild boar

rabbit

wolf

# The people of Europe

Only Asia has more people than Europe, but Asia is bigger, and Europe is the most crowded continent. It is crowded with people, and crowded with towns and villages. Many of the ideas and discoveries that have shaped the modern world had their origin in Europe.

The population of Europe, excluding the CIS, is about 480 million. (The population of the CIS is about 260 million, most of whom live west of the Ural mountains.) It is more evenly spread than the populations of the other continents. Nearly all Europeans belong to the Caucasoid race. They are divided into several racial types. Many people have ancestors from more than one group.

**Nordic people** These people are often tall and fair. Many live in Norway, Sweden, northern Germany, and the Netherlands.

**Mediterranean people** These people live mainly in countries bordering the Mediterranean Sea. They are generally shorter and darker than Nordic people.

**Alpine people** Sturdy looking, and less dark than Mediterranean people, these people live mainly in the mountain regions of central and eastern Europe. They are slightly taller than Mediterranean people.

**Other groups** These include the *Dinaric* people who live in the Balkan Peninsula in south-eastern Europe. The *East Baltic* people live in eastern Europe.

*Below: Workers tending a vineyard in France.*

**Some different children of Europe**

Mediterranean • Balkan • Alpine • Nordic

# Languages

Europeans speak about 60 different languages. Most languages belong to three main groups, but many languages have 'borrowed' words from other languages.

**Germanic languages** These are the languages of north-western Europe and part of central Europe. They include German, Danish, Dutch, English, Norwegian, and Swedish. One of these languages, English, is the most widely-spoken language in the world. The most widely-spoken language in Europe is German.

**Romance languages** These come from the Latin that was spoken by people during the Roman Empire 2000 years ago. They include Italian, French, Portuguese, Romanian, and Spanish.

**Slavonic languages** These are spoken in central and eastern Europe. They include Bulgarian, Czech, Polish, Russian, and Ukrainian.

**Other languages** These include Greek, Albanian, and the Celtic languages, such as Breton, Welsh and Gaelic.

# Ways of life

Some parts of Europe have rich mineral resources. They include petroleum, coal, iron and other metals.

**Agriculture** European farms are small, but farms in western Europe use modern machinery and methods. They are among the most efficient in the world. About half the farms grow cereals, such as wheat and barley. Other important crops are potatoes, sugar beet, vegetables, and fruits.

Many farmers keep herds of cattle and sheep. Dairy farming, for milk and milk products, is important in several countries.

**Industry** The countries of western Europe have many industries making machinery, chemicals, *textiles* (cloth), ships, cars and many other kinds of goods. Some of the eastern countries are also industrialized.

# History

Two of the great civilizations of ancient times were European. These were the civilizations of Greece and Rome. Later, many Christian kingdoms were formed in Europe. In the 1500s, much of Europe was divided between the Roman Catholic and Protestant Churches. From the 1700s onwards, a number of European countries built up empires in Asia, the Americas, and Africa. In the 1900s, millions of Europeans were killed and hundreds of cities destroyed in two World Wars.

# Australasia

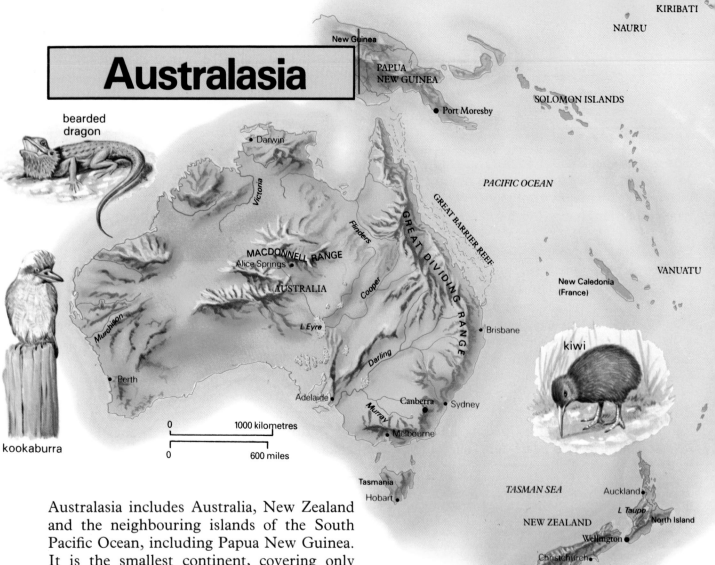

bearded dragon

kookaburra

KIRIBATI

NAURU

New Guinea

PAPUA NEW GUINEA

• Port Moresby

SOLOMON ISLANDS

PACIFIC OCEAN

• Darwin

Victoria

Flinders

MACDONNELL RANGE

Alice Springs •

AUSTRALIA

Cooper

GREAT BARRIER REEF

GREAT DIVIDING RANGE

VANUATU

New Caledonia (France)

Murchison

L Eyre

• Brisbane

kiwi

Darling

• Perth

Adelaide •

Murray

Canberra

• Sydney

0        1000 kilometres

0        600 miles

• Melbourne

Tasmania

TASMAN SEA

Auckland •

Hobart •

L Taupo

NEW ZEALAND

North Island

Wellington •

Christchurch •

South Island

Stewart Island

SOUTHERN OCEA

Australasia includes Australia, New Zealand and the neighbouring islands of the South Pacific Ocean, including Papua New Guinea. It is the smallest continent, covering only about 8 000 000 square kilometres. Another name that is sometimes used to describe this area is Oceania.

## Australia

Australia is a vast island, the largest in the world, and is often thought of as a continent on its own. The island of Tasmania in the south east also forms part of Australia. The famous coral reef, The Great Barrier Reef, lies off Queensland in the north east.

**The land** Australia is completely surrounded by water, but its centre is a huge, dry desert.

*The eastern highlands* stretch the whole way along the eastern coast. They are also known as the Great Dividing Range. About half of Australia's people live in this area of low mountains and high plains.

*The central lowlands* extend westwards from the highlands. They are dry, so many farmers depend on water from artesian wells. (See page 160.)

*The western plateau*, a high flat plain, makes up about two-thirds of Australia. It includes large, sandy deserts, where few plants grow and no people live. In the east of the plateau are the mountains of the Macdonnell Range.

**Lakes and rivers** The largest lake is Lake Eyre. Often, it is almost dry. It is the lowest point in Australia. The longest river is the Darling, about 2700 kilometres long, which flows from the Great Dividing Range to the Murray River. The Murray river is the largest in water volume, and flows south to the sea.

52

emu

UVALU

WESTERN
SAMOA

IJI

TONGA

*Above: Midway Island, one of the many small islands in the Pacific Ocean. There are thousands of islands in the Pacific, and they can be divided into three main groups: Melanesia, Micronesia and Polynesia. Some are volcanic, others are coral islands. Fishing and tourism are important.*
*Right: Some animals of Australia.*

**Climate** The northern third of Australia is in the tropics and is warm throughout the year. The whole of the centre and west have little rain, and are swept by dry winds. Further south, the climate is more temperate.

**Plants and animals** Among the commonest trees are various types of eucalyptus. The continent has some animals that do not live anywhere else. About half of the animals are *marsupials*. These animals carry their young in *pouches* (pockets of skin) on the front of the mother-animal's body. The largest marsupial is the great kangaroo, but also well-known is the koala. There are many colourful birds, but perhaps the best-known is the kookaburra.

# New Zealand

New Zealand lies about 1900 kilometres south-east of Australia across the Tasman Sea. It consists of two main islands and a number of smaller islands.

**The land** The main islands, North Island and South Island, extend about 1600 kilometres from the northern tip of one to the southern tip of the other.

*North Island* consists, in the southern part, of a fertile coastal plain rising to a central *plateau* (high plain). There is an eastern mountain range and several volcanic mountains. Some of these are active such as Ruapehu which rises 2797 metres.

*South Island*, 25 kilometres away across the Cook Strait, has a mountain 'backbone', the Southern Alps. East of the mountains is the Canterbury Plain, famous for its sheep and wheat. Mount Cook is the highest mountain, rising over 4000 metres.

**Climate** New Zealand's climate is pleasant and cool. It is warmest in the north. Most rain falls in the west.

**Plants and animals** Many of New Zealand's trees are evergreen. The country has no mammals of its own, apart from bats. People have brought mammals in from other countries. Some of its birds, such as the kiwi, are not found in any other country.

# Life in Australia

In the 1700s, people from the British Isles began to settle in Australia and New Zealand. They farmed the land, built towns, and started industries.

Australia is about three-quarters the size of Europe, but Europe has more than 30 times as many people. The population of Australia is only about 15 million. Most of the people live along the eastern and south-eastern coasts. Vast areas of the country are desert lands where nobody lives.

**The people** There are two main groups of people: the aborigines and the people of European ancestry.

*Aborigines* were the first inhabitants of Australia. They have probably lived there for 16 000 years, and may have come from Asia. When Europeans first arrived in Australia, about 300 000 Aborigines lived in the continent, but they were hunted and killed. Today, only about 40 000 live there. Most of them live on reserves, small areas set apart for them.

*Europeans* started to settle in Australia in the 1780s and 1790s. Until after the Second World War (1939–45), nearly all the settlers were from the British Isles. Four out of five of the people of Australia had British ancestors. Today, many other Europeans, from countries such as Greece, Italy and Poland have settled there.

**Ways of life** Australia has valuable natural resources, including iron, coal, aluminium, petroleum, and uranium. It is one of the world's major agricultural countries.

*Agriculture* is important with the leading products of Australia's farms being wool, wheat and meat. The country has some of the world's largest sheep and cattle stations, and vast fields of wheat and other cereals.

*Industry* is becoming more and more important. Large industries include steel-making and the manufacture of cars and other vehicles.

*Above left: A view of Sydney, Australia.*
*Below: Captain Cook charted the coastline of New Zealand and landed in Australia in 1770.*

# History

The first Europeans to see Australia were Dutch sailors. The British explorer Captain James Cook landed at Botany Bay on the east coast in 1770. Australia became a British colony, but gained complete independence in 1931.

# Life in New Zealand

New Zealand is a small country. It is a little bigger than Great Britain in area, but only has a population of about 3 million.

**The people** Maoris and people of European ancestry are the main inhabitants.

*Maoris* have probably lived in New Zealand since the 1300s. They went to New Zealand from islands in the part of the Pacific Ocean called Polynesia. The Maoris are a brave and warlike people. They speak their own language called *Maori*, as well as English. Most of the 300 000 Maoris live on the North Island.

*Europeans* from the British Isles began to settle in New Zealand in 1839. About nine out of ten New Zealanders are of British ancestry. A few are descended from settlers from other European countries.

**Ways of life** Until after the Second World War (1939–45), New Zealand traded mainly with Britain. Today, it has important trading links with other countries of the Pacific, including Japan.

*Agriculture* is modern and efficient. New Zealand's farms are famous for their sheep and cattle. The country exports much meat, and also butter and wool.

*Industry* is less important than farming, but factories make many kinds of goods, including steel and *textiles* (cloth).

Aborigine

# History

The Maoris defeated Moriori tribes who were New Zealand's first inhabitants. In the 1800s, the Maoris accepted British rule, but small wars between the Maoris and British settlers continued until 1870. New Zealand became an independent country in the mid 1900s.

*Above: Thousands of sheep being herded along a road in New Zealand.*
*Below: An Aborigine and Maori – early inhabitants of Australia and New Zealand.*

Maori

# The Arctic and Antarctic

Some animals of the polar regions

little auk

razorbill

killer whale

Adelie penguin

ringed seal

Ross seal

walrus

The polar regions, the regions around the North Pole and the South Pole, are both extremely cold. The region of the North Pole is called the Arctic. The region of the South Pole is called the Antarctic or Antarctica.

## The Arctic

The Arctic extends from the North Pole to the Arctic Circle. At the North Pole, there is nothing to tell you that you have reached it. It is just a spot in the Arctic Ocean. Its exact position has to be worked out geographically. The first person to reach the North Pole was an American explorer called Robert E Peary. He reached the Pole in 1909 by crossing the ice covering the ocean.

**Land and sea** The centre of the Arctic is the Arctic Ocean. Usually, it is covered by masses of broken ice, called the *Polar ice pack*. The ocean is surrounded by the most northerly parts of Europe, Asia, and North America. Most of the huge island of Greenland is in the Arctic.

Greenland is icy for the whole year, but some of the ice in the Arctic Ocean begins to melt in spring. It forms icebergs, some of which float out into the Atlantic Ocean and can be a danger to ships. Two famous routes through the Arctic Ocean link the Atlantic and Pacific Oceans. They are the North-West Passage and the North-East Passage.

**Life in the Arctic** Arctic animals include polar bears, whales, seals, and a few kinds of fishes. Many different peoples live in Arctic lands. They include Eskimos (in Greenland, Alaska, and Canada), Yakuta (in the CIS), and Lapps (in Lapland, northern Scandinavia).

*An eskimo from Greenland.*

## The Antarctic

The Antarctic, usually called Antarctica, extends from the South Pole to the Antarctic Circle. It is one of the world's seven continents. Many countries claim to own parts of it. No explorer succeeded in reaching the South Pole until 1911. Then, a Norwegian, Roald Amundsen, got there just one month before a British explorer, Robert Falcon Scott.

**Land and sea** Antarctica has high mountains and deep valleys. Almost everything is hidden under a carpet of ice and snow that is about two kilometres thick in some places.

The edges of the continent have cliffs and exposed mountains. They enclose two huge bays, called the Weddell Sea (part of the Southern Ocean) and the Ross Sea (part of the Pacific Ocean). A long tongue of land, the Antarctic Peninsula, reaches out towards the southern tip of South America. South America is only 650 kilometres away. The highest mountain in Antarctica rises at the southern end of the peninsula. It is the Vinson Massif, 5139 metres high.

The continent is often swept by blizzards in which it is hard for a human being to stand up. As in the Arctic, the waters around Antarctica are dangerous to ships.

**Life in Antarctica** Antarctica is larger than Australia or Europe, but most of it is empty of life. Animals and plants live mainly around the edges of the continent. The animals include penguins, seals, whales, and some kinds of fishes. Several countries have research stations in Antarctica. The only people that live in the continent are scientists and people who have to look after these stations.

*Above: A scientist from a research station in the Antarctic. He travels across the ice on a skidoo.*

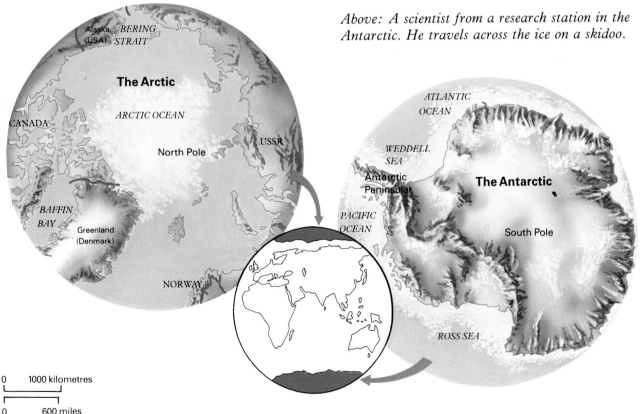

0    1000 kilometres

0    600 miles

# Races of Man

*Children of the three racial types of the world.*
*Top: Caucasoid from Europe.*
*Centre: Mongoloid from Thailand.*
*Above: Negroid from Africa.*

All human beings are alike in important ways, and are different from all other living things. Human blood is completely different to other animals' blood. The blood of an Eskimo, a European, an African or a person from any other part of the world is similar, however each race of people has definite characteristics in their blood.

No two people are exactly alike. People whose ancestors have lived in different parts of the world for hundreds or thousands of years do not look the same. The difference between them may include the shape of their heads, the colour of their skins or the shapes of their eyes or noses. Even the type of hair is different between races.

## Racial types

Many scientists divide the world's people into three basic types, based mainly on the differences in their appearance. The three types are *Caucasoids*, *Mongoloids*, and *Negroids*. The biggest group is the Caucasoids. The smallest is the Negroids. Many people have ancestors in two or even all three of these groups.

**Caucasoids** This group includes most of the people of Europe, North America, South America, and Australasia. They also include some of the people of India, Sri Lanka, Japan, and the Pacific islands. Most of them are the people usually called white. Many Caucasoids, however, have coffee-coloured, olive, or brown skins. Caucasoid people have narrow noses, and some of them have blue eyes.

Among the Caucasoids, there are many smaller groups. One group, the Nordics, are generally tall and fair. They live mainly in north-western and central Europe. Some Nordics, the Kurds, live in south-western Asia. Another group, the Mediterraneans, are shorter and darker. They live mainly around the Mediterranean Sea, and also in northern India.

## Skin colour

Skin colour depends mainly on a brown substance called *melanin* in the skin.

Melanin protects the body from harmful ultra-violet rays in sunlight. People whose ancestors have lived for hundreds of years in hot countries have more melanin granules in their skin than people belonging to cool countries. As a result, people from hot countries have darker skins.

**Melanin granules in the outer layer of the skin (epidermis).**

melanin granule

melanin-forming cell

**Mongoloids** This group includes the people of China and Mongolia. They also include the American Indians, the Eskimos, and many people in Malaysia, Indonesia, and the Philippines. Their skin colour ranges from pale yellow to light brown.

Mongoloid people have eyes that appear almond-shaped, because the upper lid has a fold in the corner near the nose. Their eyes are dark brown, and their hair is straight and black.

**Negroids** These people live mainly in Africa, where they include most of the people living south of the Sahara. They also live in New Guinea and some of the smaller islands of the Pacific Ocean.

The Negroids are the people often called black. However, they have a wide range of skin colours, from almost black to light brown. Their eyes are brown, and their hair is often very curly. They have a protruding lower jaw and some have broad noses.

**Map of the world showing main distribution of the three basic racial types**

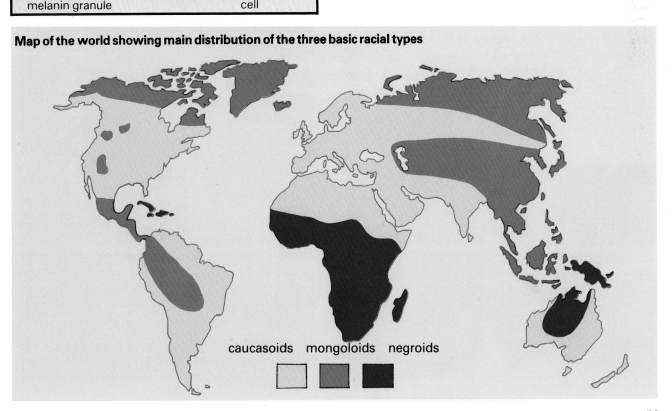

caucasoids    mongoloids    negroids

# Population

More than 4000 million people live in the world, but the spread of population is very uneven. Most of the world's people live on about one-tenth of the Earth's land surface.

The number of people in the world is increasing very quickly. Already, hundreds of millions of people have not enough to eat. Every year, many thousands die of hunger.

## Where people live

Many parts of the world have no human beings, but some parts are very crowded.

**Human settlement** People have settled wherever they can manage to live. Great civilizations have grown up in places where the climate is not too hot or too cold, and where there is fertile land to grow food.

Few people live in the world's high mountain ranges. People can only live in icy Antarctica (around the South Pole) if they bring in everything they need. A few people live in the frozen Arctic (around the North Pole) or near it.

Some other parts of the world are too hot for human settlement. Hardly anybody lives in the hot, waterless deserts. Only a few live in the hot, wet forests near the equator.

*Below: Few people live in this hilly region of China. These people live in tents and tend goats and sheep.*

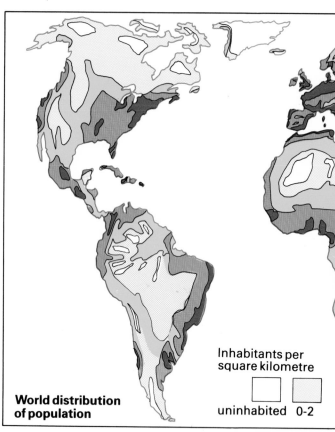

**World distribution of population**

Inhabitants per square kilometre

uninhabited    0-2

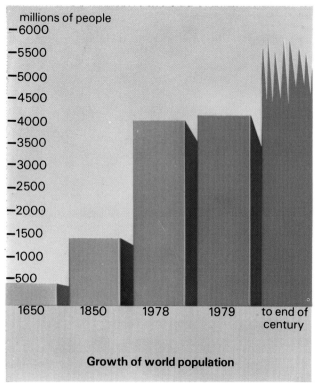

millions of people

| 1650 | 1850 | 1978 | 1979 | to end of century |

**Growth of world population**

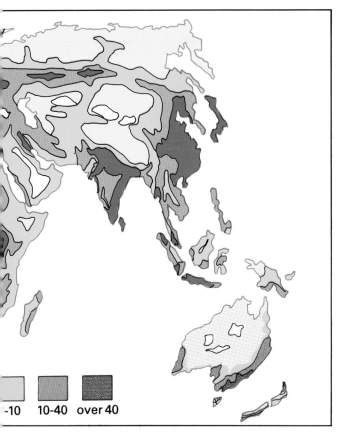

-10    10-40    over 40

**Population density** The density of population (the number of people living on each square kilometre of land) varies from place to place. The most densely-populated places are the large cities, where thousands of people live in each square kilometre.

# Growth of population

In 1650, the world population was about 500 million. By 1850, the number had risen to about 1500 million. In 1978, the world population was about 4173 million people. In 1979, it was about 4254 million. In the 1980s, the population was still increasing at the same rate. For every 100 people in the world, two more people are added every year.

The increase in population is now so fast that it is called a *population explosion*. It is bursting out like an explosion. Nothing like it has happened before.

---

# Religions of the World

Religion has been one of the strongest forces in history. It influences the way that many people think and the way they act. Millions of people have died for their religious beliefs.

Throughout history, most people have had some type of religious belief. Nearly all of them have believed that there is a Force or Power that controls the world. This Force is usually called *God*.

All religions teach that we can behave in a good way or an evil (bad) way. We should try always to do what is good.

The members of some religions believe that when we die we go to another world. There, we are rewarded with happiness if we were good on Earth. Some others believe that we return to Earth again and again, but not always as people. They believe we could return as a bird or a mammal or any sort of animal.

## The great religions

The world has hundreds of different religions. There are some major religions to which millions of people belong.

**Hinduism** This is the main religion of India. It started at least 4000 years ago. Hindus believe that there is a supreme power in the world called *Brahman*. Each person has a spirit or soul (the 'me' that is different from everyone else) that wants to be united with Brahman. This cannot usually be done in one lifetime.

**Buddhism** This religion grew out of Hinduism. It was founded by an Indian prince, Siddhartha Gautama, who died in about 483 BC. (BC means the years before Christ.) Siddhartha is known as *the Buddha*.

Buddhists believe that all creatures are born many times on Earth. People suffer because of bad things they did in the past. In time, they can reach *Nirvana* and escape from suffering.

*Bottom: Muslims praying outside a mosque in Cairo, Egypt.*
*Opposite right: Jews praying at the Wailing Wall in Jerusalem, Israel.*
*Opposite left: Buddhist monks in a temple in Bangkok, Thailand.*
*Below: Muktesvara Temple, a Hindu temple in India.*

**Islam** This religion was founded in Arabia by Muhammad in the AD 600s. (AD means the years after Christ.) The word Islam means peace by submitting to God. Muslims (followers of Islam) call God *Allah*. The teachings of Islam are written down in a book called the *Koran*.

**Judaism** This is the religion of the Jews, developed in Palestine more than 3000 years ago. Its early prophets included Abraham and Moses. Judaism teaches that there is one God, who is all-powerful and just. Jews follow the laws and teachings of the Hebrew *Bible* (the *Old Testament*) and the *Talmud*.

*Above: A crowd in St Peter's Square, Rome, waiting to hear the Pope, head of the Roman Catholic Church, a Christian Church.*
*Below: A Christian wedding.*

**Christianity** This religion developed from Judaism. Its beliefs are based on the life of a Jewish teacher named Jesus, who lived 2000 years ago. His teachings were written down in the *New Testament* by his followers. These followers were given the name Christians because they followed Jesus *the Christ (the Anointed)*. They believed he was the Son of God. Jesus followed many Jewish teachings, and stressed the importance of love.

**Shinto** This is an important religion in Japan. Most Shintoists believe in a large number of gods and spirits. These include dead heroes and emperors, and nature spirits. Shinto means 'way to the gods'.

**Confucianism** This religion was founded by the Chinese thinker Confucius, who died in 479 BC. He taught that goodness shows itself in good behaviour.

**Taoism** A Chinese thinker, Lao Tzu, is said to have founded this religion in the 500s BC. Taoists believe that good people should live quietly, in agreement with nature.

# Plants and Animals

*African elephants.*

# Living and Non-living Things

Dogs are living animals, oak trees are living plants, but rocks, flames and motor cars are not alive. What is the difference? Living things, or *organisms*, breathe and eat to get energy to grow and move. Yet we could say that motor cars eat petrol and breathe air so that they can move along the road.

Living things are made of the complicated materials called organic substances. The main ones are sugars, proteins and fats.

## Reproduction

All living things can *reproduce* by making copies of themselves. Dogs have puppies which grow up into adult dogs like their parents. Oak trees make acorns which grow into new oak trees. Rocks, flames and motor cars cannot reproduce.

Most living things reproduce by *sexual reproduction*. This means that they grow from an egg, made by a female parent, once the egg has joined with a sperm from a male parent. This is called *fertilization*. Another way that some organisms reproduce is by *asexual reproduction* – growing new individuals. A tulip plant grows new bulbs which break off and grow into separate plants.

Clostridium tetani *bacteria, which cause tetanus by paralysing the muscles.*

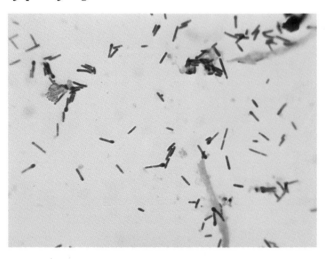

A variety of fungi

morel

fly agaric

fairy ring toadstool

puff ball

cup fungus

helmet cap

sulphur tuft

purple stereum

## Kinds of living things

There are four main sorts of living things. These are bacteria, viruses, plants and animals.

**Bacteria** These are tiny organisms which can be seen only with a high-power microscope. Some are less than one thousandth of a millimetre across. They reproduce by asexual reproduction and split into two identical halves. Bacteria can be found in every part of the world, including places where no other organisms can live. They are important in making soil fertile. Some bacteria are useful – they turn milk into cheese and yoghurt. Other bacteria cause diseases. Acne, tuberculosis, bubonic plague and blood poisoning are caused by bacteria.

66

chanterelle
moss pixy cap
inkcap
amethyst agaric
boletus
cup fungus
earth ball
death cap

**Viruses** These are even smaller than bacteria and cannot be seen with an ordinary microscope. They can live in many places but only grow and reproduce when they are inside bacteria, plants or animals. Many diseases, for example colds, measles, polio and smallpox, are caused by viruses.

**Plants and animals** These are made up of basic units called cells. Each cell has a nucleus which controls it. Many cells joined together make up tissues. Bones, muscles and nerves are animal tissues. Plants also have different sorts of tissues made from cells joined together.

The main difference between plants and animals is that most plants make their own food substances but animals have to eat plants, bacteria or other animals. Plants use energy from the Sun to turn water and carbon dioxide into sugar. This is called *photosynthesis*. Oxygen is given off during photosynthesis. The Sun's energy is trapped in the plant by a substance called *chlorophyll* which gives plants their green colour.

Another difference between plants and animals is that nearly all animals can move, but all except the simplest plants are fixed to one place. Animals usually have to move to find their food. This means that they need limbs to move, and sense organs to guide the movements of these limbs.

*Fungi* are plants which do not have any chlorophyll. Some fungi form a large cap or stalk on the top of the ground or on tree trunks. These are the toadstools and mushrooms.

Fungi can cause a great deal of damage. They form mould and mildew on food and plants and dry rot in wood. But others are very useful. For example, yeast is used for making bread and alcoholic drinks, and penicillin comes from a kind of fungus.

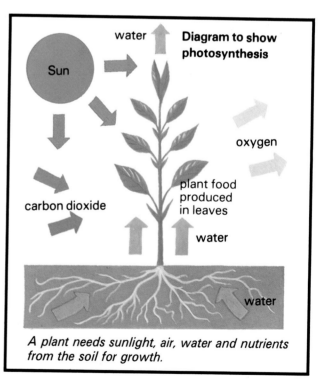

Diagram to show photosynthesis

Sun
water
oxygen
carbon dioxide
plant food produced in leaves
water
water

*A plant needs sunlight, air, water and nutrients from the soil for growth.*

# Evolution

Life began over 3000 million years ago, but very little is known about the first living things. Ever since life began on Earth, the kinds of living things have been changing. Plants and animals of the past are not the same as those living today. New kinds have appeared and others have died out. This process of change takes hundreds and thousands of years and is called *evolution*. Because the process is so slow we cannot watch one kind of animal or plant turn into another. But we can see that this has happened by studying fossils. Fossils are the remains of plants and animals which have been buried in soil or mud which has then become rock. Sometimes only an impression of the plant or animal is left in the rock. Older fossils are buried deeper than new ones. By arranging fossils according to their age, the way that living things have changed over the years can be seen. (See also pages 26 and 27.)

*These birds are known from fossils.*

## From bacteria to birds

The first living things were very simple organisms like bacteria and viruses. They changed very slowly but, eventually, simple plants and animals evolved from them. All the earliest organisms lived in the sea. The plants were simple kinds called algae. Later, some plants developed that were able to grow on land. From these, the mosses, ferns and flowering plants evolved.

**The first animals** These probably evolved from the simple plants and many of them were like the jellyfishes, sponges and worms which live in the sea today. The fishes were the first animals with backbones and they have ruled the seas ever since. About 400 million years ago, some fishes managed to come out of the sea on to the land and from them evolved the first amphibians. They lived in swamps where huge ferns grew. The first insects also appeared at this time.

Archaeopteryx

Dinornis

Phororharaos

**Conquest of the land** The reptiles evolved from the amphibians and very quickly became the most important animals. Some were very large. The dinosaurs walked on the land; the plesiosaurs and ichthyosaurs swam in the sea; and the pterodactyls flew in the air. These giant reptiles disappeared suddenly after 100 million years. No one knows exactly why they died out, but the smaller snakes, lizards and crocodiles have survived. The birds and mammals had already evolved from some reptiles millions of years earlier and they now became the most important animals on land. Meanwhile, the modern flowering plants, including trees and grasses, took over from the ferns and other simple plants.

The scales on the legs of birds are a sign that they are descended from reptiles and their feathers have evolved from scales. The first birds could not fly well. They hopped through the branches and glided from tree to tree.

# Mammals

The first mammals were small mouse-like animals that came out at night to escape from the reptiles which hunted by day. When the large reptiles became extinct, many more kinds of mammals evolved.

Man is one of the newest mammals. The first kinds of men evolved from apes about 6 million years ago. Modern humans appeared no more than 150 000 years ago.

*Archaeopteryx*

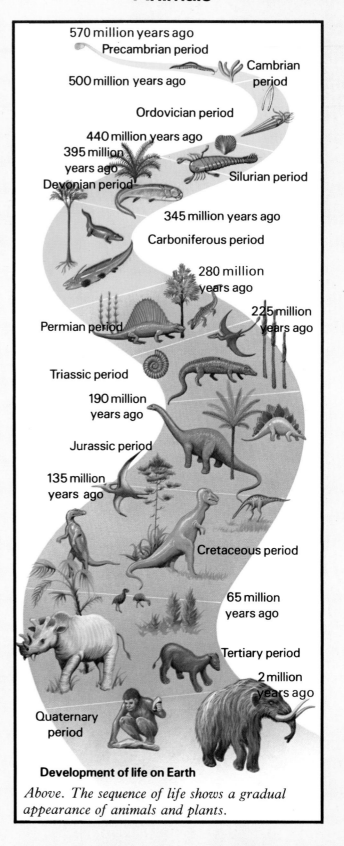

570 million years ago
Precambrian period

Cambrian period

500 million years ago

Ordovician period

440 million years ago

395 million years ago

Devonian period

Silurian period

345 million years ago

Carboniferous period

280 million years ago

225 million years ago

Permian period

Triassic period

190 million years ago

Jurassic period

135 million years ago

Cretaceous period

65 million years ago

Tertiary period

2 million years ago

Quaternary period

**Development of life on Earth**

*Above. The sequence of life shows a gradual appearance of animals and plants.*

# Algae, Lichens, Mosses and Ferns

*Above: A lichen growing on a bare rock.*

## Algae

These are simple plants which do not have stems, roots or leaves. Some algae are tiny and consist of single cells which can only be seen under a microscope. The largest algae are giant seaweeds which grow to over 50 metres long. Nearly all algae live in the sea or fresh water but a few live in damp places on land. The green substance that can be scraped off many tree trunks is an alga. Some of the smallest algae swim by beating whip-like threads called flagella (singular – flagellum). A simple 'eye' guides them towards the light.

Tiny, single-celled algae can be so abundant that they stain the water green or pink. These algae are very important because they are the main food of fishes and many other water animals. Diatoms are algae with shells of glassy silica. The shells have two halves which fit together like a box and its lid. Over millions of years, the shells of dead algae have gathered on the sea bed and turned into thick layers of chalk and other rocks. Oil also comes from the remains of algae which died long ago and became buried under rocks.

The seaweeds growing on the shore are large algae. Most kinds are brown but there are also green and red seaweeds. They are fastened to rocks and, when the tide is in, their fronds float like underwater forests.

A variety of algae, lichens, mosses and ferns

## Lichens

Lichens, which grow on walls and trees, are an alga and a fungus growing together so closely that they behave like a single plant. Lichens grow extremely slowly. Some lichens in the Antarctic are over 1000 years old. These grow only 2–3 centimetres in 100 years.

## Mosses and liverworts

The mosses and liverworts are plants without roots but some do have leaves. They grow in damp places and often form thick clumps. Sometimes they can be found in places where no other plants can survive. One liverwort flourishes on ground where there has been a fire. Bog-moss or *Sphagnum* is the main plant in wet bogs. Its tissues can absorb large quantities of water, like a sponge. When bog-moss dies, its remains slowly rot, become compressed and form peat.

*Above: A clump of ferns shows the withered remains of last year's fronds. The new fronds develop spores on the underside.*

# Ferns

The ferns are like the mosses and liverworts but the second stage or spore-producing stage (see box) is very large and is the plant you are most likely to see, whereas the first stage is tiny. The second stage of a fern has roots, stems and leaves. (A stem and its leaves is called a *frond*.) You can find small bumps on the underside of the leaves which is where the spores are developing.

Most ferns grow in woods where it is dark and moist, and they are most common in tropical countries. The smallest ferns are only 2 millimetres long, but the tree ferns of tropical countries grow to 15 metres high. Bracken is a fern which prefers open ground. Its underground stems, called *rhizomes*, spread rapidly. Farmers do not like bracken because animals cannot eat it and it quickly covers fields and kills the grass.

Horsetails and clubmosses are similar to ferns and they are also common in tropical countries. About 300 million years ago, ferns, horsetails and clubmosses were the most important plants. Some types were very tall and formed forests. Their remains rotted into peat and then turned into coal. (See page 144.)

## Two-stage plants

A moss or liverwort goes through two stages in its life. The first stage has male and female sex organs. Then the fertilized egg develops into the second stage which produces spores. Spores are like tiny seeds and are carried away by the wind. When one settles on the ground, it grows into a new first stage plant.

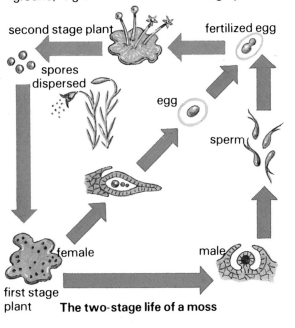

second stage plant      fertilized egg
spores
dispersed
egg
sperm
female      male
first stage
plant      **The two-stage life of a moss**

# Cone-bearing Plants

## Conifers

Trees which grow cones are called conifers. The cones are either male or female. Male cones are small and soft and they produce pollen. The pollen is blown by the wind to fertilize the female cones, which then produce seeds. It sometimes takes two or more years for the cones to grow.

Most conifers have long, narrow leaves called needles. The monkey-puzzle tree, however, is a conifer which has flat, triangular leaves. Conifer leaves live for up to 20 years and most of these trees are called *evergreens* because they do not lose all their leaves in winter. Instead, a few leaves at a time are lost throughout the year. The larch is one of the few conifers which does shed its leaves every winter.

## Pine trees and spruces

There are many sorts of conifer, including over 80 kinds of pines. Pine needles are very long and grow in pairs. The Scots pine is the common kind in Europe. It is shaped rather like an umbrella, with a flat top but most other conifer trees have a conical shape. The lodgepole pine from western North America is often grown in Europe for its timber.

**Spruces** These are rather like the pines but the needles grow on short stalks which are left behind when they fall. The Norway spruce is used for Christmas trees in Europe but Americans use the Douglas fir.

**Timber** The timber of conifers is called softwood because it is easily cut. It is very important for use in buildings and for making crates, fences and plywood. Conifer timber is also used for making paper for newspapers and some trees give turpentine and pitch. The timber of yew trees was once important for making bows.

male cone

pollen

young female cone

one-year-old female cone

mature female cone

seeds

Welwitschia

European larch

Scots pine

cycad

Douglas fir

lodgepole pine

# Other cone-bearers

**Cycads** They live in warm countries around the world and they look rather like palm trees. The trunk is up to 20 metres high and has a clump of long leaves, like the fronds of a palm tree, at the top. When the leaves fall, they leave a stump. Stumps of old leaves can be seen all the way up the stem. One large cone grows at the top of the stem. Sago is extracted from the trunk of cycads.

**Maidenhair tree** It grows wild only in one part of China but it used to live all over the world. It is now grown in parks and gardens, and it can be recognized by its leaves. They are shaped rather like fans.

**Welwitschia** The strangest cone-bearing plant is *Welwitschia* which lives in the deserts of south-west Africa. It looks like a giant radish growing 30 centimetres out of the ground, 120 centimetres across, and has two broad leaves 3 metres long. It can live for hundreds of years.

## The largest living things in the world

Three kinds of American conifer are the largest living things in the world. The redwood or sequoia grows in California, near the coast. The tallest redwood is over 110 metres high and 6 metres across the base. The wellingtonia, a relative of the sequoia, is found in the mountains of California. It is not as tall as the redwood and grows only to 90 metres high but its base may be 9 metres in diameter. The Douglas fir also grows over 90 metres high.

*The sequoia, a giant tree.*

**A variety of cone-bearing plants**

maidenhair    Norway spruce    monkey-puzzle    Lebanon cedar

# Flowering Plants

Most plants have flowers. Flowering plants are the most advanced and complicated plant forms. There are about 250000 species and they include garden and countryside flowers, vegetables and crops, grasses and many trees. They range in size from duckweed, 3 millimetres across, to giant eucalyptus or gum trees. The algae, mosses, ferns and cone-bearers do not have flowers.

*Right: Flowers are pollinated by many different insects.*

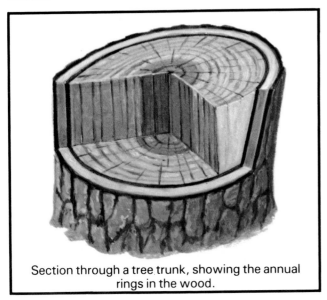

Section through a tree trunk, showing the annual rings in the wood.

**Diagram to show the parts of a flower**

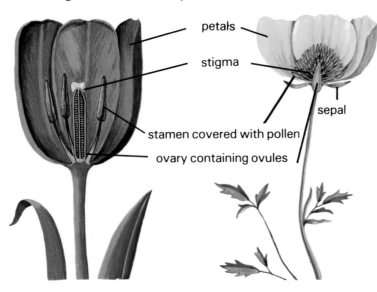

petals

stigma

sepal

stamen covered with pollen

ovary containing ovules

## Plant structure

Large flowering plants have woody stems. Large woody plants are called trees; smaller ones are bushes and shrubs. The wood helps to support the plant and transports water from the roots to the leaves. The wood grows in rings. Because one new ring is formed each year, you can tell the age of a tree by counting the rings on a stump. The wood is covered with *bark*. The inner layer of bark carries food up and down the stem. In cooler parts of the world, many trees and shrubs lose all their leaves in winter. They are called *deciduous* plants.

The flower is the reproductive part of the plant and it produces seeds. It has a ring of colourful *petals* and small, usually green, sepals. The *sepals* protect the flower when it is a bud. Inside the petals there are stalked *stamens* surrounding a single *pistil*. The stamens are the male part of the flower and release pollen. The pistil is the female part and seeds develop from egg-cells in the *ovary* at the base. Not all flowers have both male and female parts together. Some species have either all male or all female flowers on one individual, or on different parts of the same plant.

# Pollination and growth

The seeds develop when the egg-cells are fertilized by pollen grains which land on the stigma. This is called *pollination* and pollen may be carried from one flower to another by the wind, by insects, or other animals. Wind-pollinated flowers are small and dull, as in the grasses and many trees. Most flowers are pollinated by insects, especially moths, butter-flies, bees and flies. The flowers are brightly coloured and contain sugary nectar to attract the insects.

**Fruit formation** The petals fall off after pollination and the pistil starts to swell as the seeds inside begin to grow. The pistil becomes the *fruit*, which may be hard like an acorn, or soft and juicy like a plum or orange. An apple is a 'false fruit' because the juicy part comes from a swollen part of the stalk growing round the pistil. The pistil becomes the apple core containing the seeds.

Juicy fruits and nuts are eaten by animals and this helps to spread the seeds since they are scattered in the animals' droppings. Small grass seeds are spread by the wind and the sycamore seed has a 'wing' so that it is carried in the wind.

## Animal help for plants

Flowers are usually pollinated by the wind or by insects, but some are visited by other kinds of animals. In warm countries birds are often as important for pollination as insects. Hummingbirds and parrots are among the birds which feed on nectar contained in some brightly coloured flowers. They pollinate cacti (singular: cactus), hibiscus and eucalyptus.

Fruit bats are the most usual mammal pollinators as they feed on the nectar in flowers of fruit-bearing trees, but small lemurs, bushbabies and opossums visit some flowers.

*A hummingbird which is a pollen carrier.*

**Growth** Plants usually grow from the tip of the stem but grasses grow from the base. This means that they can be nibbled by animals or cut with a lawnmower and still continue to grow. There are over 10 000 species of grasses. The world's most important food sources are grasses, such as wheat, rice, barley, maize and sugar cane. Bamboo is the largest grass.

# Asexual reproduction

Flowers and seeds are not the only way that plants reproduce. Some develop special organs which split off and grow into new plants. A tulip or daffodil grows from a *bulb*, which sprouts new bulbs from its base. The potatoes we eat are *tubers*. These are swollen stems. The 'eyes' are buds which sprout into new plants.

# Useful Plants

## Food plants

The world's main food plants are grasses. Wheat, rye, barley and oats are grasses called *cereals*. (See also page 153.) Their ripe seeds or grain are ground into flour.

Other grasses are millet, rice and corn. Millet and rice are grown in hot countries. Rice is the main food for half the world's people. It is grown in flooded fields called *paddies*. Maize or corn gives us corn-on-the-cob, cooking oil and cornflour. Short grasses are used for feeding farm animals. Cut grass can be stored as dry hay or moist silage.

Peanuts or groundnuts are roasted and salted for eating but they are more important for the oil they produce. It is used for cooking and making margarine and soap. Soya beans give an oil which has the same uses as peanut oil but they are also used to make flour. This is a very important food in some countries. Soya beans are grown mainly in China and the United States of America.

**A variety of plants used for food**

**Palm trees** Date palms have been grown for over 5000 years. They flourish in dry places and, as well as giving sugary dates for eating, their leaves are used for thatching roofs and making mats. A coconut palm can give 300–450 'nuts' each year. The coconuts we buy in shops are the seeds. They grow inside a thick husk used to make mats and ropes. As well as being a food, coconuts are a source of oil. The oil is used for cooking and for making soap and margarine. Like the leaves of the date palm, coconut leaves are used for making roofs.

**Vegetables** Cabbages were developed from a wild flowering plant which grows on European coasts. The part we eat is a huge bud of many leaves packed together. If the cabbage is not cut, the leaves grow and unfold. Other varieties of cabbage are broccoli, kale, brussel sprout and cauliflower. We eat the young flowers of cauliflower. Turnips, swedes, watercress and radishes are also members of the cabbage family. We eat the leaves of watercress, but the roots of turnips, swedes and radishes.

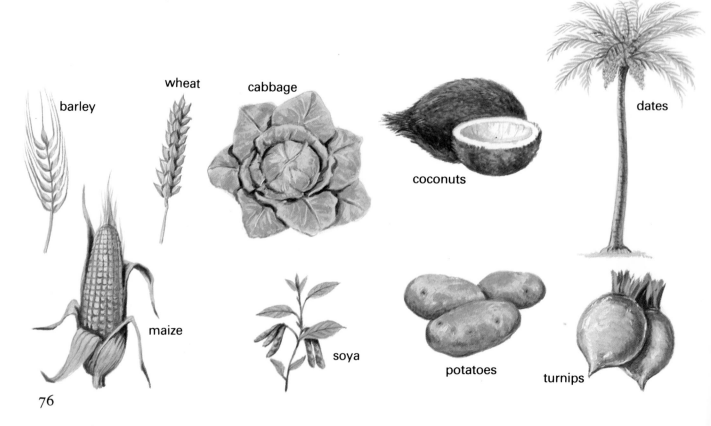

barley
wheat
cabbage
coconuts
dates
maize
soya
potatoes
turnips

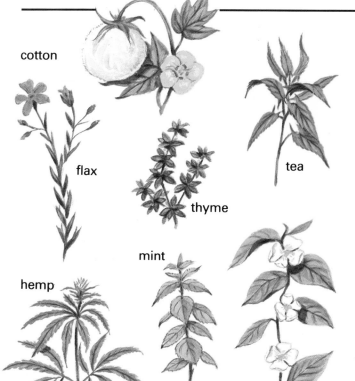

cotton

flax

thyme

tea

mint

hemp

jute

**More useful plants**

# Other useful plants

Natural rubber comes from the sap of a tree. Cuts are made in the bark of the tree. A sticky liquid called latex oozes out and hardens into solid rubber. It has to be treated before it can be used to make tyres and other rubber articles.

Products made from plants are used for many other purposes. Food is flavoured with herbs, such as thyme, sage and mint, or with spices, such as pepper, nutmeg and cinnamon. Drinks are made from tea leaves, coffee berries and cocoa seeds. Quinine, used for curing malaria, comes from the bark of the cinchona tree, and pain-killing morphine and codeine come from the opium poppy.

*Below: Rubber trees are 'tapped' by cutting grooves. Sticky latex oozes out and is collected in a cup tied to the tree below the cut.*

# Fibres

Several plants are grown for their long fibres. Linen cloth is made from the flax plant which grows in many parts of Europe. The stems are allowed to rot. Then they are beaten to separate the long fibres which will be woven into linen. The fibres are also used to make high quality paper and the seeds give linseed oil.

Hessian is a coarse cloth used for making sacks. It is made from the stems of the jute plant. Sisal is made from the leaves of agave plants which come from the deserts of Mexico. It is used for making string and matting. Fibres from hemp plants are used for making rope.

Cotton has been used for making cloth for thousands of years. It is now grown in Egypt, India and the United States of America. The plants grow large, fluffy fruits called cotton-bolls. The fluff is spun into cotton thread. (See also page 164.)

# Unusual Plants

## Desert plants

Plants cannot live without water. They dry up because water escapes from their leaves. Desert plants can survive with very little water because their leaves are usually very small and a layer of wax on the leaves stops water escaping.

Cacti are desert plants which do not have leaves. Photosynthesis takes place in the skin of their large, swollen stems, which also have an extra thick waterproof covering. The roots of a cactus spread over a wide area so they can collect as much water as possible when it rains. The water is stored in tissues of the stem for use during a dry spell and some cacti can swell up when there is plenty of water. Plants which store water are called *succulents*.

The mesquite bush of American deserts gets its water by sending its roots to a depth of over 50 metres where the soil is always moist.

## Growing on trees

In the dense growth of tropical rainforests, the tree trunks are covered with small plants called *epiphytes*. Some get their water and salts from dirt which gathers around their roots. Others make a bowl from their leaves and trap rain-water. Many kinds of animals live in the water. Frogs even lay their spawn in the bowls.

*Above right: Epiphytes on a tree.*
*Left: Desert cacti.*

## Salt-water trees

The shores of tropical seas are sometimes hidden by dense forests of mangrove trees. Mangroves grow in the mud and they are surrounded by sea water at high tide. Other kinds of trees cannot live in salt water.

Mangrove trees have *prop* roots which make arches to support their trunks. The roots send up special shoots out of the mud to help the tree to breathe. This is because it cannot get enough oxygen from the waterlogged mud through its underground roots.

*Above: A venus fly-trap with a captured insect.*

# Meat-eating plants

Some plants feed on small animals which they trap and digest. The leaves of pitcher-plants fill with water and make a trap to drown insects. The sides are slippery so that the insects cannot get out and their bodies are digested by juices produced by the leaves.

Butterwort and sundew have sticky blobs of glue on their leaves which catch insects that wander on to them. As an insect struggles, it gets caught in more glue. Then digestive juices are poured on to it and it is absorbed into the plant.

The Venus fly-trap has special leaves which fold in half to make a trap. The trap snaps shut when an insect walks on it and long bristles form 'prison bars' to prevent it escaping.

Bladderwort lives in ponds and gets its name from leaves which are like hollow bladders. Each bladder has a trapdoor and some bristles which act as a trigger. When an insect or water flea bumps into the trigger, the trapdoor flies open and the animal is sucked in.

# Poisonous plants

Many plants make poisons to discourage animals from eating them. Stinging nettles are one example. They are armed with tiny hollow hairs. When we brush against them, the hair tips are broken off. The hairs then penetrate our skin and poison is pumped in. Nettle poison causes itching and a rash which soon disappear, but the American poison ivy can cause serious inflammation.

Common plants which are poisonous include buttercups, yew, ivy and privet berries, laburnum, hemlock and deadly nightshade. They are harmful when eaten. Foxgloves contain a poison, called digitalis, but this can be used for treating heart disease. South American Indians poison their arrows with curare which they get from plants. Tapioca comes from poisonous cassava plants which have to be boiled for a long time or else ground and washed to make them safe to eat.

**A variety of poisonous plants**

hemlock

laburnum

nettle

yew

foxglove

Australian nettle

privet

deadly nightshade

buttercup

ivy

# Simple Animals

*Above: A sea anemone is a bag with tentacles.*

## Protozoans

The simplest animals are microscopic, single-celled protozoans which are usually less than one tenth of a millimetre in size. They live in water and the soil, or in the bodies of bigger animals. The disease malaria is caused by a protozoan which lives in the blood. Mosquitoes in hot countries spread malaria when they bite.

## Sea anemones, jelly-fish and corals

**Sea anemones** These are many-celled animals which have a soft body with a mouth at the top, like a bag. The mouth is surrounded by a ring of tentacles. The tentacles seize and sting small fishes and shrimps and push them into the mouth. If a sea anemone is disturbed, it quickly folds away its tentacles. It also does this at low tide so that it does not dry up.

**Jellyfish** Jellyfish are like upside-down sea anemones. The mouth is underneath. Some jellyfish are dangerous because they can sting badly.

**Corals** The corals are also similar to sea anemones, but they are protected by hard skeletons which grow around their bodies. They can retreat into their skeletons when disturbed. Many corals grow together in colonies and, when they die, their skeletons remain. Over the years, millions of skeletons have piled up to make coral reefs on which the new coral grows.

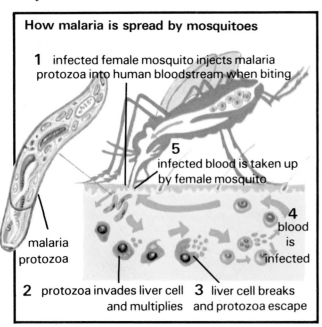

**How malaria is spread by mosquitoes**

**1** infected female mosquito injects malaria protozoa into human bloodstream when biting

**5** infected blood is taken up by female mosquito

**4** blood is infected

malaria protozoa

**2** protozoa invades liver cell and multiplies

**3** liver cell breaks and protozoa escape

*Above: Corals have fantastic shapes.*

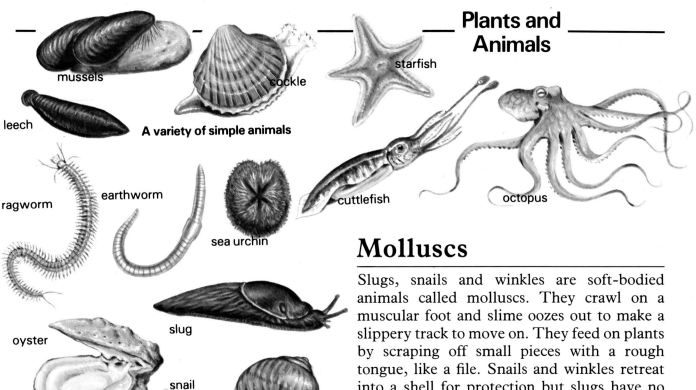

mussels

cockle

starfish

leech

A variety of simple animals

ragworm

earthworm

sea urchin

cuttlefish

octopus

oyster

slug

snail

# Worms

Many kinds of animals are called worms. They are long, thin animals with soft bodies. Earthworms are made up of about 150 rings, or segments, and burrow through the soil. There can be a million earthworms in 100 square metres of soil and they make the soil more fertile by churning it up and eating it. They also pull dead leaves into the soil, where they eat them. The leaves are broken up and digested, then pass out of the worm as a fertilizer.

Leeches are segmented worms which suck blood. They live among damp vegetation in warm countries, or in water, and fasten on to passing animals by means of a sucker. The leech's jaws cut a hole in the animal's skin and it sucks up blood until the body is swollen like a balloon. The animal does not feel anything because the leech injects an anaesthetic.

Ragworms are also segmented worms and they live on the seashore. They crawl and swim using their rows of bristly 'paddles'.

# Molluscs

Slugs, snails and winkles are soft-bodied animals called molluscs. They crawl on a muscular foot and slime oozes out to make a slippery track to move on. They feed on plants by scraping off small pieces with a rough tongue, like a file. Snails and winkles retreat into a shell for protection but slugs have no shell, or only a very small one.

Cockles, mussels, oysters and clams are molluscs with shells in two parts. They are usually attached to rocks or burrow in sand or mud, but scallops swim by clapping their shells together.

The octopuses, squids and cuttlefish swim by squirting out jets of water and the octopuses can also crawl on their arms. The arms have rows of suckers which help to catch their prey. The prey is crushed with a beak like a parrot's. Octopuses eat crabs, and squids and cuttlefish eat shrimps and other animals. Giant squids can be up to 20 metres long.

# Spiny animals

Starfish have five arms bearing rows of suckers, called *tube feet*, and sharp spines which help them to move and seize small animals. A starfish can pull open a mussel or oyster with its tube feet. The starfish then pushes its stomach through its mouth and folds it around its food.

Sea urchins are closely related to starfish and also crawl on tube feet and spines, but feed on seaweed.

# Jointed-legged Animals

Like the animals described on the previous pages, none of the animals described here have bones. They are *invertebrates* – animals without backbones. But the animals on these two pages do have a hard skin, like a suit of armour. This skin supports the body in the same way that our skeleton does. These animals also have many pairs of legs. Each leg has several joints.

## Insects

There are more than a million species of insects in the world. All have six legs and most have two pairs of wings. Their bodies are divided into three sections – the head, the thorax, and the abdomen. The *head* is small and has a pair of sensitive antennae. The *thorax* is the middle section and has the wings and legs. The *abdomen* is the largest section.

**Butterflies and moths** These are some of the most brightly coloured and patterned insects. They have two pairs of wings. Butterflies fly by day but most moths fly at night. There are four stages in their lives: egg, caterpillar, pupa, adult. The caterpillar, which hatches from the egg, is the young insect, or larva. It then changes into an adult inside the pupa.

**Flies** They have only one pair of wings. Instead of the second pair, they have a pair of tiny, club-shaped stalks. These help to balance the fly when it is flying.

**Grasshoppers and crickets** These grow up in a different way to the butterflies, moths and flies. The young insects, called nymphs, look like their parents but they do not have wings. As they grow they shed their hard skins several times and the wings become fully developed only when they become adults. Locusts are kinds of grasshoppers which live in huge swarms that can destroy crops. (See also page 121.)

## Social insects

Bees, wasps, ants and termites are called the social insects because they work to help each other. They also live in large nests. (A bees' nest is called a hive.) Each nest has a queen who does nothing but lay eggs. Worker insects collect food, look after the nest and care for the young insects.

Bees eat pollen and turn nectar into honey. Wasps and ants eat animals and plants. Termites eat wood and they can destroy buildings.

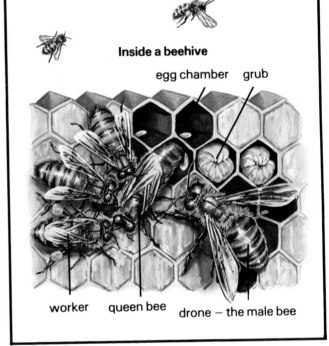

**Inside a beehive**

egg chamber    grub

worker    queen bee    drone – the male bee

## Spiders and scorpions

Spiders are eight-legged and their bodies are in two parts. The best known ones spin webs which trap unwary insects, but some spiders chase their prey. Both types kill the victim with a poisonous bite and suck it dry. The largest spiders can give humans a very nasty bite and some can catch small birds.

Scorpions are eight-legged relatives of the spiders. They are armed with two claws and a sting at the end of the tail.

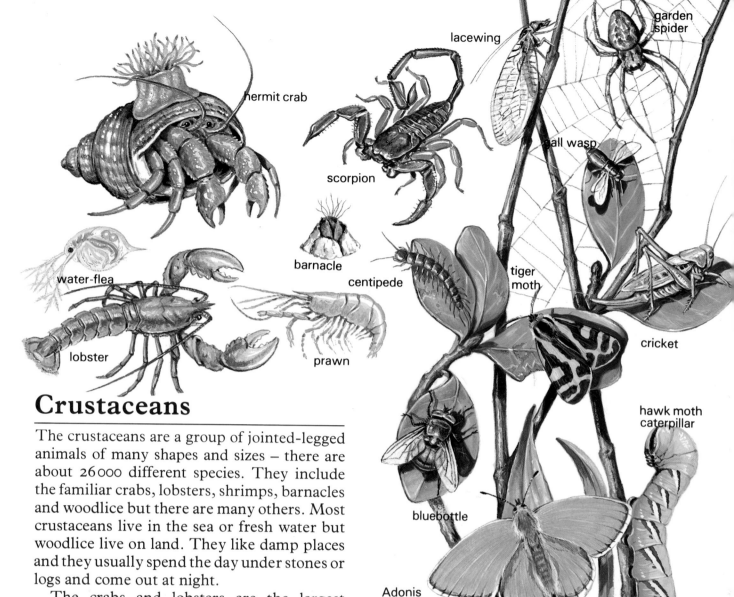

labels in image:
hermit crab
scorpion
barnacle
water-flea
centipede
lobster
prawn
lacewing
garden spider
gall wasp
tiger moth
cricket
hawk moth caterpillar
bluebottle
Adonis blue butterfly
sand wasp
millipede
woodlouse

A variety of jointed-legged animals

# Crustaceans

The crustaceans are a group of jointed-legged animals of many shapes and sizes – there are about 26000 different species. They include the familiar crabs, lobsters, shrimps, barnacles and woodlice but there are many others. Most crustaceans live in the sea or fresh water but woodlice live on land. They like damp places and they usually spend the day under stones or logs and come out at night.

The crabs and lobsters are the largest crustaceans. They have five pairs of legs including a pair of claws for tearing up their food and defending themselves. The largest crab is the giant spider crab of Japan which is 3·5 metres from claw to claw. The robber crab weighs as much as 2 kilograms. It spends most of its time on land and climbs trees. Hermit crabs are unusual because they have no shells of their own. Instead they carry empty seashells on their backs and retreat into them when disturbed.

There is an enormous variety of shrimps, prawns, water-fleas and other small crustaceans living in fresh and salt water. Many are active swimmers. Barnacles are small crustaceans which settle on rocks and are protected by their shells.

# Many-legged animals

Centipedes and millipedes are famous for their many legs. Centipedes have one pair of legs under each body segment and catch small animals with their poison claws. Millipedes, however, have two pairs of legs on each segment and eat plants.

# Fishes

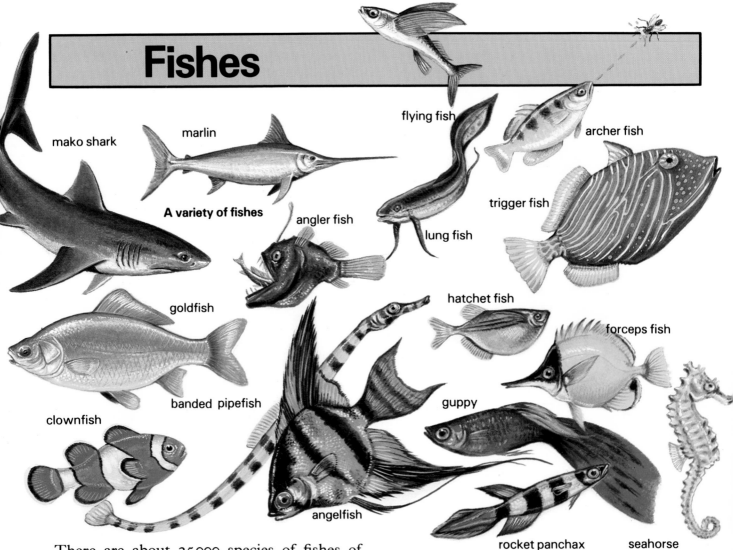

mako shark

marlin

flying fish

archer fish

**A variety of fishes**

angler fish

trigger fish

lung fish

goldfish

hatchet fish

forceps fish

banded pipefish

guppy

clownfish

angelfish

rocket panchax

seahorse

There are about 25 000 species of fishes of many different shapes and sizes. Fishes, like the birds, reptiles and mammals, are *vertebrates* – animals with backbones. All fishes live in water, although a few can come on to land for a short time. Some live in the sea and others live in fresh water.

## Breathing and Swimming

Fishes get their oxygen from the water and they use *gills* to breathe instead of having lungs as we do. They gulp water into the mouth and through a gill chamber on each side. The gills look like pink feathers and they take oxygen from the water, which then passes out through a slit behind the head. A few fishes can also get oxygen by gulping air. Fishes have nostrils but they are used only for smelling, and not for breathing.

Nearly all fishes swim by wriggling the rear part of the body and their tail fins from side to side. The other fins are used for balancing and steering. Other fishes have special ways of swimming. Rays swim by flapping their fins like wings and the seahorse swims upright and is pushed along by waving a little fin on its back.

A fish slips through the water easily because it has a smooth surface and a slender body with a pointed head. The smooth surface is made by a layer of shiny scales that overlap, like the tiles on a roof. These scales protect the fish's skin. The trunkfish has strong scales which fit together to make a strong box. The puffer fish is unusual because it has scales like spines and it blows itself up to make a prickly ball. Sometimes you can tell the age of a fish by counting the rings on one of its scales, like counting the rings on a tree trunk.

# Fishes with strange habits

Very deep parts of the ocean are always pitch dark. They are the home of very strange-looking fishes. Some have rows of lights on their bodies, which they use to find food or to recognize each other or perhaps to frighten enemies. The angler fish has a long spine which hangs over its mouth like a fishing rod. There is a light on the tip of the spine which attracts prey animals so that the angler fish can catch them.

A few fishes can come out of the water. The mudskipper lives in tropical seas and it comes up on to the beach to look for food. It carries a supply of water in its gill chambers to help it breathe, but it cannot stay out of water for long. The lungfishes have a kind of lung as well as gills. When the rivers they live in dry up, the lungfishes burrow into the mud and breathe with their lungs.

The flying fish can glide through the air for hundreds of metres. If it is chased by a hunting fish, it shoots out of the water and spreads its large fins like wings.

*Above: Mudskippers can survive out of water.*
*Below left: Pufferfishes blow up their bodies.*
*Below right: Rays have skeletons of gristle.*

# Boneless fishes

Sharks and rays have skeletons of gristle instead of bone and the scales covering their bodies are like tiny teeth. Most sharks are fast swimmers and hunt other fishes. The basking shark and whale shark are the world's largest fishes and grow to over 12 metres long. They eat only the tiny animals (see page 114) which float in the sea. These are strained out of the water as it passes through the gills.

# Amphibians and Reptiles

## Amphibians

Amphibians are animals which spend part of their lives on land and part in water. There are about 2400 species of frogs, toads, newts, and salamanders, together with other unfamiliar amphibians such as the legless caecilians, the olm and the mudpuppies. Most adult amphibians live on land, but their skins are not fully waterproof so they lose water from their bodies. Therefore they have to live in damp places. Some toads live in deserts but they survive by burrowing deep in the ground and storing water in their bodies. They also have more waterproof skins.

Tropical forests are the home of the tree frogs. They have long toes and fingers with pads at the tips to help grip. They are also very good at jumping, which helps them move from tree to tree. The flying frog of tropical Asia has huge webbed feet to help it to glide.

**Reproduction** Adult amphibians return to water to lay their eggs since the eggs and tadpoles would dry out on land. Some make use of small puddles or hollows in trees that gather water. The masses of eggs (spawn) hatch into *tadpoles*. Like fishes, tadpoles have gills and swim by wriggling their tails. Eventually they develop into adults with lungs and legs, and come on to the land. Some differ, however. The axolotl spends its life in water and never loses its gills. The greenhouse frog of America lays its eggs on moist earth and they hatch straight into tiny frogs.

The eggs are usually abandoned after they have been laid, but the male midwife toad wraps strings of spawn around his legs and the female Surinam toad carries her eggs on her back in little pits in her skin.

**Newts and salamanders** These look like lizards, but they have soft, moist skins. The largest is the Japanese giant salamander which measures 150 centimetres. Newts and salamanders keep their long tails when adult and many of them spend most of the summer in water.

**Life cycle of the newt**

adult newt – gills have disappeared

eggs laid in early spring

external gills

tadpole hatches after 1-2 weeks

back legs appear at 7-8 weeks

front legs appear at 3 weeks

A variety of amphibians and reptiles

bearded dragon

chameleon

fire salamander

green toad

sand lizard

# Reptiles

Reptiles (such as lizards, snakes and crocodiles) have fully waterproof skins, so they can live in dry places. Their eggs have tough, leathery shells so they can be laid on land.

**Lizards** There are 3000 species of lizards. Most are fast runners and the basilisk of South America can run across water. The chameleons are slow-moving, climbing lizards. They can change colour either to match their surroundings or to show that they are angry.

Geckoes are the expert climbers among lizards. Their toes have minute hooks which let them cling to smooth surfaces such as windows and ceilings. The flying dragon glides from tree to tree by stretching flaps of skin to act as wings.

**Snakes** These are legless reptiles and there are about 3000 species. They move by wriggling to push the body against the ground or by pushing with their scales.

Snakes eat animals by swallowing them whole. The egg-eating snake swallows birds' eggs and crushes them in its throat. Boas and pythons kill their prey by *constriction* – wrapping the body around the prey so it cannot breathe. Poisonous snakes inject venom into their prey through hollow teeth called fangs. The vipers and rattlesnakes have long fangs which fold back when not being used. Kraits, sea snakes, cobras and rattlesnakes are the most dangerous of the poisonous snakes.

**Crocodiles** These live near water and some live in the sea. The largest crocodiles grow up to 9 metres long. Alligators are a sort of crocodile. One kind lives in the United States of America, another in China. Caimans are like small alligators and live in South America. The gharial has a long slender snout and lives in India.

**Tortoises** They have a bony shell covered with horn. The shells of land tortoises are very heavy. Giant tortoises' shells can be 1 metre long and 200 kilograms in weight. Sea turtles are like tortoises with lighter, flat shells and their legs are flat flippers for swimming.

green tree boa

tortoise

gharial

crocodile

# Extinct Reptiles

Brachiosaurus

Brontosaurus

Allosaurus

Rhamphorhynchus

Diplodocus

The Age of Reptiles was the time when reptiles were the most important animals. It lasted from 260 million to 70 million years ago. There were many different kinds of reptiles, including tortoises and crocodiles like those alive today. Other kinds have completely died out but their fossils have been found in the ground. No one knows exactly why they died out.

## The 'terrible lizards'

The largest extinct reptiles are called dinosaurs, a word meaning 'terrible lizards'. *Brachiosaurus* was 24 metres long and must have weighed 80 tonnes, perhaps much more. This is equal to the weight of 10 elephants. Not all dinosaurs were huge – some were only the size of a chicken.

*Above: The dinosaurs were the most important animals for millions of years, but suddenly and mysteriously died out.*

**Walking on four legs** Dinosaurs like *Brachiosaurus* and *Diplodocus* walked on four legs and had long necks and tails. They walked slowly through the forests of ferns and cycads (see page 73). Their long necks let them munch soft leaves from the tops of the plants, in the same way that giraffes feed. *Stegasaurus* was smaller and measured only 7 metres long. Its back was protected with rows of triangular bony plates and its tail had two pairs of spikes which it used to attack its enemies. *Triceratops* was another armoured dinosaur. It looked like a rhinoceros with three horns and had a frill to protect its neck.

**Walking on two legs** Other dinosaurs stood on their back legs and had very small front legs. They looked rather like kangaroos. Their long tails helped to balance them when they ran. *Iguanodon* and the duck-billed dinosaurs, or hadrosaurs, were of this type and were plant-eaters. One kind had 3000 tiny teeth in its mouth for chewing tough food.

*Tyrannosaurus* was a meat-eater. It hunted smaller dinosaurs and killed them with its teeth which were 15 centimetres long.

# Giant sea reptiles

Several kinds of giant reptiles lived in the sea. The plesiosaurs swam with their flippers, like the present-day turtles. Some plesiosaurs had long necks and hunted fish and squid. Others, the pliosaurs, had short necks and large heads. They ate other reptiles.

The plesiosaurs may have come ashore to lay eggs but the ichthyosaurs could not come on land. They looked like dolphins and gave birth to live young in the sea.

## Studying fossils

Scientists learn how extinct animals lived by studying their fossils. They can tell what an animal ate by looking at the shape of its fossilized teeth. Sometimes they find the remains of a meal inside a fossil. A few fossils show the outlines of skin. The fossil below shows that the fish-like ichthyosaurs had a fin on the back and a tail fin. If just the bones had been fossilized, we would not have known this. Other ichthyosaur fossils have been found with tiny skeletons inside. So we know that they must have given birth to live young.

*Fossil ichthyosaur.*

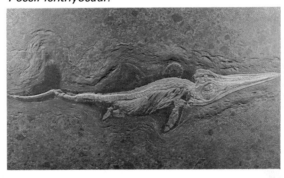

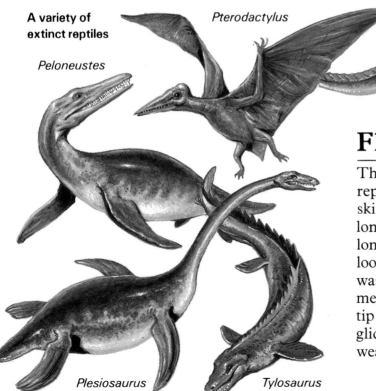

A variety of extinct reptiles

*Peloneustes*

*Pterodactylus*

*Nothosaurus*

*Plesiosaurus*

*Tylosaurus*

# Flying reptiles

The pterodactyls or pterosaurs were flying reptiles. Their wings were thin folds of leathery skin which stretched from their single, very long fingers to the hindlegs. Some kinds had a long tail but others had a very short tail and looked like bats. The smallest pterodactyl was the size of a sparrow but the largest measured 15·5 metres from wingtip to wingtip. The long wings were very good for gliding but the pterodactyls' muscles were too weak for them to fly well by flapping.

# How Birds Live

Birds are the only animals with feathers. There are about 8600 different species. The feathers keep them warm and they help the birds to fly. A feather is made of the same substance as our hair. There are two kinds of feather. *Down* is soft and fluffy. A baby bird is covered in down and the adult feathers grow over the down as the bird grows up. Adult feathers are very strong and light. They are made up of a central shaft and flat vane.

The birds' wings are the 'arms' and they do not have hands. They have to hold their food and build their nests with the beak, or bill. The beak is part of the jaws and has a horny covering. Birds do not have teeth so they cannot chew their food. You can tell what sort of food a bird eats by looking at its beak. Hawks and owls have hooked beaks for tearing flesh. Sparrows and finches have stout beaks for cracking seeds. Tits and robins have thin beaks for picking up insects.

## Flying

A bird flies by flapping its wings up and down. On the downstroke, the wings are pushed firmly down and back, so that the bird moves forwards and upwards. On the upstroke, the wings are raised and twisted so that they keep pushing the bird forward. The tail is used for steering and braking. The shape of a bird's wings shows how it flies. A swift has long, narrow wings for high-speed flight, and a pheasant has short but broad wings for taking-off almost vertically among trees. A humming-bird flaps its wings so fast that they can hardly be seen. It can hover and even fly backwards.

A bird needs strong muscles to fly. It has very large breast muscles for working its wings and a strong heart for pumping blood around the body. Its bones are light and also hollow to save weight. Its lungs have extra parts to increase the amount of oxygen it can get when breathing, so that it can produce more energy needed for flying.

## Nesting

All birds lay eggs. They are kept warm, or *incubated*, by the parents sitting on them. The eggs are usually kept in a nest of twigs and leaves, but the nest of some birds is only a small hollow in the ground. Kingfishers make burrows in the ground and woodpeckers dig holes in trees. The emperor penguin of the Antarctic has no nest. It carries its egg on its feet.

A nest of eggs is called a *clutch*. They hatch into a *brood* of chicks. Many baby birds stay in the nest until they can fly and their parents have to feed them. Others, like ducklings and chicks, can walk and find their own food only a few hours after they have hatched.

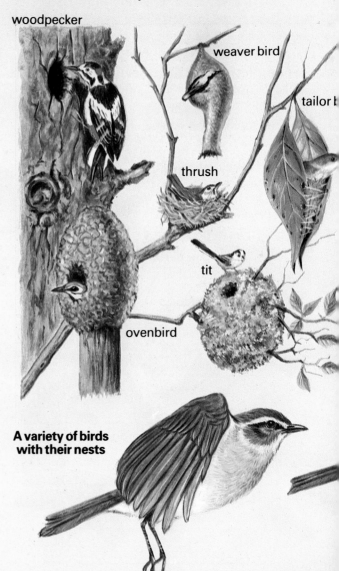

woodpecker

weaver bird

tailor b

thrush

tit

ovenbird

**A variety of birds with their nests**

sparrow

avocet

toucan

kestrel

teal

wagtail

**A variety of beaks and feet**

## Migration

Some birds travel long distances between the place where they nest in summer and the place where they spend the winter. The journey is called a migration.

Swallows come to Europe to nest in the summer, then fly to Africa for the winter. They cannot stay in Europe because the flying insects, which they eat, disappear in winter. So they migrate to a warm country where they will find plenty of food. When they migrate, birds find their way with the help of the sun and stars. The Arctic tern nests in the Arctic and spends the winter in the Antarctic, so it travels more than 30 000 kilometres in a year.

gull

heron

falcon

crow

**Two kinds of feathers with a close up of a flight feather**

**Migration route of swallows**

down feather

flight feather

A wood warbler, showing how a bird moves its wings when flying

# Different Kinds of Birds

## Flightless birds

Some birds have lost the ability to fly. The ostrich is the largest living bird. It has long legs and can run at over 50 kilometres per hour. Its wings are very small but help to steer the ostrich when it is running fast. Ostriches live on the plains of Africa and eat mainly plants. The rheas of South America and cassowaries and emu of Australia are rather like the ostrich.

The kiwi of New Zealand is about the size of a chicken and its wings are so small that they are hidden under the feathers. It is unusual amongst birds because it has a very good sense of smell which it uses to find the worms it eats. Penguins are flightless birds which spend most of their lives at sea. Their wings have become flippers for swimming.

*An ostrich, which has long, powerful legs enabling it to run fast.*

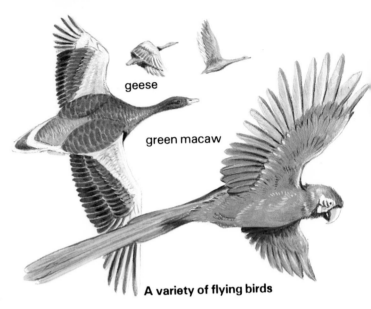

geese

green macaw

**A variety of flying birds**

## Flying birds

**Ducks, geese and swans** These birds are sometimes called wildfowl or waterfowl. They have webbed feet for swimming and water-proof feathers. Some, like the eider and shelduck, live in the sea, but most kinds live in rivers, ponds and lakes. Swans and ducks get most of their food from the water but geese feed on land. Swans use their long necks to reach below the surface and some of the ducks dive for their food.

**Seabirds** Many seabirds spend most of their lives far out to sea and come back to the land only to nest. Albatrosses have long, narrow wings and they can glide over the sea for many kilometres without flapping their wings. They live in the Pacific Ocean and the Antarctic. The auks, such as the guillemot, puffin and razorbill, swim underwater using their wings but cormorants and shags swim underwater using their feet. Gannets dive for fish from a great height. The gulls are probably the best-known seabirds. They usually live near the shore but some nest inland.

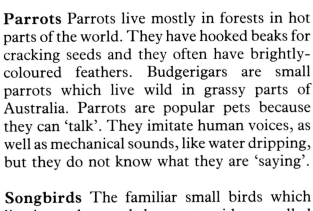

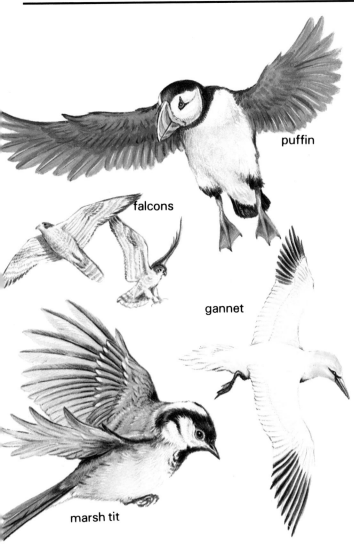

puffin

falcons

gannet

marsh tit

**Parrots** Parrots live mostly in forests in hot parts of the world. They have hooked beaks for cracking seeds and they often have brightly-coloured feathers. Budgerigars are small parrots which live wild in grassy parts of Australia. Parrots are popular pets because they can 'talk'. They imitate human voices, as well as mechanical sounds, like water dripping, but they do not know what they are 'saying'.

**Songbirds** The familiar small birds which live in gardens and the countryside are called songbirds. There are about 5000 species around the world. Robins, thrushes, tits, finches and wrens are all songbirds.

Not all songbirds sing well. Sparrows and crows are songbirds with poor voices. Usually only male birds sing. The song drives other males away but attracts females.

**Hunting birds** The eagles, hawks and falcons are called *birds of prey*. They hunt living animals and kill them with their long claws, or *talons*, and sharp, hooked beaks.

The falcons have narrow, pointed wings and fly very fast. The peregrine can dive at over 160 kilometres per hour, but the kestrel hovers in one place. The eagles and hawks have broad wings. Some of them glide effortlessly in search of food. Others, like the sparrowhawk, chase among the trees. The osprey is a hawk which specializes in catching fish.

The vultures are birds of prey which eat dead animals. The owls are a group of birds which hunt mainly at night. They fly noise-lessly and have very good hearing and eyesight for finding their prey in the dark.

## Cuckoos

There are 127 kinds of cuckoos in the world and 47 kinds have the strange habit of getting other birds to rear their young. They lay their eggs in the nests of smaller birds and then leave them. When the young cuckoo hatches, it throws the other eggs out of the nest. The birds that laid these eggs now look after the cuckoo and so they are called foster parents. They feed the cuckoo until it has grown larger than them and is too big to fit in the nest.

*Young cuckoo removing eggs from a reed warbler's nest.*

# Mammals

*A pony with her foal.*

Mammals are animals with fur or hair. There are about 5000 species. Both birds and mammals are '*warm-blooded*'. This means that the temperature of their bodies stays the same all the time. This is because their fur or feathers and the way their bodies work help to keep them warm. Except in very hot places, the body temperature is higher than the surroundings. A high body temperature helps the muscles and other parts of the body to work well. All the other kinds of animals, such as reptiles and amphibians, are *cold-blooded*. They have no way of controlling their body temperature unless they can bask in the sun. So they are always at about the same temperature as that of their surroundings.

## Reproduction

Nearly every mammal gives birth to live babies. They grow inside their mother's body and receive nourishment through her blood. Some baby mammals, like some baby birds, are blind and helpless when they are born. They are kept in a snug nest and their mother keeps them warm. Puppies and kittens are like this. Other babies, like foals and calves, are born in the open and can walk and run when they are only a few hours old.

All baby mammals are fed on milk made in their mother's body until they are old enough to eat solid food. When they can feed themselves, they are said to be *weaned*. Only mammals feed their babies in this way.

# Monotremes and marsupials

**Monotremes** Two kinds of mammals lay eggs, like the reptiles from which the mammals have evolved. One is the platypus of Australia which is a strange-looking animal with a flat, horny beak like a duck. It lives in rivers and lakes where it catches insects and other small animals. The other egg-laying mammal is the echidna, or spiny anteater, which looks rather like a hedgehog and lives in Australia and New Guinea. It eats insects, which it catches with its long, sticky tongue.

**Marsupials** There are many different kinds of marsupials. Millions of years ago, they lived all over the world but now most marsupials live only in Australia and New Guinea. A few kinds live in North and South America.

The kangaroos and their other marsupial relatives keep their babies in a pouch on the mother's body. A baby kangaroo is tiny. A 2-metre red kangaroo has a baby only 2 centimetres long. When it is born, it crawls through its mother's fur and into her pouch.

It stays there and feeds on her milk until it is much larger.

The largest kangaroos are the red and the grey kangaroos. They all move by hopping on their hindlegs and they can jump over 3-metre high fences. There is no particular difference between kangaroos and wallabies, but smaller kinds are generally called wallabies. The tree kangaroos are good climbers and live in trees.

The koala is another well-known marsupial and looks like a friendly bear. It is also a good climber and eats only the leaves of eucalyptus, or gum, trees. The wombat looks rather like a badger and lives in burrows. There are also many small marsupials which are mouse-sized and there are meat-eating marsupials like the Tasmanian devil and the dasyures.

The most famous American marsupial is the opossum. It is the only kind which lives in North America. When it is frightened, it pretends to be dead. Its body goes limp and its eyes close. When the danger has passed it runs away. The yapok or water opossum is the only marsupial which spends much of its life in water. It has webbed feet, and rests and breeds in burrows in river banks. The mouth of its pouch closes so that the babies do not drown.

echidna

koala

kangaroo

wombat

**A variety of monotremes and marsupials**

platypus

common opossum

striped opossum

# Plant-eating Mammals

## Rodents

The rodents are gnawing mammals. They have two pairs of long teeth, like chisels, one each in the front of the upper and lower jaws. These teeth, called *incisors*, grow continuously so they never wear down despite continually gnawing hard food.

There are more kinds of rodents than any other sort of mammal. They are found all over the world and in many different places. The brown rat, black rat and house mouse live in buildings. Voles and lemmings are like mice but they have small ears and round heads. They usually live in burrows in the ground. Many squirrels, however, live in trees and have bushy tails to help them balance, but gophers, marmots and chipmunks are squirrels which live on the ground.

*Below: A grey squirrel uses its sharp incisor teeth to open the hard shell of a nut.*

## Dam builders

The beaver is a rodent and it is the greatest engineer in the animal world. It cuts down trees with its sharp teeth to build dams across the river. A deep pool forms behind the dam and the beaver builds a lodge of mud and sticks in the middle. This means that the beaver has a very safe place to live in.

As well as using trees for building, the beaver eats the bark of the twigs.

*A beaver lodge.*

## Rabbits and hares

These are also gnawing animals but they are different from rodents because they have two pairs of incisor teeth in each jaw. Rabbits and hares have long ears and are good runners. Baby rabbits are born in a burrow. They are naked and helpless at first. Baby hares are born in a nest on top of the ground. They have a coat of fur and soon leave the nest.

## Hoofed mammals

A hoof is a large toenail, so hoofed mammals are walking on tiptoe. There are two sorts of hoofed mammal. The even-toed or cloven-hoofed mammals have a pair of hoofs on each foot. Cattle, sheep, pigs and deer are cloven-hoofed. The odd-toed mammals have one or three toes on each foot. Horses and zebras have a single toe; rhinoceroses and tapirs have three toes.

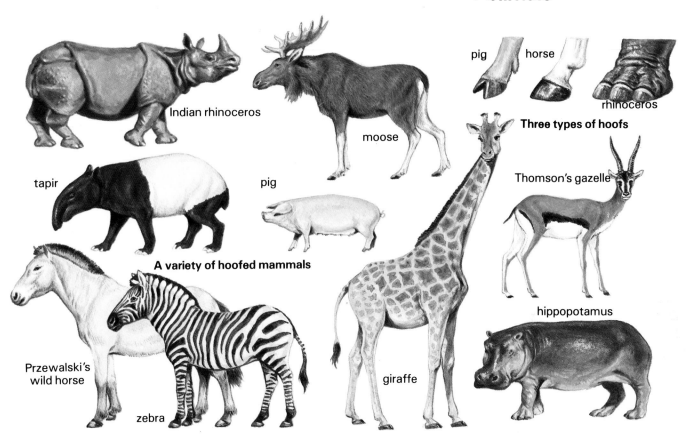

Indian rhinoceros

moose

pig    horse

rhinoceros

**Three types of hoofs**

tapir

pig

Thomson's gazelle

**A variety of hoofed mammals**

Przewalski's wild horse

zebra

giraffe

hippopotamus

**Even-toed mammals** The 40 species of deer live mainly in woods. Most adult males have a pair of antlers. These are made of bone. Each year the antlers are shed and a new pair are grown. Both sexes of reindeer and caribou wear antlers. The moose or elk is the largest deer and has enormous antlers.

Antelopes look like deer but they have horns instead of antlers. Most antelopes live in Africa but the blackbuck lives in India and the saiga lives in Central Asia. Oryx live in deserts, but dik-diks and duikers live in the forests. Wildebeests (or gnus), elands and gazelles live on the open, grassy plains. They live in huge herds and rely on their speed to escape from enemies.

The giraffe is nearly 6 metres tall and can feed on leaves near the tops of trees. The much bulkier hippopotamus lives in the water and comes out at night to eat grass. It can swim but it also walks on the bottom of lakes and rivers.

**Odd-toed mammals** Horses are nearly extinct in the wild. There are a few wild relatives of the domestic horse alive in Mongolia and some of their other relatives, the asses, in Africa and Asia. Asses are wild kinds of donkey. The zebras are the only wild horses that are not rare.

There are five species of rhinoceros (see also page 126). The black and the white rhinoceroses live in Africa and have two horns. The Sumatran rhinoceros also has two horns but the other Asian rhinoceroses – the Indian and the Javan rhinoceroses – have a single horn.

# Elephants

The elephants are the largest living land animals. The African elephant has larger ears and tusks than the Asian elephant. The tusks are very large teeth. The trunk is a very long nose and it is used for picking things up.

# Flesh-eating Mammals

Flesh-eating mammals are called carnivores. They have long teeth, called fangs, for holding and tearing the flesh of their prey. The cheek-teeth are used for slicing meat and cracking bones.

## Cats

There are about 40 species of wild cats. Most are about the size of our pet cats, which are descended from one kind of African wild cat. The lion is the only truly sociable cat. It lives in groups called *prides*. Each pride consists of several females, with their cubs, and one or two males. They hunt together, usually at night.

Lions live in Africa and India but the tiger lives only in Asia. It is found in mountains and forests. The leopard of Africa and Asia is distinguished from the jaguar of South America by the pattern of its spots. The African cheetah is the fastest running animal. It hunts gazelles and reaches speeds of up to 120 kilometres per hour.

## Dogs

All the breeds of domestic dog have come from the wolf. Wolves live in small groups called *packs*, in North America, Europe and Asia. By hunting together wolves can kill big animals like caribou. The coyote is a small relative of the wolf and lives in North America. The jackals of Africa and Asia are small wild dogs which live in ones or twos. They hunt mice and other small animals, and often eat the left-overs from large carnivores' meals.

The red fox is very common in America, Europe and Asia and it often lives in towns. In the cold north, the Arctic fox turns white in winter. Its thick fur helps it to survive the cold weather. The fennec is a small fox with huge ears which lives in deserts. The ears act as radiators and help the fennec to keep cool.

*Below: A cheetah with its prey, which it caught after a furious sprint. It will now eat a huge meal, then go to sleep.*

# Other meat-eaters

Although bears are the largest carnivores, most of them do not hunt large prey. They eat mice, fish, insects and berries. Small bears, like the black bear, are good tree climbers but the large brown and the grizzly bears stay on the ground. The polar bear lives among ice and snow in the Arctic, where it hunts seals.

The hyaenas of Africa and Asia are powerful animals with big jaws for crushing bones. They live in packs and eat the remains of other carnivores' meals, but the spotted hyaena also hunts its own prey. The spotted hyaena is sometimes called the laughing hyaena because it makes a noise like people laughing and shouting.

Mongooses and civets look rather like stoats and they are very good hunters. The Indian mongoose is famous for killing snakes, but many kinds are fond of fruit.

A variety of flesh-eating mammals

# The weasel family

There are many members of the weasel family. The weasels and stoats are slender, agile carnivores. They are expert hunters and can kill animals larger than themselves. In northern countries they turn white in winter. A white stoat is called an ermine. The polecats, minks and martens are similar animals, but martens are tree climbers and the minks are swimmers. The otters are also expert at swimming. They swim with their webbed feet and by beating their strong tail up and down. Most otters live by lakes and rivers but the sea otter lives in the sea.

Badgers look like small bears. They eat worms and insects, but their relative the wolverine of the Arctic is strong enough to kill reindeer. The skunks of America are famous for making a terrible smell which drives away enemies.

## A vegetarian bear

The giant panda is an unusual sort of bear. It is very rare and lives only in forests in one part of China. Its favourite food is young bamboo shoots and it has a sort of extra thumb on each front paw to help hold the bamboo while it is eating. Wild giant pandas are hardly ever seen and no one knows why they are black and white.

# Sea Mammals

Four kinds of mammals live in the sea. The sea otter lives along the shores of western North America and very rarely comes on land. The seals spend most of their lives at sea but they must come ashore to breed. The whales and sea cows spend their whole lives in the water, breeding there too.

## Whales

The whales include the largest animals alive today. Blue whales grow to over 30 metres long and weigh over 100 tonnes. The body of a whale is beautifully streamlined (smooth and curved) so that it can move easily through the water. It swims by beating its tail up and down. The tail has two broad *flukes* which act as paddles. Whales have no fur and they are kept warm by a thick layer of fat, called *blubber*, under the skin. A whale's nostrils, called the *blowholes* are on top of its head. As the whale breathes out, or 'blows', a puff of vapour appears. This is rather like the way your breath 'steams' on a cold day. There are two main sorts of whales: the whalebone whales and the toothed whales.

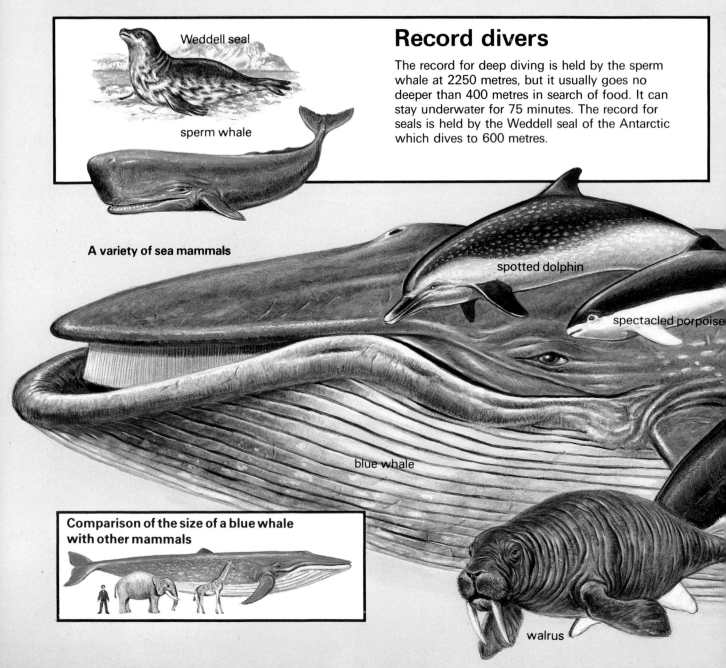

Weddell seal

sperm whale

## Record divers

The record for deep diving is held by the sperm whale at 2250 metres, but it usually goes no deeper than 400 metres in search of food. It can stay underwater for 75 minutes. The record for seals is held by the Weddell seal of the Antarctic which dives to 600 metres.

**A variety of sea mammals**

spotted dolphin

spectacled porpoise

blue whale

**Comparison of the size of a blue whale with other mammals**

walrus

**Whalebone whales** The whalebone whales have two rows of bristly plates of whalebone, or baleen, which hang like curtains on each side of the mouth. The whalebone plates are used to strain small shrimp-like animals and fishes from the water. The whale takes a gulp of water or swims with its mouth open. The water pours out through the plates and leaves the animals in the whale's mouth. The largest whales, such as the blue whale, are whalebone whales.

**Toothed whales** The toothed whales eat fishes and squid. Most kinds have rows of teeth to help grasp their slippery prey. The sperm whale is the largest toothed whale. The narwhal has a long tusk, but no one knows its purpose.

Dolphins and porpoises are small, toothed whales. There are many kinds of dolphins and some can swim at more than 50 kilometres per hour. The killer whale is a large dolphin which eats seals as well as fish.

## Seals

The seals evolved from carnivores which lived on land, and they still have to come out of the water to have their babies, called pups. Seals living in the Arctic and Antarctic give birth to their pups on the pack ice. A few seals live in lakes and rivers.

There are three types of seals. The true seals swim with their hind flippers. When they are on land they crawl on their bellies. The elephant seal is the largest seal. It weighs up to 3500 kilograms.

The second type of seal are the eared seals which swim with their front flippers. On land, they can turn their hind flippers forwards, lift their bodies off the ground and gallop along. The popular circus and zoo sealion is an eared seal. It comes from California.

The walrus is the third type of seal and it lives in the Arctic. It has long ivory tusks which it uses for digging shellfish out of the mud.

## Sea cows

The dugong of the Indian Ocean and the manatee of the Atlantic are peaceful animals which live near the shore, where they eat sea plants. The manatee also swims up rivers.

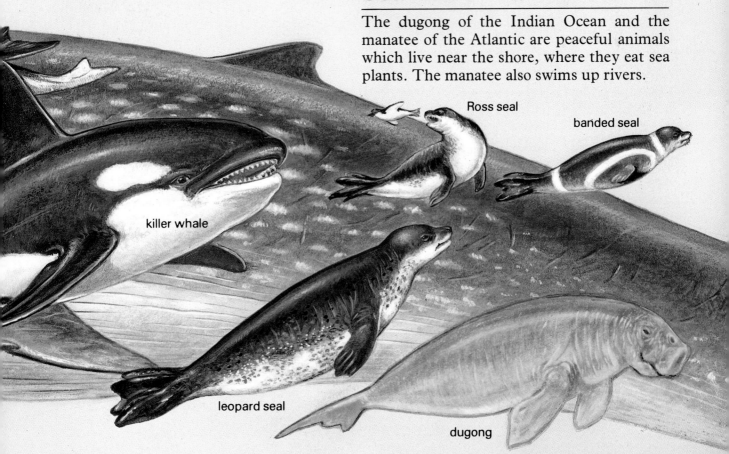

killer whale · Ross seal · banded seal · leopard seal · dugong

# Unusual Mammals

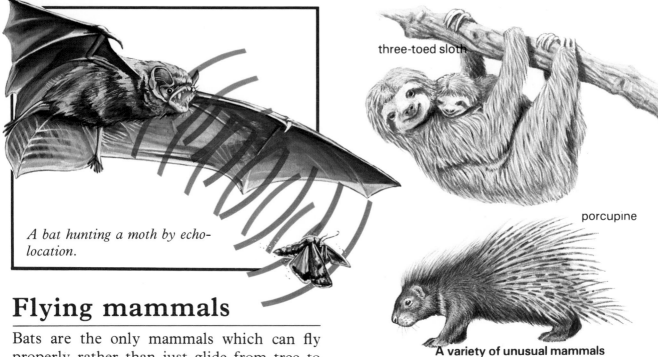

three-toed sloth

porcupine

*A bat hunting a moth by echo-location.*

A variety of unusual mammals

## Flying mammals

Bats are the only mammals which can fly properly rather than just glide from tree to tree. All bats fly at night and most of them hunt for flying insects, such as flies and moths. They find their prey by *echo-location*. As it flies, a bat squeaks continuously, but the sound is too high-pitched for us to hear. The bat listens for echoes of its squeaks as they bounce off an insect showing its position.

In tropical countries, the fruit bats feed on nectar and ripe fruit. They do not use echo-location but instead they have very large eyes to see in dim light. The largest fruit bat has a wingspan of 1·5 metres. The vampire bat of South America drinks the blood of other animals, especially farm animals, and a few bats catch fish, birds and even other bats.

Several mammals seem to fly from tree to tree, but they are not proper fliers because they do not have wings which they can flap. Flying squirrels, flying phalangers and the flying lemur have wings of thin skin stretched along their sides between their front and back legs, like a kite. They can only glide from tree to tree, but they can change direction in mid-air. The flying lemur can glide for 135 metres between trees.

## Sloths, anteaters and armadillos

These mammals come from Central and South America. Only the nine-banded armadillo has spread to North America.

**Sloths** Sloths spend their lives upside down in the forests of Central and South America. They hang by their hooked claws and walk slowly along the branches, but they spend most of their time resting. If a sloth comes down to the ground, it cannot stand properly and has to drag itself along on its belly.

**Anteaters** The anteaters of South America have long sticky tongues which they use for wiping up ants and termites, after they have torn open the nests with their strong claws.

**Armadillos** The 21 species of armadillo are protected by rows of small bones set in their heads and backs. Some armadillos have flexible armour so that they can roll up for added protection.

# More anteating mammals

The African aardvark breaks open termite nests with its strong claws and pulls out the termites with its long tongue. The pangolins of Africa and Asia are anteating mammals which look like enormous pinecones. Their bodies are covered with horny scales and pangolins protect themselves by rolling up.

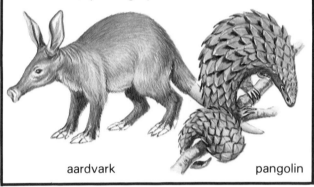

aardvark                    pangolin

giant anteater

hedgehog

giant armadillo

armadillo rolled up        nine-banded armadillo

# Spiny mammals

Hedgehogs have a coat of sharp spines and they roll into a prickly ball when frightened. Baby hedgehogs are naked when they are born and the spines poke through the skin when they are a few days old.

Porcupines have longer spines than hedgehogs. Those of the American porcupines are hidden under the long fur. They are barbed so that they stick in an enemy's skin and cannot be removed. The porcupines of Africa and Asia have very long spines. When these porcupines are attacked, they rattle their spines and push them into the attacker's skin.

# Burrowing mammals

Moles spend their lives underground. They dig a network of tunnels with their powerful, spade-shaped front paws and push the earth to the surface, to make 'molehills'. When the tunnels have been finished, the moles run along them to catch worms which have fallen in.

Mole-rats are rodents which dig burrows with their long incisor teeth. They eat the roots of plants.

*Below: A mole shows the huge, spade-shaped paws which it uses for digging.*

# Monkeys, Apes and Man

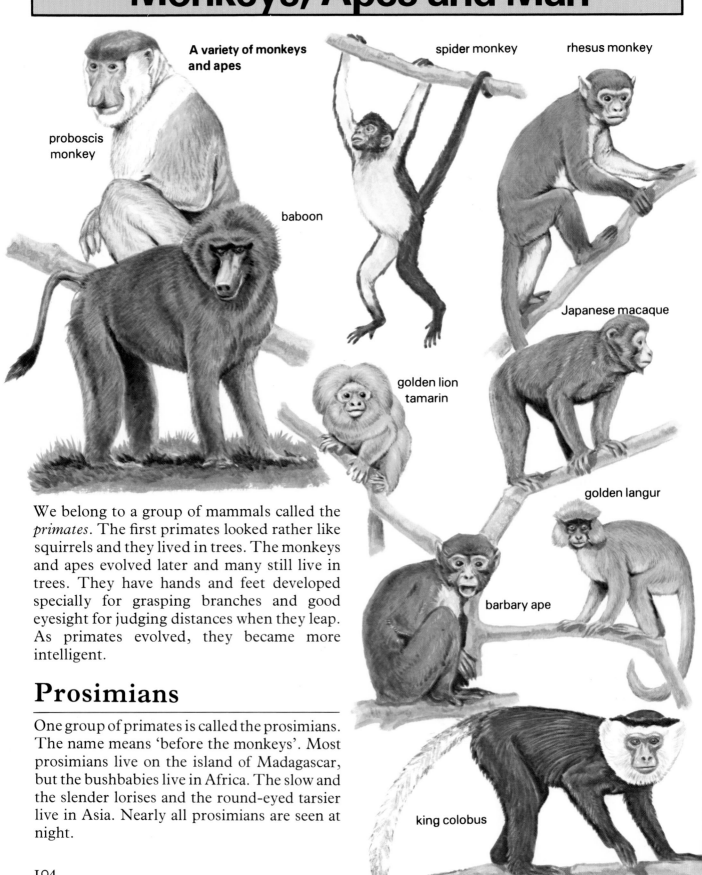

A variety of monkeys and apes

proboscis monkey

spider monkey

rhesus monkey

baboon

golden lion tamarin

Japanese macaque

golden langur

barbary ape

king colobus

We belong to a group of mammals called the *primates*. The first primates looked rather like squirrels and they lived in trees. The monkeys and apes evolved later and many still live in trees. They have hands and feet developed specially for grasping branches and good eyesight for judging distances when they leap. As primates evolved, they became more intelligent.

## Prosimians

One group of primates is called the prosimians. The name means 'before the monkeys'. Most prosimians live on the island of Madagascar, but the bushbabies live in Africa. The slow and the slender lorises and the round-eyed tarsier live in Asia. Nearly all prosimians are seen at night.

douroucouli

howler monkey

# Monkeys and apes

The monkeys and apes are called anthropoids, which means 'man-like' animals. There are many kinds of monkeys living in the warm regions of the world. In South America, there are woolly monkeys and spider monkeys which hang from branches by their tails. There are also the tiny marmosets, and the douroucouli which is the only monkey to come out at night.

Families of howler monkeys hoot loudly to each other. Adult howler monkeys hold on to each other and make a living bridge so that young monkeys can cross from tree to tree.

The langur and colobus monkeys live in Asia and Africa and eat leaves. The proboscis monkey is a langur with an enormous nose. In Asia, langurs are sacred in the Hindu religion and they wander undisturbed around temples.

The rhesus monkey is a macaque which is used in medical research. The Japanese macaque lives in places where it snows in winter. The Barbary ape is a macaque which lives in Gibraltar. It is the only monkey living in Europe.

Baboons are large monkeys which are found in open country. They live in large groups called *troops*. The males have large teeth and can defend the troop against attacks by leopards.

## Man's ancestors

The ancestors of Man were apes that lived in the trees. Then they left the trees and lived in open country, as do the baboons. They started to walk on two legs, which other apes can do for only a short distance. This means that the hands were free for carrying things. The apes' hands had developed specially for swinging in the trees, but they could now be used for many tasks. The long fingers and thumb, which are so different from an animal paw, could be used for holding tools and weapons. Good eyesight was useful for life in the trees. We also need good eyesight for doing difficult jobs with our hands.

Intelligence is the most important difference between Man and the apes. Humans are much more intelligent and no other animal has learned to use fire or to speak with a proper language.

**The evolution of Man**

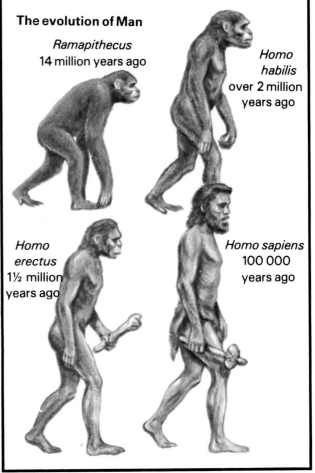

*Ramapithecus*
14 million years ago

*Homo habilis*
over 2 million years ago

*Homo erectus*
1½ million years ago

*Homo sapiens*
100 000 years ago

# Domestic Mammals

*Horses, dogs and cattle have their uses.*

Our lives would be very different without domestic animals. Our ancestors tamed them and kept them for food, instead of hunting them. Other animals were used for carrying loads or for riding. Animals were first domesticated 10000 years ago. They have been bred for special purposes and they often do not look like their wild ancestors.

## Dogs

The wolf (see page 98) is the ancestor of dogs. The first domestic dogs probably helped to hunt other animals. Later, they were used to guard flocks of sheep against wild animals. The Alsatian is such a guard dog. The husky is a dog used for pulling sledges. Nowadays, dogs are used to guide blind people and to search for lost objects, as well as helping in hunting and guarding.

## Horses

At one time horses were very important because they were the main form of transport. Large horses were used for pulling carts and ploughs, or for carrying knights in armour.

Ponies are small horses. The Falabella pony is only 76 centimetres tall. In some parts of the world, donkeys are more important than horses, perhaps because they are tougher. A mule is the offspring of a horse and a donkey and combines sure-footedness, patience and hardiness.

## Cattle

Farm cattle are descended from a wild animal called the aurochs. It lived in the forests of Europe and Asia but it died out in 1627. The zebu of Africa and Asia is another kind of domestic cattle and has a hump on its shoulders. It survives well in hot climates.

Cattle are sometimes used for pulling carts and ploughs, but there are now two main uses. Dairy cattle are kept for their milk. Some cows give 13 000 litres of milk in a year. Beef cattle are kept for their meat.

# Sheep

The fur of most mammals is made up of two kinds of hair: long hairs and short, soft underfur. The underfur is usually hidden under the long hairs, but sheep's wool is extra-long underfur. The Merino sheep has unusually fine wool.

Some sheep are kept for their milk, which is made into cheese. Their meat is also important.

# Goats

Goats often look very much like sheep but they have shorter hair and longer legs. The male goat, or *billy*, has a beard. Goats are kept for their milk, meat and skins. They are most often found in hot, dry countries. They can eat almost anything and will even climb trees to eat the leaves. In some places goats have turned forests into deserts by eating all the plants.

*Goats sometimes climb trees so that they can get at the highest leaves.*

*Shearing a sheep. Wool is extra long underfur.*

# Pigs

Domestic pigs come from both the European wild boar and the Chinese wild pig. Pigs are bred mainly for their meat and fat. Their skins are also used for leather and their bristles are made into brushes. Pigs are often popular because they are easy to keep. They eat all sorts of scraps and they can find their own food if they are left to run around in the country.

# Other mammals

Several other mammals have been domesticated, in various parts of the world, for carrying loads. Indians use elephants, the Tibetans use yaks, and reindeer are used by the Lapps of the Arctic for pulling sledges. Camels carry people and loads in deserts. They are also used for ploughing. The llama of South America is a relative of the camel. It is used for carrying loads and for providing meat and wool.

# The Workings of Nature

## Food chains

Energy for life comes from the Sun. Plants use this energy to make their own food by photosynthesis (see page 67). Some animals eat plants and they are called *herbivores*, or plant-eaters. Other animals eat the herbivores. They are *carnivores*, or meat-eaters. There are other animals which eat dead animals and plants. They are called *scavengers*. A rabbit is an example of a herbivore because it eats grass and flowers. The fox which eats the rabbit is a carnivore. If you find a dead rabbit, you may notice small beetles and maggots on it. These are scavengers eating the remains of the body. Vultures are also scavengers which eat the remains of prey left by lions and other carnivores.

The way that energy is passed from plant to herbivore, and then to carnivore and scavenger is called a *food chain*. Sometimes one kind of carnivore eats another, so the food chain is longer. In a lake, for example, the plants at the bottom of the chain are tiny algae which are eaten by water-fleas and water insects. These animals are eaten by small fishes, such as sticklebacks. The stickleback, a carnivore, is eaten by a larger carnivore, the pike. Sometimes pike are eaten by otters.

*Above: Vultures eating another animal's left-over prey.*

**Two examples of a food chain**

goshawk

Sun

fox

algae

stickleback

water insects

rabbit

# The balance of nature

There are always more animals at the bottom of the food chain than at the top. There are, for example, more rabbits than foxes and more sticklebacks than pike. During its lifetime, a fox or pike needs to eat many animals. If the food animal (called prey) becomes scarce, the animals that eat it (the predators) starve and die. At another time there may be too many predators and they kill off all their prey. Usually there is the right number of prey and predators. This is called the balance of nature.

A pair of robins lays about 10 eggs each summer. If 10 baby robins grew up and had their own families, our gardens would become crowded with robins. But some of these babies die in cold weather or because they are injured. Their bodies are eaten by scavengers. Other robins are eaten by predators. Some will move away to a new area. Just enough robins survive in one place for their numbers to stay the same. This is a balance because there are not too many robins, eating too much food, nor too few to support the predators.

## Omnivores

Some animals eat both plants and animals. They are called *omnivores*. Humans are omnivores because we eat plant food, such as bread, rice and vegetables, and may also eat animal food, such as meat and fish. This means that our food chain is more complicated. Farmers may plant a field with crops like wheat or potatoes, or they may let grass grow. Cattle and sheep eat that grass and then we 'prey' on them.

# Ecology

The study of the way that animals and plants depend on each other is called *ecology*. A person who studies ecology is called an ecologist. One ecologist may study an animal to find out what it eats and what preys on it. Another ecologist may look at a place, such as a pond, a wood or a desert, to see what animals and plants live there, and why they live there. For instance, animals and plants in deserts have to be able to survive very hot and dry weather. Each place, called a *habitat*, is the home of particular kinds of animals and plants, which can live in those particular conditions. A tropical forest is very different from a desert and it has different plants and animals.

pike

otter

Sun

grass and flowers

# Deserts

Deserts are places where less than 25 centimetres of rain falls each year. Parts of some deserts get no rain for years. Then there may be a storm and a large amount of rain falls in a short time. Most deserts are very hot, as well as dry, but there are cold deserts. The Gobi desert in Asia, and the Arctic and Antarctic are cold deserts. Even in hot deserts, it can get cold at night. Deserts are not all sand. There may be large areas of flat rocks and gravel.

## The desert in bloom

Desert animals and plants must cope with hot sun and very little water. Some plants, such as cacti, store water and grow long roots to use the small amount of moisture in the soil (see also page 78). Other plants survive dry periods as seeds. When it rains, the seeds sprout very quickly and the plants grow before the soil dries up again.

*Below: The fennec fox has huge ears which act as radiators to lose heat.*

## Keeping cool

Small desert animals escape the fierce heat by hiding during the day. They crawl under stones or burrow into the soil, and come out to feed at night. Some mammals and birds do not burrow but they sit in the shade of plants and rocks. The jack rabbit of America and the fennec fox of Africa have enormous ears. The ears act as radiators for losing heat.

Large animals, like camels, cannot hide from the sun. Their coats of thick hair help to protect them from the sun. They have to sweat to keep cool, but these desert animals can bear much higher temperatures than other animals before they get uncomfortable and have to sweat.

*Below: Some of the animals that live in American deserts.*

gila monster (lizard)

scorpion

beetle

# Finding water

Carnivores such as scorpions, snakes and foxes, get enough water from the blood of their prey, but herbivores have to live with very little water. Whenever possible they eat succulent plants, like cacti, or they eat leaves which have been moistened with dew. The addax, a kind of antelope, travels long distances in search of fresh plants. It gets all its water from its food.

The deserts are the home of many kinds of rodents. They include gerbils and the jerboas. Jerboas look like mouse-sized kangaroos. They have long back legs and move by jumping. These animals live on seeds and they never need to drink. There is a little water even in dry seeds, and they also breathe the moist air in their burrows at night.

The sandgrouse nests a long distance from water. It flies to a pool every day and soaks its feathers with water. When it returns, its chicks suck the water from the feathers.

# Moving across the desert

Camels and addax have broad feet so that they can walk easily on soft sand without sinking. Some lizards and insects have fringes on their feet for the same purpose. The sidewinder is a snake which gets its name from the way it crawls sideways over the sand so that it can get a proper grip. Other lizards and beetles do the opposite. They burrow through the sand, as if they are swimming.

*Below: The camel and addax are desert specialists.*

camel

addax

jack rabbit

road runner

rattlesnake

kangaroo rat

JOHN GREEN

# Polar Regions and Mountains

The polar regions surround the North and South Poles. They are very cold because the Sun sets at the beginning of the winter and does not rise again until spring. At the exact poles, there is a six month period of darkness followed by a six month period of light. It becomes extremely cold in winter and it does not get much warmer in summer because the Sun does not heat up the ground enough to melt all the ice and snow.

*Polar animals, like the Weddell seal and her pup, below, and the polar bear family, bottom, are often unafraid of people.*

Arctic hare

Norwegian lemming

snowy owl

## The Arctic

The Arctic region consists of the Arctic Ocean surrounded by the land of America, Europe and Asia. The Arctic Ocean is the home of walruses and seals which live among the ice floes. Polar bears also live there and, although they are strong swimmers, they can only catch seals when they come out of the water on to the ice.

The land thaws out in summer and is full of life. Plants come into flower and insects appear in swarms.

Musk-oxen, Arctic hares and foxes spend their whole lives in the Arctic. They lead a very hard life in winter. The musk-oxen and hares scrape away the snow to find food. Lemmings, which are rodents rather like voles, live a snug existence in tunnels under the snow. Foxes and lemmings turn white in winter. Musk-oxen have very thick coats of wool and hair to keep them warm. When they are attacked by wolves, they huddle together for protection.

Ducks, geese, snow buntings and other birds migrate north to the Arctic in summer to feed on the plants and insects. They nest and rear their young quickly then fly south before winter starts again.

A variety of animals that live in polar regions and mountains

snow leopard

musk oxen

Arctic fox

mouflon

emperor penguin

ibex

*Below: Mountain goats are surefooted climbers.*

# The Antarctic

The Antarctic region is a continent, Antarctica, surrounded by the Southern Ocean. The continent is covered with a sheet of ice hundreds of metres thick. Nothing can live there except around the coasts where the snow melts in summer. The rocks are bare except for patches of lichens and moss. A few insects and other invertebrates live among them.

The sea surrounding Antarctica is the home of millions of seals and penguins. Whales migrate to the Southern Ocean for the summer. Most whales eat a shrimp called krill which lives in large swarms.

Penguins are flightless birds and they spend most of their lives in the sea. They return to land every summer to nest. The emperor penguin is unusual because it breeds on the frozen sea and carries its egg on its feet. The egg is laid in winter when it is extremely cold.

# Mountains

If you climb a mountain you will find it gets colder as you get higher. The tops of high mountains are covered with snow and ice. On the way up, the plants and animals change in the same way as if you were walking towards the poles. The trees disappear and only tough flowers, lichens and mosses survive.

Mountain animals have to withstand very cold weather. The snow leopard has thick fur and it climbs high into the mountains in search of prey. Many mountain animals belong to the cloven-hoofed group (see page 96). For example, the chamois, ibex and mountain goats jump agilely around the rocks.

113

# The Seas

Seawater covers nearly three-quarters of the Earth's surface. It is divided into five large oceans: Atlantic, Pacific, Indian, Arctic and Southern (Antarctic). There also are many smaller seas such as the North Sea, Mediterranean Sea and Caribbean Sea. Oceans are extremely deep. The average depth is 4000 metres and it is much deeper in the vast oceanic trenches. The Mariana Trench in the Pacific Ocean is 11 033 metres deep.

## Sea life

Sunlight penetrates only a few hundred metres into the sea, so most living things are found near the surface. At the bottom of the food chain are masses of microscopic algae, such as *diatoms*. They can live only near the surface where the light is strong enough for photosynthesis. They are eaten by small animals which float in the water. The animals are called *zooplankton*, a word which means 'floating animals'. The diatoms are part of the *phytoplankton* – 'floating plants'.

Zooplankton includes many kinds of shrimp-like crustaceans, jellyfish and baby fishes. They are eaten by fishes, squid, seabirds and some kinds of whales and seals. At the top of the ocean food chain, there are meat-eating sharks and killer whales.

The plankton-eating fishes often live in large crowds, called *shoals*. They include the herring, sardine, and anchovy which are caught in huge numbers by fishing boats. Other important food fishes, like tuna and cod, feed on these fishes.

## Flatfish

When a plaice is young, it looks like an ordinary fish. Then it settles on the bottom of the sea and starts to change into a flatfish. It lies on its side and its body becomes flattened. Its head twists so that both eyes are on the upper side.

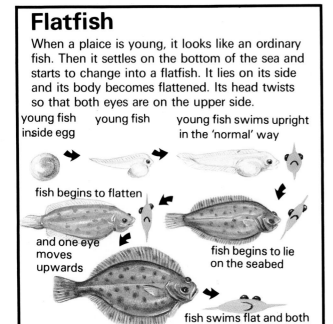

young fish inside egg

young fish

young fish swims upright in the 'normal' way

fish begins to flatten

and one eye moves upwards

fish begins to lie on the seabed

fish swims flat and both eyes are on the upper side of the head

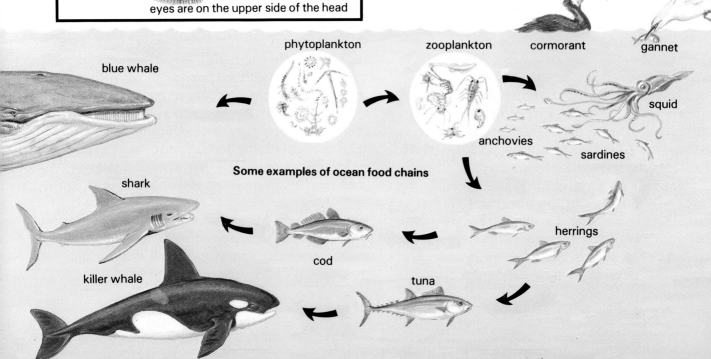

Some examples of ocean food chains

blue whale

phytoplankton

zooplankton

cormorant

gannet

squid

anchovies

sardines

shark

herrings

cod

tuna

killer whale

*Above: Different animals live at different depths in the sea. Some stay at the surface, others live on the bottom. Below 750m it is always dark.*

Labels in illustration:
- Portuguese man o'war
- flying fish
- surface
- basking shark
- marlin
- 1000m
- giant squid
- garfish
- 3000m
- angler fish
- viper fish
- rat-tail
- prawn
- brittlestar
- 6000m

# Shallow seas

The shallow seas are the home of fishes and other animals which live on the seabed. The plaice, sole, rays and skates are flatfish which hide by pressing their flat bodies against the bottom. They are coloured so that they do not show on the seabed. They feed on shrimps, worms and shellfish that live among the sand and rocks.

# Coral reefs

Coral reefs grow in warmer seas. Generations of coral animals have left their limestone skeletons to make a reef (see page 80). Coral grows where the water is clear and its temperature is above 18°C. It also needs plenty of sunlight, so it can grow only in shallow water. The Great Barrier Reef of Australia is 1600 kilometres long.

Coral reefs are the home of an enormous variety of animals. Many of the fishes are brightly coloured, but the stonefish is well camouflaged. It is one of the world's most poisonous animals. It is easy to step on it and be stung. The giant clam is found on coral reefs and has shells which grow up to 1·25 metres wide.

# Ocean deeps

Although it is completely dark in the deep parts of the ocean, special kinds of animals can live there. They feed on the bodies of dead animals and plants which sink from the surface. They also eat each other. Strange worms and shellfish live on the ocean bed and weird-looking fishes swim through the water. Some are blind but others have huge eyes. They usually have big mouths so they can catch prey as big as themselves. The deep-sea angler fish (see also page 85) has a light on a sort of 'fishing rod' which attracts prey towards the angler fish's mouth.

# Seashores

The seashore is the strip of ground between the high and low tide marks. It is uncovered as the tide goes out and flooded again as the tide comes back. So the shore is sometimes land and sometimes sea. The animals and plants have to be able to live in two different conditions. Most seashore organisms come from the sea and they can live a few hours in the air, while the tide is out. Land animals come down to the shore to eat them at low tide.

## Sandy and muddy shores

Sandy and muddy shores often look as if nothing is living on them. The animals are hiding in the damp sand or mud. When the tide is in, shrimps and crabs come out into the water and search for food. Worms and molluscs also become active.

The lugworm lives in a U-shaped burrow in the sand or mud. It sucks water through the burrow to strain out tiny particles of food. Cockles, razorshells and other molluscs push tubes to the surface of the sand to suck in water. The water brings oxygen for breathing, as well as food.

## Rocky shores

Rocky shores are more interesting to visit and study. The rocks are covered with seaweeds, barnacles, limpets and mussels.

A variety of animals live among the seaweeds, and rock pools hold shrimps, lobsters and fishes, which have been left behind when the tide fell.

**Seaweeds** As you walk down a rocky shore, the kinds of plants and animals change. There will be green seaweeds like long hair at the top of the shore and flat, strap-like or round 'bootlace' brown weeds at the bottom. Seaweeds are algae and their position on the beach depends on their ability to survive drying up. The seaweeds at the bottom of the shore die if they spend long in the air, but those at the top can survive for days.

*Below: There are plenty of animals to be seen in a rock pool, but the animals on a sandy shore hide when the tide is out.*

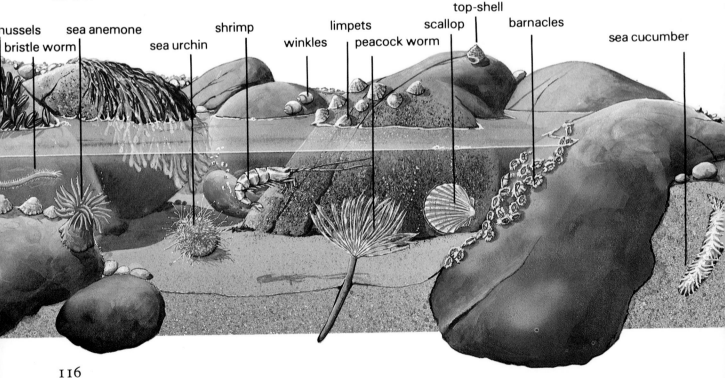

mussels · bristle worm · sea anemone · sea urchin · shrimp · winkles · limpets · peacock worm · top-shell · scallop · barnacles · sea cucumber

**Some animals of tropical seashores**

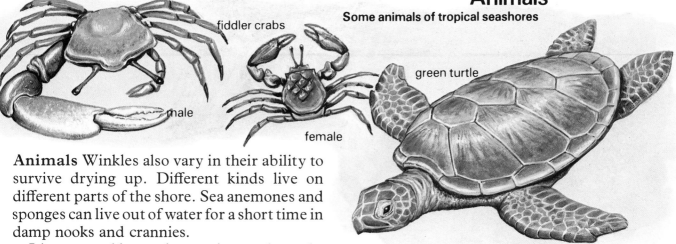

fiddler crabs

male

female

green turtle

**Animals** Winkles also vary in their ability to survive drying up. Different kinds live on different parts of the shore. Sea anemones and sponges can live out of water for a short time in damp nooks and crannies.

Limpets and barnacles survive on the rocks because they are protected by their shells. When the tide is in, barnacles open their shells and rake in food particles with their feathery legs. Limpets let go their tight hold and crawl across the rock. Limpets are a kind of snail. They move in the same way and scrape up algae with a rough tongue. Before the tide goes out again, the limpets return to their old positions, where the shell fits the rock exactly.

Seashore animals and plants also have to survive being pounded by waves. Storms can tear seaweeds from the rocks and wash animals away or smash them. The sheltered sides of large rocks have more living on them than the sides facing the open sea.

# Tropical seashores

In tropical countries the seashores look like those in cooler places but they may have different animals living on them. Turtles crawl up beaches to lay their eggs during the night and the baby turtles hatch out later and scamper down to the sea. Tropical beaches swarm with fiddler crabs which find their food in mud. The male fiddler crab has one enormous claw which it waves to attract females. The mudskipper (see page 85) is a fish which crawls out of water on its stout fins, and even climbs trees.

*Below: Limpets and barnacles clinging to rocks. You can see the underneath of one limpet.*

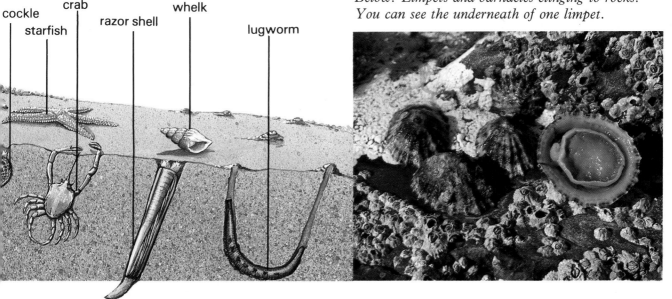

cockle

crab

starfish

razor shell

whelk

lugworm

# Rivers and Lakes

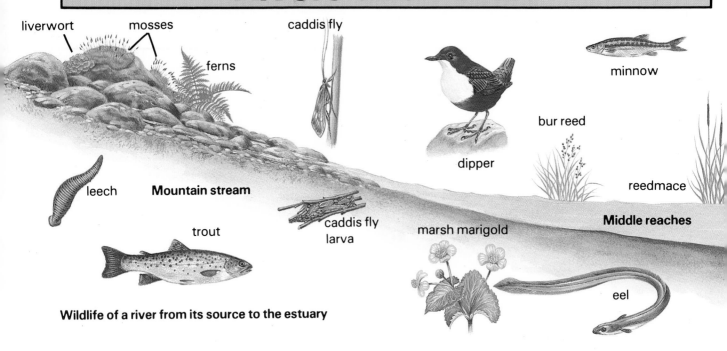

liverwort
mosses
caddis fly
ferns
minnow
bur reed
dipper
reedmace
leech
**Mountain stream**
**Middle reaches**
trout
caddis fly larva
marsh marigold
eel

**Wildlife of a river from its source to the estuary**

*Below: A water vole at home on the river bank.*

In large countries, rivers can be very long. The River Nile in Africa is the longest river in the world. It is over 6600 kilometres long. The Amazon is about 6500 kilometres long and it has a thousand branches, or *tributaries*, while its mouth is 240 kilometres wide. The world's largest freshwater lake is Lake Superior, one of the Great Lakes of North America. It is 616 kilometres long.

Many animals make their homes in or near fresh water. Fishes cannot live out of water, but some animals, such as herons and ducks, only come to water to find food. Others, such as frogs, only come to breed.

## River life

A river is made up of several sections, called *reaches* (see page 21). If it rises in the mountains, it starts as a stream that rushes over the rocks. The only animals and plants living here are those that can cling to the rocks or find sheltered places. Some animals have flat bodies and strong claws for holding on, so that they are not swept away.

When the stream reaches the valley it becomes deeper but it is still fast-flowing. Farther on, the river winds slowly through flat country and it then becomes full of life. Reeds and other plants grow along the bank and water lilies grow in the middle. Fish such as eels, minnows and pike, and a variety of insects live in the water. Coots, moorhens and ducks, as well as water voles and otters, are often found here. The winter is a particularly good time to see flocks of birds.

When the river nears the sea at its estuary, salt water is brought up by the tide. Crabs and sea fish appear but the number of living things is smaller.

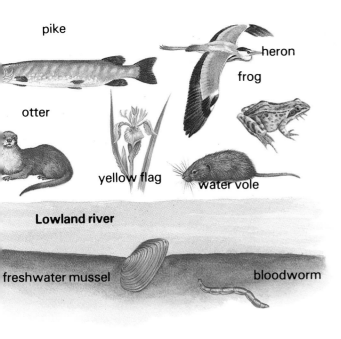

pike

heron

frog

otter

yellow flag

water vole

**Lowland river**

freshwater mussel

bloodworm

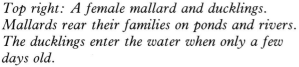

*Top right: A female mallard and ducklings.*
*Mallards rear their families on ponds and rivers.*
*The ducklings enter the water when only a few*
*days old.*
*Right: A dragonfly. Dragonflies spend their early*
*lives in water, but the winged adults may travel*
*far afield.*

# Lakes and ponds

A lake is like a small, freshwater sea. The edge can be full of life but the bottom is cold and dark. Near the surface there are microscopic algae which feed plankton animals. These are eaten, in turn, by fishes. A pond is a small lake which is so shallow that plants can take root even in the middle.

Ponds and the shores of lakes are very good places for looking at wildlife. It is easy to watch the waterbirds, which may have their chicks with them. Small water animals can be caught with a net, or even watched if the water is clear. If you catch anything with a net, treat it carefully and return it to the water so it does not die.

**Insects** Dragonflies, caddisflies and mayflies like places where there are water plants growing out of the water. They perch on the plants as they lay their eggs under the water surface and the larvae live in the water. Dragonfly larvae are fierce predators of other small animals and caddis larvae protect themselves with a tube made of tiny pebbles or pieces of twig. Eventually, the larvae crawl out of the water and become adults with wings. Water beetles and water boatmen spend their adult lives in the water but they sometimes fly to new ponds.

**Return to life** Ponds sometimes dry up in hot summers. When it rains again and the pond fills up, life quickly returns. Some of the animals have survived as eggs which hatch when they become wet. Others fly in, or are carried on the feathers of visiting birds.

If you take some mud from a dry pond or ditch and keep it in a bowl of water, you will be surprised how many animals appear.

# Grasslands

Where there is not enough rain to support forests of trees, the land becomes covered with grasses. Some grasslands are very extensive. There are the prairies of North America, the steppes of Europe and Asia, the pampas of South America, the grasslands of Australia and, largest of all, the savannahs of Africa. Many other plants live with the grasses and, at certain times of the year, the ground is covered with bright flowers. There are often some trees, especially along the banks of rivers and lakes where the soil is damper. The trees are often destroyed by fire, started in hot dry conditions, but the grass quickly grows again.

Large areas of the world's grasslands have been taken over for agriculture so that the natural plants and animals have become rare. Elsewhere, forests have been cut down and turned into grassland for domestic animals.

## Animal herds

Grasslands provide food for many animals because of the way that grass grows (see page 75). It can grow rapidly after it has been cut. The vast savannahs of Africa were once the home of great herds of antelopes and zebras. Most of the herds have gone because the animals have been killed, either by hunters or by poachers, but they still exist in the National Parks. In the Serengeti Plain in Tanzania, there are hundreds of thousands of wildebeests, gazelles and zebras. They migrate around the grassy plains each year in search of the freshest grass. By keeping on the move, they avoid destroying the grass. The herds of herbivores are followed by their predators: lions, leopards, cheetahs, hyaenas and jackals.

The American prairies were the home of big herds of bison, and pronghorns, a relative of the antelopes. These animals moved around the grasslands in the same way as the African animals. At one time there were 60 million bison but they were slaughtered by settlers until only 500 were left. They are now protected in reserves, but most of the prairies have been ploughed up to grow wheat.

**A variety of animals that live on the grasslands of East Africa**

elephant

hyaenas

eland

zebra

impalas

wildebeests

buffaloes

## Animal towns

The prairies are also the home of the prairie dog. This is a kind of squirrel which lives in burrows. Prairie dog 'towns' spread over many hectares of land where millions of the animals have their burrows. The steppes are the home of other ground-living squirrels, like the marmots.

*A prairie dog town.*

## Bird life

Grass seeds attract flocks of birds which travel around the grasslands as they ripen. Budgerigars flock in large numbers in Australia, and African savannahs are occupied by weaverbirds. These little birds are like sparrows and they use grass stems to weave elaborate nests. The nests hang from the branches of trees so that it is difficult for predators to get to them.

## Locusts

Locusts are grasshoppers which suddenly appear in swarms. For most of the time they are hardly seen. Then rain or floods provide bare mud for them to lay their eggs. When the grass sprouts, the young grasshoppers hatch out and grow quickly. They form swarms which walk or fly in search of more food. Wherever they go, they destroy the vegetation. A swarm of desert locusts moves 50 kilometres a day and can be 50 kilometres across.

*Below: A locust. Locusts cause great damage by eating plants and so destroying crops.*

giraffes

lion

guineafowl

# Rainforests

In the tropical regions near the equator, it is hot all the year. In some parts, it is also very wet. There may be 200 centimetres of rain every year. Plants grow well in warm, damp conditions and thick forests cover large areas of the tropics.

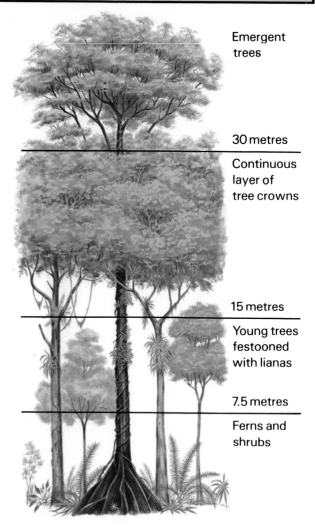

Above: The four levels of the rainforest.

---

Emergent trees

30 metres

Continuous layer of tree crowns

15 metres

Young trees festooned with lianas

7.5 metres

Ferns and shrubs

---

## Amazing birds

The forests of Australia and New Guinea are the home of two birds which have amazing habits.

The birds of paradise get their name from their beautiful feathers. The males gather in one place where they show off their colours and elaborate plumes to attract the females. They flap their wings and shake their plumes, and the king bird of paradise even hangs upside down from a branch.

The bowerbirds attract their mates to a 'bower' of sticks. It is decorated with stones, feathers or flowers, and the satin bowerbird even uses a frayed twig to paint its highly-decorated bower with mud.

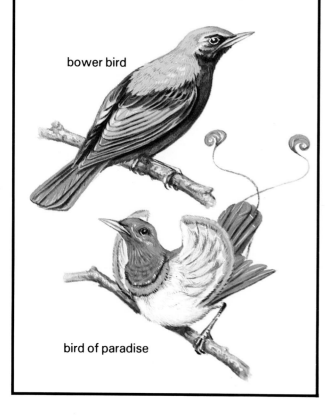

bower bird

bird of paradise

## A variety of life

Rainforest trees grow up to 30 metres or more tall and their leaves form a dense canopy which cuts down the amount of light reaching the ground. It is so dim there that few low plants can grow, unless a big tree falls down and lets in the light. Climbing plants, such as lianas, stretch up the tree trunks to reach the light, and the branches are covered with epiphytes (see page 78).

When a tree does fall down in a tropical forest, it soon disappears. Armies of ants and termites quickly attack the leaves and wood, and fungi eat into the trunk.

The variety of life in a rainforest is immense. There may be several hundred kinds of trees in a hectare and Malaysia has over 2000 kinds of trees in its forests. There are no seasons like the summer and winter of cooler climates. So plants produce fruits and flowers all the year round and the birds and mammals find plenty to eat. The canopy is full of birds, mostly with brightly coloured feathers. There are parrots, pigeons, toucans, hornbills and humming-birds. The monkeys and other mammals are more difficult to see among the leaves.

The warmth and moisture also suits insects and other invertebrates which grow to a great size. There are giant millipedes, leeches, beetles and spiders, and butterflies and moths the size of small birds.

*Below: Many strange animals live in the trees of the rainforests. Some never come to the ground. These animals live in different parts of the world.*

# Life in the canopy

The canopy of the rainforest is the home of many kinds of animals which clamber or leap around the branches. In America, the spider monkeys and marmoset monkeys use their tails as an extra 'hand' for grasping branches. The same trick is used by tree porcupines, the kinkajou (a relative of the raccoon), por-cupines, anteaters, chameleons and the mar-supial cuscus of Australia. Tree frogs, lizards and squirrels have claws or pads on their toes to get a good grip on the bark of trees as they climb about in them.

Monkeys, tree frogs, squirrels and tree kangaroos are good at jumping, so that they can easily move from tree to tree. Some glide greater distances by developing 'wings' from flaps of skin (see page 102). There are flying frogs, flying lizards, flying lemurs and even flying snakes in the rainforests.

# Temperate Forests

Above: Coniferous forests grow in cold places because they are not damaged by snow.

butterfly
bumblebee
deer
jay
snail
stoat

The temperate regions lie between the tropics and the polar regions. They are never very hot nor very cold, but there is a big temperature difference between summer and winter. The temperate regions of North America, Europe and Asia were once covered with forests, but they have now mostly been cut down.

There are two main kinds of forest. Coniferous trees, such as firs, pines and spruces, make up the *evergreen* forests in the north (see page 72). Conifers can stand long winters because their shiny needles shed snow and ice without breaking the branches. Farther south, the forests have *deciduous* trees, such as oak, elm and ash, which lose all their leaves in winter.

Nearer the equator, where the winters are warmer, forests become evergreen again. Around the Mediterranean, there are forests where cork oaks grow. Corks for bottles are made from their thick bark. China has bamboo forests which are the home of the giant panda. The eucalyptus or gum forests of Australia are the evergreens in the southern hemisphere.

A female koala and young one. Koalas live in the eucalyptus forests of Australia.

## Coniferous forests

The thick, green foliage makes coniferous forests very dark and few plants grow under the trees. There is more plant life in clearings and around the many bogs and lakes. The elk, called the moose in America, lives in these wet places.

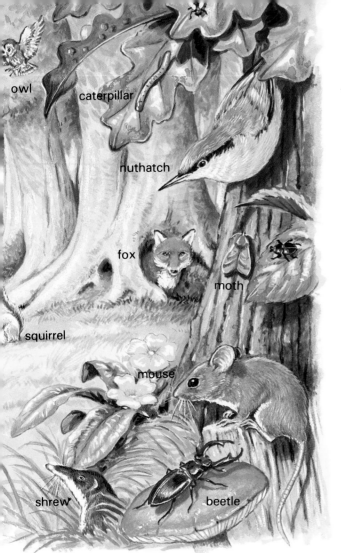

owl

caterpillar

nuthatch

fox

moth

squirrel

mouse

shrew

beetle

*Above: A variety of animals that live in
deciduous forests.*

**Animal life** The animals in the coniferous
forests of Europe and Asia are often the same
or similar to those living in North America.
The moose, wolf, lynx, brown bear and
wolverine live in both places. American
squirrels, martens and beavers are very like
those in Europe and Asia. This is because,
many years ago, land joined Europe and Asia to
America and animals could cross from one
continent to the other.

Conifer trees are inhabited by many animals
which feed on their cones. Crossbills are small
birds which crack open cones to get the seeds.
The two halves of their beaks cross over and
make good cutters. Red and grey squirrels,
flying squirrels, spruce mice and chipmunks
live among the conifers. Spruce grouse, black
grouse and capercaillies are birds which eat
conifer shoots.

# Deciduous forests

More light comes between the branches of
deciduous trees than of conifers, so bushes and
low plants can carpet the ground. They flower
mainly in the spring, before the trees grow
their leaves. The plants attract a great variety
of butterflies and moths, bees, beetles and flies.
Birds eat the insects, as well as the buds and
fruits. They are joined by squirrels, mice and
voles, and deer feed on the lower leaves of the
trees. The birds and mammals are hunted by
foxes, weasels, hawks and owls. Wolves, pumas
and bears were once common, but they have
almost died out.

## Leaf fall

When deciduous trees are ready to lose their
leaves in the autumn, a wall of cork grows
across the base of the leaf stem. After the leaf
has fallen off, the cork makes a plug to
prevent sap escaping. Before this happens,
photosynthesis stops. The green chlorophyll
disappears and reveals yellow and red
substances which give leaves their autumn
colours.

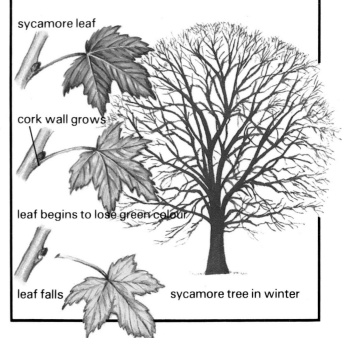

sycamore leaf

cork wall grows

leaf begins to lose green colour

leaf falls

sycamore tree in winter

# Endangered Wildlife

Animals and plants are in danger in nearly every part of the world. Animals are hunted for pleasure or because they attack domestic animals and crops. They are also killed for food.

There are 250 000 flowering plants in the world and 25 000 are in danger. Plants disappear because they are poisoned by weed-killers or because collectors are too enthusiastic. Tigers, leopards and other cats are hunted for their furs, and *Rafflesia*, which is the biggest flower in the world, is becoming rarer because of people picking it.

*Above:* Rafflesia, *the largest flower in the world.*

# The changing countryside

A much more common reason for plants and animals disappearing is that there are fewer places for them to live. Forests are cut down, grasslands are ploughed up and wet places are drained. The countryside is needed for farms to help feed the world's growing human population. The island of Madagascar has lost 80% of its forests, endangering the lemurs and other animals that live nowhere else in the world. People are even worried that the huge forests of Brazil may disappear.

Once the countryside has been changed, there is nowhere for the animals and plants to live. We can see this even when a hedge is cut down to make a field larger. The birds lose their nesting places and some of the delicate plants cannot survive in the open.

The number of animals and plants in danger is increasing all the time. When tropical forests are cut down, some kinds may become extinct before anyone has ever seen them. Even familiar animals such as elephants, zebras and crocodiles have disappeared from many of their old homes.

## Rhinos in danger

Of the five species of rhinoceroses, three live in Asia and two live in Africa. All five have become rare. Much of the countryside where they used to live has been destroyed, and they are hunted for their horns. Laws protect the rhinos from being hunted, but the horns are so valuable that poachers still kill them illegally.

The white rhinoceros of Africa became very rare but it was saved by careful protection. Meanwhile the African black rhinoceros suddenly became very scarce because of hunting. The Asian rhinoceroses are in even greater danger. There are only about 20 Javan rhinoceroses left.

Sumatran

Indian

Javan

African white

African black

**Diagram to show how poison is passed along a food chain**

crops sprayed with insecticide

birds of prey poisoned by accumulated insecticide after eating smaller birds

caterpillars contaminated

caterpillars eaten by birds

small birds eaten by birds of prey

# Poisoning

Poisoning is another danger to wildlife. Chemicals used to kill weeds and animal pests also kill other plants and animals. The poisons are passed along the food chains (see page 108) and gather in the bodies of predators. Sparrow-hawks and peregrine falcons die when they catch and eat birds which have been feeding on seeds treated with poisons for killing pests.

# Protection for wildlife

Many people are becoming worried by the disappearance of our wildlife. Laws have been passed in most countries to protect various animals. Hunting may be forbidden and people are not allowed to buy or sell rare plants and animals. The use of dangerous chemicals is kept under control. Parts of countries are made into reserves where the wildlife must not be disturbed. Some reserves are as big as a small country so that all kinds of wildlife are preserved. Others are small patches of land where one kind of rare animal or plant lives.

*Below: A new road allows people into a forest which is being cut down even more.*
*Bottom: Polar bears were killed for these skins.*

# Wildlife Saved

Although so many animals and plants are in danger of becoming extinct, some are being saved by conservationists.

**The Arabian oryx** used to live in the deserts of the Middle East but so many were shot by hunters that none were left alive in the wild. Luckily, some oryx had been captured and kept in zoos. Descendants of these captives have been taken back to the desert. They now live a wild life under protection.

**The whooping crane** nests in Canada and migrates to the southern United States. It became rare when its summer and winter homes were turned into farmland. The surviving birds were shot during their annual 7000 kilometres migration. In 1952, there were only 21 left. Then people living on the migration route were asked not to shoot the cranes, and they are becoming more common.

**The tiger** has become rare because it was hunted for its fur or for sport and it was also killed because it attacked farm animals. Its natural prey of deer and antelope was also disappearing. In 1973, Project Tiger was started to save the tigers in India. Large areas of country are now kept specially for tigers. Even villages have been moved out of the reserves so that the tigers can live in peace. They are guarded very closely and their numbers are increasing.

The protection given to tigers means that many other animals benefit from living in the reserves and Project Tiger has helped to save all sorts of wildlife in India.

*Left: Arabian oryx were saved in zoos.*
*Below left: The whooping crane's numbers are rising through protection.*
*Below: Tigers are now safe in reserves.*

# How we live

*Water cooling towers in Birmingham, England.*

# Shelter

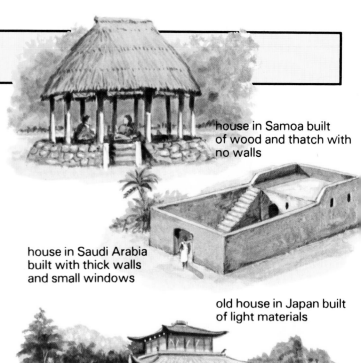

house in Samoa built of wood and thatch with no walls

house in Saudi Arabia built with thick walls and small windows

It is very important for us to have shelter. Early people sheltered, wherever they could, from the cold, the burning sun, and bad weather. Usually, the best shelter they could find was in trees or in caves. After they discovered how to make a fire, they lit large fires at night to frighten away the wolves and other animals that they feared.

Later, people started to build their own shelters. They used such materials as the branches of trees, thick grasses, piles of stones, and the skins of animals that they had eaten for food. As people developed skills, and began to live together in villages and towns, they tried to make their homes comfortable and happy, as well as safe.

In time, people started to put up buildings that were not just needed for shelter. They built meeting places, theatres, places for selling goods, and places of worship.

old house in Japan built of light materials

house in the Alps in Europe built with a pointed roof

house in a river in Malaysia built on stilts

*Below: A castle in Germany built for the King of Bavaria in 1869–81.*

## Houses around the world

When people build houses, the first thing they have to think about is the weather. If they live in a place where there is much rain, the most important thing is to keep out the water. If there is hot sunshine for much of the year, houses will have to keep out heat. In very cold places, the most important thing is to stay warm. People also have to think about the materials they can find for building, and use the best and easiest material available.

**Weather** The appearance of a house tells us a lot about conditions in the country it belongs to. Rainy countries usually have houses with high, pointed roofs, so that the rain runs off. In some snowy countries, houses also have pointed roofs, so that the snow does not pile up on the roof. In some hot countries, houses have thick walls to keep out the heat. They also have small windows. In other hot places, the houses have roofs but no walls, so that cooling breezes can blow through them. Some countries have frequent earthquakes. The people use light materials for building so that nobody will be hurt if houses fall down.

block of flats built of concrete

house built of bricks

**Materials** Usually, people use building materials that they can find easily. In Scandinavia and northern Canada, where there are large forests, many houses are made of wood. In parts of Africa, long thick grasses are woven together to make huts, similar to the way that baskets are made.

Mud is a common building material. In some African countries, people plaster it on to a wooden framework to form walls. The mud bakes hard and dry in the hot sunshine. People in northern Africa use mud in a different way. They mix it with straw, and shape it into bricks. When the bricks have dried, they are built together to make walls. Bricks made in a similar way are also used in Mexico, the south-western United States, and parts of South America. There, they are called *adobe*.

In cold or wet climates, adobe bricks crumble. Clay can be made into harder bricks by *firing* (burning) it in very hot ovens called *kilns*. Bricks of this type are used all over the world. Stone is also used in many countries, but usually only for certain parts of houses.

Today, new types of man-made materials are available. Both large and small buildings are made of concrete (a mixture of water, stone and sand with a 'binder', usually cement). Plastics (see page 170) are also used in building making it easier than in the past.

*Below: A hut in a village in Ethiopia, Africa.*

# Famous Buildings

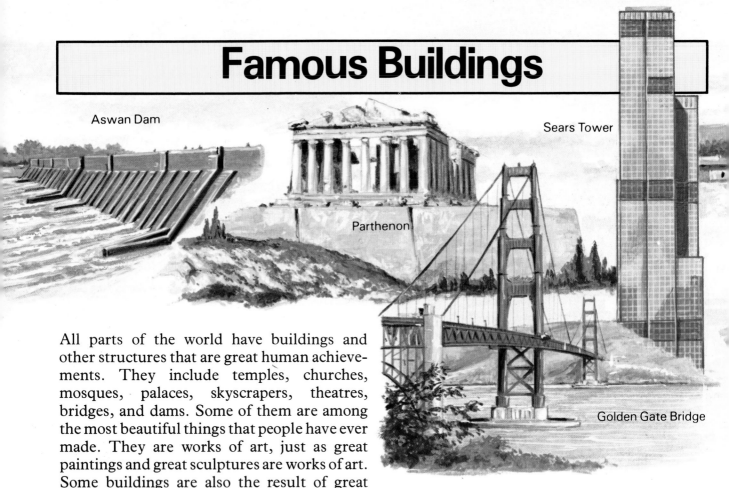

Aswan Dam

Parthenon

Sears Tower

Golden Gate Bridge

All parts of the world have buildings and other structures that are great human achievements. They include temples, churches, mosques, palaces, skyscrapers, theatres, bridges, and dams. Some of them are among the most beautiful things that people have ever made. They are works of art, just as great paintings and great sculptures are works of art. Some buildings are also the result of great technical skills, as remarkable as the skills that have landed men on the Moon.

## Great building achievements

**The Pyramids of Egypt** These huge stone structures in the desert were built more than 4000 years ago. They were tombs for the *pharoahs* (kings) of Egypt. One of them, the Great Pyramid, is nearly 140 metres high. Nobody knows exactly how the pyramids were built. But it is certain that thousands of workmen must have laboured for years on each of them.

**Angkor** This city was abandoned by its people 500 years ago. It stands in the jungle in Kampuchea, a country of South-Eastern Asia. Near it is the ruined Hindu temple of Angkor Wat, the largest religious building in the world. One of the carvings in the *wat* (temple) is 800 metres long. At one period, more than 300 000 people worked on the buildings of Angkor.

**Golden Gate Bridge** Many bridges are great engineering achievements. One of the most admired is the Golden Gate Bridge, which spans the entrance to San Francisco Bay in the United States of America. This graceful suspension bridge is nearly 2 kilometres long.

**Dams** The Aswan High Dam, is a concrete barrier built across the River Nile in Egypt, creating a huge artificial lake. It helps to store the river's water for *irrigating* (watering) the land and making electricity. The world's first dam was probably also built across the Nile, in 3000 BC. A dam in the Soviet Union, the Rogunsky Dam, is 327 metres high.

**Skyscrapers** Some of these are among the wonders of the modern world. The highest of them is the Sears Tower in Chicago, in the United States of America. It is 443 metres high, and has 110 storeys. The most impressive group of skyscrapers is on Manhattan Island in New York City, also in America.

Canterbury Cathedral

Pyramids of Egypt

Angkor

**Palace of Versailles** In a city near Paris in France, is one of the world's most famous palaces. It was begun in the 1600s by the 'Sun King' Louis XIV. The French Revolution, which began in 1789, broke out partly because life at the palace was so rich, when most people were so poor. In the *Galerie des Glaces* (Hall of Mirrors), the Treaty of Versailles was signed to end the First World War (1914–1918).

**Canterbury Cathedral** This cathedral in England is one of the many wonderful cathedrals in Europe dating from the Middle Ages. It was begun in 1070. It is mainly in the *Gothic* style, as are many famous cathedrals in France, such as Notre-Dame in Paris.

*Below: The bedroom of Louis XV in the Palace of Versailles, near Paris.*
*Bottom: The beautiful Taj Mahal at Agra.*

# Buildings as works of art

The world is full of buildings famous for their beauty, their history, or their unusual design.

**Taj Mahal** Some people consider the Taj Mahal, at Agra in India, to be the most beautiful building in the world. It was built in the 1660s by the Emperor Shah Jahan as a tomb for his wife Mumtaz-i-Mahal. It is made of white marble.

**Parthenon** The Parthenon, in Athens, the capital of Greece, is also built of white marble. Some people think it is even more beautiful than the Taj Mahal. It was begun in 447 BC, and is part of the wonderful group of buildings called the Acropolis.

# Building Techniques

Many different kinds of workers take part in the construction of a building, whether it is a small house or a huge skyscraper. They include architects, surveyors, engineers, carpenters, bricklayers, electricians, plumbers, factory workers, and the people who do the hard jobs of digging and carrying. In many countries, particularly highly-developed countries, building is the biggest single industry.

Every building must be suitable for its purpose. A house for example, is not built in the same way as a hospital. A building must be strong, because it has to support two kinds of loads. It has to support its own weight, and the weight of the people and objects in it.

## Building support

A building may be supported by *load-bearing walls*, by a *frame*, or by a *shell*.

**Load-bearing walls** In most houses and other small buildings, certain walls carry all the weight. Usually, these are the outside walls, and a small number of interior walls. Other walls in a house are *screen walls*, built to divide the house up into rooms.

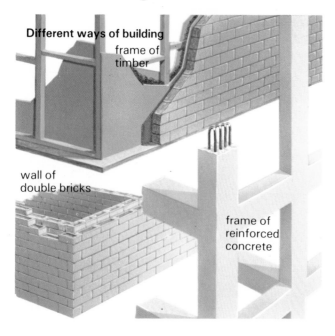

**Different ways of building**
frame of timber

wall of double bricks

frame of reinforced concrete

**Frame** A tall building would need extremely thick load-bearing walls. Instead, builders make a frame of steel or *reinforced concrete* (concrete with strengthening steel rods set in it) to carry the building's weight. The walls can then be made of light materials.

**Shell** Some buildings are supported by a 'shell' of reinforced concrete or wood. Inside, the shell is divided up by light walls.

## Building methods

**Traditional building** Methods include the use of wood, stone, brick and concrete. The walls are put together piece by piece.

To build brick walls, the bricks are laid in regular patterns, and are held together with *mortar*. Mortar is a mixture of cement, sand, and water. It is used when it is wet and soft, and quickly sets hard.

*Above: A busy building site in London, England. The workers have dug deeply into the ground to make the foundations of the building.*

**Prefabricated building** Some buildings today are constructed of walls, roofs, floors and other parts that have been made in factories. At the building site, they are merely joined together to form a building. This method of building is called *prefabrication*.

Prefabrication has many advantages. The sections can be made to standard sizes, and can be *mass-produced* (made in large numbers). This saves money. Money is also saved on the building site, because work can be done quickly and simply, and is not delayed by bad weather.

The sections are sometimes called *modules*. They can be put together in many different ways, so that the finished houses do not all look the same.

# Building construction

**Design** The first stage in building is design. An *architect* draws plans for the building, showing what it will look like. A *structural engineer* helps, to make sure that the building will be strong. A *quantity surveyor* advises on the amount of materials and work needed.

**Foundations** These are the first part of the building to be prepared. They are the parts of the building below the ground. They make sure that the building's weight is safely supported.

**Superstructure** The main part of the building is then constructed. Walls, floors, and roof are built, or, if the building is prefabricated, joined together. Doors and windows are put in.

**Fittings and decoration** These complete the building. Workers install heating, lighting and plumbing. Wall surfaces are papered, or finished in some other way. Painters make sure that doors and windows look bright and new.

# A Modern House

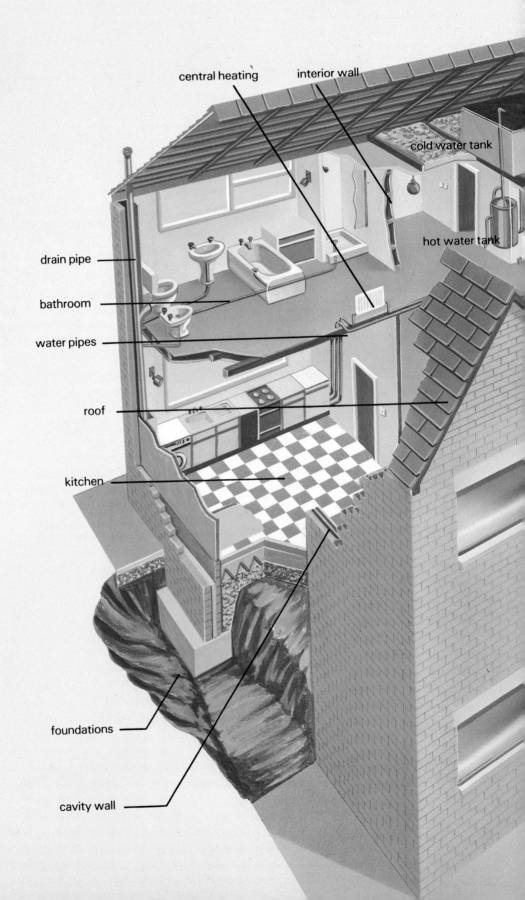

central heating

interior wall

cold water tank

hot water tank

drain pipe

bathroom

water pipes

roof

kitchen

foundations

cavity wall

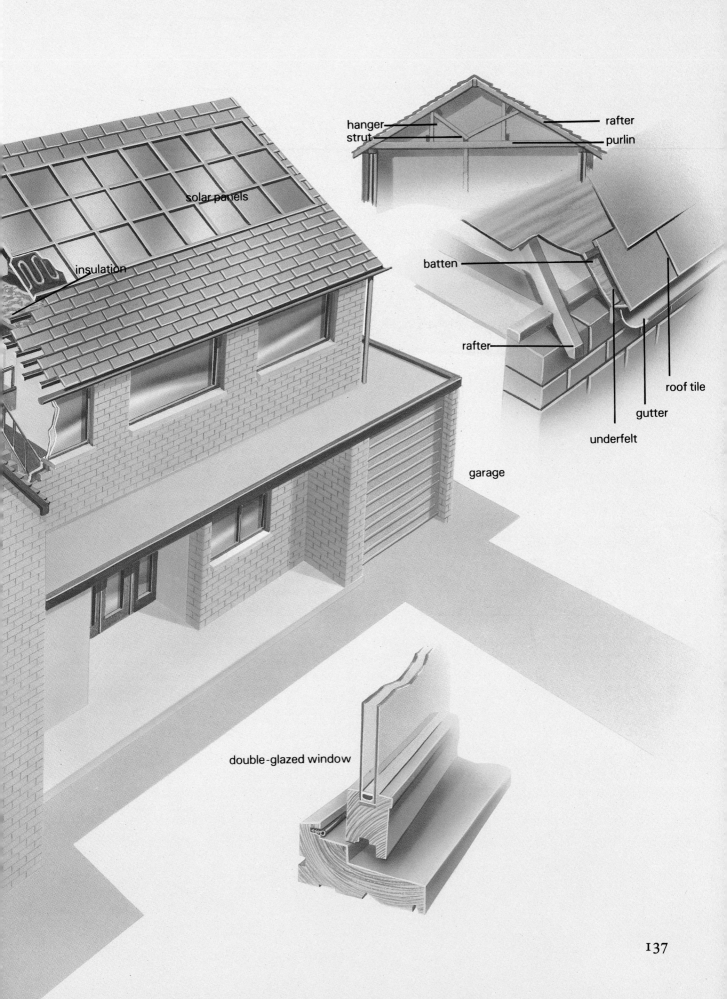

hanger
rafter
strut
purlin

batten

rafter

roof tile

gutter

underfelt

solar panels

insulation

garage

double-glazed window

# Services to the House

People who live in modern houses take many useful services for granted. They know, for example, that the light will come on when they press an electric switch, and that water will start to flow when they turn a tap. Without such services, life would be less comfortable. Millions of workers are employed in making sure that they are always there. The most important services are the plumbing system, electricity, and gas.

## Plumbing

The plumbing system in a house consists mainly of pipes carrying water. Some of them supply clean water for drinking, washing, or heating. Others carry dirty water, called *sewage*, away from the house.

**Water supply** Water from rivers, lakes, and reservoirs (see page 160) is *purified* then carried in large underground pipes called *water mains* to towns and villages. Smaller pipes branch from the mains to carry it into each house.

In a house, some pipes carry water directly to the drinking-water taps. Another pipe carries water to a storage tank at the top of the house.

The storage tank supplies the hot-water system. Water from the tank is piped to a *boiler* heated by coal, electricity, oil, or some other fuel. The hot water from the boiler goes to taps in basins, baths, and sinks. It is also used in the radiators of central heating systems.

**Sewage** This is carried away by pipes from sinks, wash basins, baths, and lavatories. It flows into large underground pipes called *drains* and *sewers*. These pipes lead to *sewage works*, where the sewage is treated.

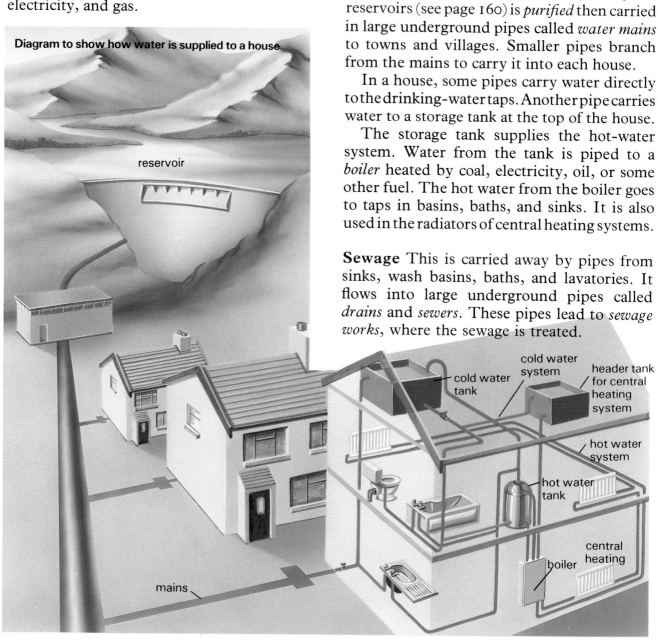

Diagram to show how water is supplied to a house

reservoir

mains

cold water tank

cold water system

header tank for central heating system

hot water system

hot water tank

central heating

boiler

138

How an electric appliance is connected
to the electricity supply

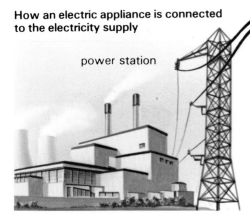

power station

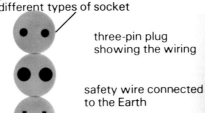

different types of socket

three-pin plug
showing the wiring

safety wire connected
to the Earth

fuse, for safety,
breaks if too much
electricity flows
through it

neutral wire        live wire

two-pin plug
which has no
earth wire

electric heater

# Electricity

Many common household things work by
electricity. (See also page 148.) Important
appliances are lights and heaters. There are
also many others, including refrigerators,
washing machines, vacuum cleaners, cookers,
food mixers, electric blankets, hair driers,
shavers, radios, and television sets.

**Power supply** Electricity is produced in
power stations, and then carried through
*cables* (wires) to houses and other buildings,
where it is used. The cables may be underground, or may be strung high overhead.

**Electric wiring** The wiring distributes electricity throughout a house. The wires are
usually hidden in the walls. *Switches* are
placed near doors and at other convenient
spots, so that the electricity can be turned on
or off. Switches work by completing or breaking
an *electric circuit*.

Lights, cookers, and some other electric
appliances are connected permanently to the
electricity supply. They can, of course, be
switched off when they are not in use. Other
appliances, such as hair driers and television
sets, can be plugged into the electricity supply
when wanted. A *plug* attached to the appliance
fits into a *socket* or *outlet* carrying electricity.
The appliance can be moved from place to
place, and plugged into a convenient socket.

# Gas

In some houses, coal gas and natural gas take
the place of electricity for heating and cooking.
They can also be used for lighting. Underground pipes carry the gas to houses from the
huge tanks in which it is stored. Unlike
electricity, gas burns with a flame.

**Coal gas** This is made by heating coal (see
page 144). Gas is given off, leaving coke
behind. Coal gas is really a mixture of several
gases. One of them, carbon monoxide, is a
deadly poison. A strong-smelling substance is
added to coal gas to warn people of leaks.

**Natural gas** This is found deep down in
underground rocks. Often, natural gas is found
near petroleum (see page 146).

# Energy

Everything we do depends on energy. We could not live without energy, and nor could animals or plants. Most of the energy in the world comes from the Sun. It reaches the Earth in rays of sunlight. Sunlight enables plants to make their food. Human beings and animals eat plants to gain the energy they need for life. They also obtain energy by eating meat, but the energy in meat comes from plants that those animals have eaten.

Energy from food enables our muscles and other parts of our bodies to work. But other forms of energy are also useful to us. We use them for many of the things that make our lives comfortable. For example, we depend on energy to heat and light our homes, to cook our food, and to make motor cars and aeroplanes work.

*Athletes using energy to race over hurdles. They get their energy from the food they have eaten.*

## What is energy?

Energy is the ability to do work of some kind. It has many forms. The most important are heat and light. Sound is also a form of energy. *Mechanical energy* comes from machines. *Chemical energy* is released when chemical changes take place.

Energy can be changed from one form into another. For example, the chemical energy stored in a torch battery can be changed into light. Your hands can work like a machine. If you rub them together in cold weather they become warm. The mechanical energy released by the action of rubbing has been changed by *friction* into heat.

The amount of energy in the world is always the same. Energy cannot be created or destroyed. When energy seems to have been used up, it has really only been changed into another form.

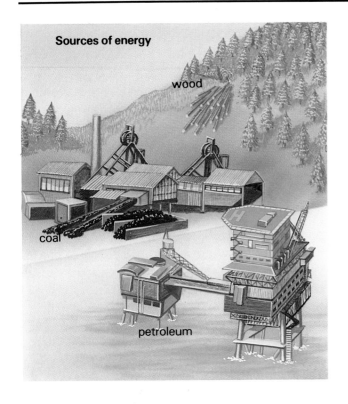

Sources of energy

wood

coal

petroleum

**Natural gas** Formed in much the same way as petroleum, it lies deep underground between layers of rock. It is used for heating and cooking.

**Electricity** This is a very useful type of energy because it can be *conducted* (moved) from place to place along wires. Electricity can easily be made from other forms of energy. For example, the energy in a waterfall can be used to drive a *generator* that produces electricity. This is a form of *hydro-electricity*.

**Other sources of energy** These include the wind, the waves of the ocean, and the hot water that gushes up from the earth as *geysers* in some parts of the world. Most geysers occur in New Zealand, the United States of America and Iceland.

# Sources of energy

As well as energy that comes directly from the Sun, we use energy from sources that store the Sun's energy, such as coal and petroleum. Nuclear energy is released from atoms.

**Nuclear energy** Within the last fifty years, scientists have learnt to release this from the atoms of such minerals as uranium and plutonium.

**Wood and coal** These both release energy in the form of heat and light when they are burnt. Coal consists of the remains of plants that lived millions of years ago. The energy in wood and coal comes from the food that trees and other plants made by means of the Sun's rays.

**Petroleum** This is one of the most important sources of energy. It gives us petrol (gasolene), diesel oil, paraffin (kerosene) and thousands of other products. It is formed from the remains of tiny sea plants and animals.

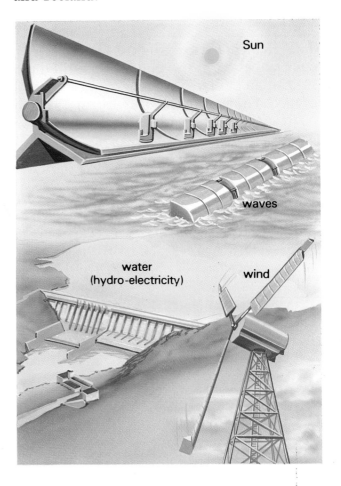

Sun

waves

water (hydro-electricity)

wind

# Nuclear Energy

Nuclear energy or *atomic energy* is energy released when the *atoms* (the smallest particles into which anything can be broken down) of one chemical element change into those of another. The change may be *nuclear fission*, when the atoms of a heavy element split into the atoms of two lighter elements. Or it may be *nuclear fusion*, when parts of two atoms join.

Nuclear energy could become the world's greatest source of power for lighting, heating, operating factories, driving ships, and countless other uses. However, some people fear it because it is also used to make bombs and other weapons that are the most terrible and destructive in the history of the world. Also, some of the products of the fission process are extremely poisonous.

## Producing nuclear energy

The elements used to produce energy by nuclear fission are uranium and plutonium. Each atom of uranium and plutonium (and of every other element) has a *nucleus* at its centre made up of *protons* and *neutrons*.

*Right: A nuclear power station at Dungeness, Kent. Atoms are split in a nuclear reactor.*
*Below: A march protesting against nuclear weapons.*

**Nuclear fission** When a loose neutron is made to collide with an atom of uranium or plutonium, the atom's nucleus 'captures' the neutron. The nucleus then splits into two parts, releasing a great amount of energy. It also releases two or three neutrons. These neutrons collide with other atoms, and the same fission happens each time, in what is called a *chain reaction*.

Millions of millions of fissions can take place in one-millionth of a second. This is what happens when an atomic bomb explodes. When nuclear energy is produced for ordinary peaceful purposes, the chain reaction has to be slowed down. To produce energy for ordinary purposes, the fissions take place in a machine called a *nuclear reactor* or *atomic pile*. The speed of the fissions is controlled in various ways. One way is by the use of *control rods* that take away some of the neutrons.

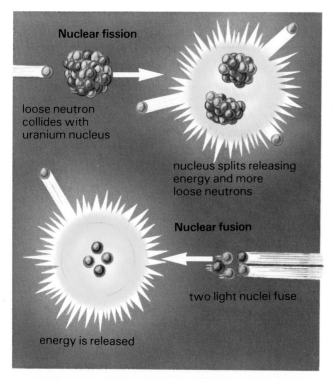

Nuclear fission

loose neutron collides with uranium nucleus

nucleus splits releasing energy and more loose neutrons

Nuclear fusion

two light nuclei fuse

energy is released

**Nuclear fusion** This is also called *thermo-nuclear reaction*, because it occurs only at very high temperatures. It is the opposite of nuclear fission. Two light nuclei *fuse* (join) together to form a heavier nucleus.

The Sun's tremendous energy comes from nuclear fusion. The nuclei of light hydrogen atoms fuse to form the nuclei of heavier helium atoms. As this happens, huge amounts of energy are released in the form of heat.

Nuclear fusion produces the destructive energy of the hydrogen bomb. In the future, however, nuclear fusion may be one of the most valuable sources of peaceful energy, because it can use the water in the sea and in lakes and rivers to produce power.

# Using nuclear energy

Nuclear energy is already used in many ways. It generates electricity, drives ships, and is used in factories and hospitals.

**Electricity** Nuclear power stations produce some of the electricity that people use every day. Each station has a nuclear reactor in which nuclear fission takes place. The nuclear fission releases energy in the form of heat. This heat is passed to a gas or liquid called a *coolant*. The coolant goes to a *heat exchanger*, where it heats water and turns it into steam. The steam is then used to turn a turbine. The turbine drives a generator, which produces electricity.

**Other uses** Turbines powered by nuclear fission are also used to drive ships and submarines. Because nuclear reactors need no oxygen, nuclear submarines can remain under water for long periods.

Certain kinds of atoms produced during nuclear fission help doctors to diagnose (identify) diseases, and to fight them. These atoms are called *radio-active isotopes*. They also have many uses in industry and agriculture.

# Coal

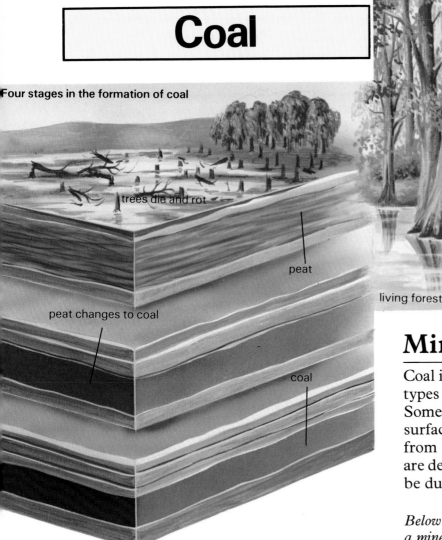

Four stages in the formation of coal

trees die and rot

peat

peat changes to coal

coal

living forest

## Mining coal

Coal is a rock that lies in layers between other types of rock. The layers are called *seams*. Sometimes a seam slopes upwards to the surface. Then the coal can be *quarried* (dug) from it by *open-cast mining*. Most coal seams are deep underground, and long shafts have to be dug in the earth to reach them.

*Below: A machine called a shearer cutting coal in a mine. It also loads coal on to a conveyor.*

Coal is the remains of forests and swamps that covered much of the Earth hundreds of millions of years ago. When the trees and other plants in the forests died, they rotted and slowly turned into *peat*. Pressure and heat caused the peat to lose some of the gases it contained. It gradually became the thickly-packed mass of carbon that we call coal. Coal is one of our most valuable fuels for producing heat and light.

Coal is often called a *fossil fuel* because it formed, like fossils, from the remains of plants that lived long ago. You can still see the shape of ferns and other plants in some pieces of coal. These plants used sunlight to make food. When we burn coal today, we are releasing energy from sunlight that shone on the Earth millions of years ago.

**Open-cast mining** This is also called *strip mining*. Huge power shovels and bulldozers dig away any earth and rock covering the coal. The coal is broken up, and is then dug out and carried away.

**Underground mining** An underground coal mine, or *pit*, has to be carefully planned. At least two *shafts* are dug down towards the coal seams. Fans at the *head* (top) of one shaft draw fresh air into the mine and remove stale air. A *cage* (lift) travels down and up the main shaft to take miners to their work and to raise the coal as it is dug out.

The miners dig tunnels or *galleries* out from the shafts to reach the coal seams. They cut into the seams, removing the coal as they go. The part of a seam that is being cut at any particular time is called the *coal face*.

In modern mines, the coal is cut from the face by special machines. Explosives are sometimes used to break up the face. As the coal is cut, it is carried back to the shaft on a conveyor belt or in small trucks that run on rails. The coal is then taken up to the surface in the lift.

## Mine safety

Mining is a dangerous job. Tunnel roofs have to be carefully propped up to prevent falls of rock. One of the greatest dangers is the accidental explosion of natural gases in the mine. Miners carry special lamps to test for gas.

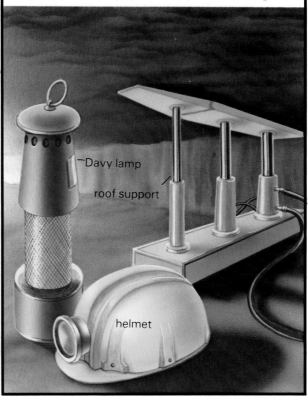

Davy lamp
roof support
helmet

# Uses of coal

Coal first became important in the 1700s, at the beginning of the Industrial Revolution in Europe, the period when people started building factories and using machines. Coal was burnt to heat water for the steam engines that had recently been invented. It is still used to make steam for factory machinery and for *generating* (making) electricity. Coal is used to heat buildings, and to make coal gas for heating and cooking. It is also used in making iron and steel. Among the hundreds of things made from coal are perfumes, dyes, drugs, and plastics.

# Petroleum

Petroleum is one of the most useful materials in the world. It provides about half of the world's energy, in the form of petrol and other fuels. It is also used to make hundreds of things that we use every day. Petroleum is found deep in the ground as a thick brownish or green-black oil. It is often just called *oil* or *crude oil*.

The modern world is so dependent on petroleum that many people wonder what will happen when the known supplies of petroleum are used up. Petroleum is also becoming more and more expensive. Scientists are searching for new ways of powering motor cars, aircraft, trains, and ships without having to use petroleum fuels.

Like coal, petroleum is a *fossil fuel*. It is made, like fossils, from the remains of tiny animals and plants that lived long ago. The energy it contains is energy that came from the Sun millions of years ago.

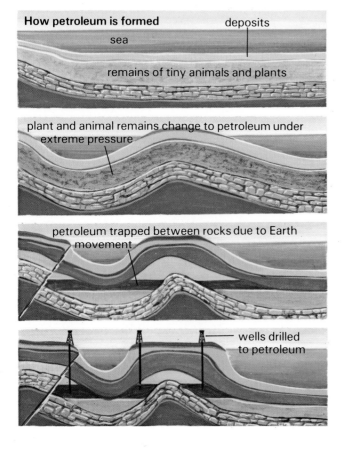

How petroleum is formed

deposits

sea

remains of tiny animals and plants

plant and animal remains change to petroleum under extreme pressure

petroleum trapped between rocks due to Earth movement

wells drilled to petroleum

*Above: An oil rig in the North Sea.*

## Where petroleum is found

Petroleum has been found in most parts of the world. It lies in certain types of underground rock formations. These may be under deserts, forests, farm lands, or anywhere else; even under the sea.

## The oil well

When a spot has been chosen for drilling, a *derrick* or *rig* is erected over it. This metal framework supports the *drill* that bores a hole deep into the ground.

**The Christmas tree** When the bit reaches the petroleum, pressures in the Earth usually force the petroleum to the surface. Workers fix a complicated group of valves called a Christmas tree to the top of the bore hole. In this way, they can control the flow of petroleum. If the petroleum does not come up naturally, a *pump* is used to suck it up.

# Refining petroleum

Before petroleum can be used, it has to be *refined*. It is taken from the oil well to a refinery. There, it is heated to separate the various substances it contains. Each of them boils and vaporizes at a different temperature. Petrol, for example, boils first. Its vapour is drawn off. When the vapour is cooled, it condenses to form pure petrol.

## Petroleum products

The chief petroleum products are petrol and fuel oils. Fuel oils include diesel fuel for diesel-engined locomotives, ships, and road vehicles. They also include heating oils, and oils used in factories and power plants. *Petrochemicals* (chemicals made from petroleum) are used in making plastics, paints, cosmetics, medicines, fertilizers, and some kinds of cloth.

**Drilling** The drill revolves (turns) at a fast speed, and its sharp point gradually cuts down through the rock.

The main parts of a drill are its *stem* and the *bit*. The upper part of the stem is a hollow steel tube called a *kelly*. A *rotary table*, driven by an engine, turns the kelly. The bottom of the kelly is attached to a steel tube called the *drill pipe*. The drill pipe ends in the bit, the cutting tool. This is often made even harder by implanting diamonds into its cutting edge.

The drill pipe is made in 10-metre lengths. As each length bores into the ground, another length is added.

As the hole is drilled, it is lined with a steel pipe called a *casing*. While work is going on, mud is pumped through the casing to cool the drill and to remove little pieces of rock.

# Electricity

Electricity is one of the most plentiful sources of energy. There is electricity in everything.

Electricity provides us with heat and light. It powers motors that drive trains, trucks, and machinery. Without it, we would not have radio, television, or telephones.

## What is electricity?

Electricity is a force that is contained in all matter: in all solids, liquids, and gases. Matter is made up of *atoms* (the smallest particles into which anything can be broken down). A single grain of sand contains thousands of millions of atoms. The outside of an atom contains one or more particles called *electrons*. Inside, at the centre, is a tiny *nucleus* made up of particles called *protons and neutrons*.

**Electrons and protons** Electrons are said to be *negatively charged*, and protons are said to be *positively charged*. Usually, the amount of electrons and protons is evenly balanced. In some materials, however, chiefly metals, the atoms have electrons that are free to move between atoms.

**Electric current** The electricity we use for heating, lighting, and other purposes is called *electric current*. It flows through a wire as electrons move between the atoms of metal in the wire. Each electron has an electric charge. As they move, electric charges travel along the wire at very high speed.

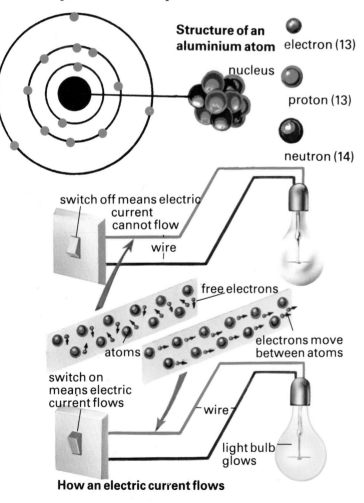

**Structure of an aluminium atom**
electron (13)
nucleus
proton (13)
neutron (14)

switch off means electric current cannot flow
wire
free electrons
atoms
electrons move between atoms
switch on means electric current flows
wire
light bulb glows

**How an electric current flows**

## Electricity in industry and the home

Electricity powers machines and tools in factories, and is used for lifts, cranes and conveyor belts. In offices, it operates typewriters and computers. Hospitals use it for X-ray machines, life-support machines, and other apparatus. Radio, television, telegraph, telephone, radar, and sonar all depend on electricity. Engines for cars, locomotives, ships, and aircraft have electrical components (parts). Refrigerators, vacuum cleaners, food mixers, irons, washing machines, and shavers are among the electrical items used in the home.

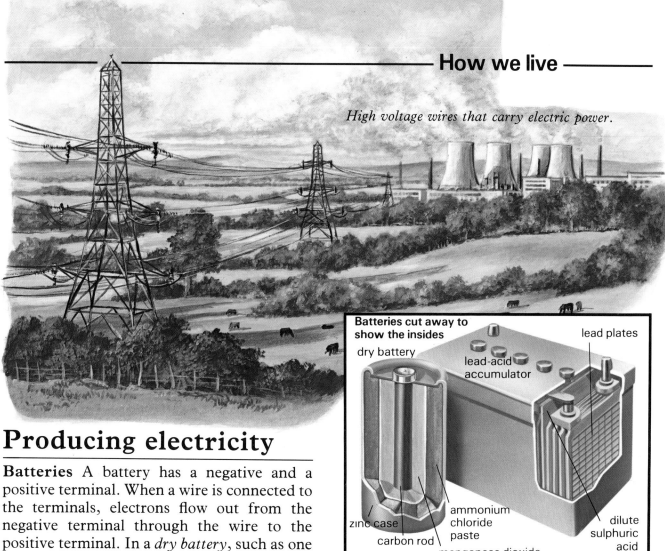

*High voltage wires that carry electric power.*

**Batteries cut away to show the insides**
dry battery
lead-acid accumulator
lead plates
zinc case
carbon rod
ammonium chloride paste
manganese dioxide
dilute sulphuric acid

# Producing electricity

**Batteries** A battery has a negative and a positive terminal. When a wire is connected to the terminals, electrons flow out from the negative terminal through the wire to the positive terminal. In a *dry battery*, such as one used in a torch or transistor radio, electrons are released by the chemical action of ammonium chloride on zinc. As the battery is used, the chemicals change until no more electrons are released. The battery is then dead. In a *lead-acid accumulator*, the sort of battery used in a car, a chemical reaction takes place between lead and sulphuric acid. This sort of battery can be recharged. A supply of electricity is connected to the battery, and electrons are fed back into the atoms.

**Generators** These produce most of the world's electric power in *power stations*. Generators work because of the close connection between magnetism and electricity. When a magnet is moved past a coil of wire, an electric current is *induced* (produced) in the wire. Many power-station generators have huge magnets that spin round past thick copper coils, or coils that move past magnets.

Most generators are driven by *turbines*. Turbines are wheels rather like the wheels of a paddle steamer. They are turned by steam, water, or gas.

# Transmitting electricity

Electric power may have to be *transmitted* (carried) for hundreds of kilometres from a power station to houses, factories, schools, and other buildings where it will be used. It travels through underground *cables* or through *high-voltage* lines high above the countryside. On its way, it passes through several *transformers*. Some transformers increase its voltage, so that electricity is not lost during long-distance transmission. Others, farther along, decrease the voltage to what is needed for use.

149

# Minor Sources of Energy

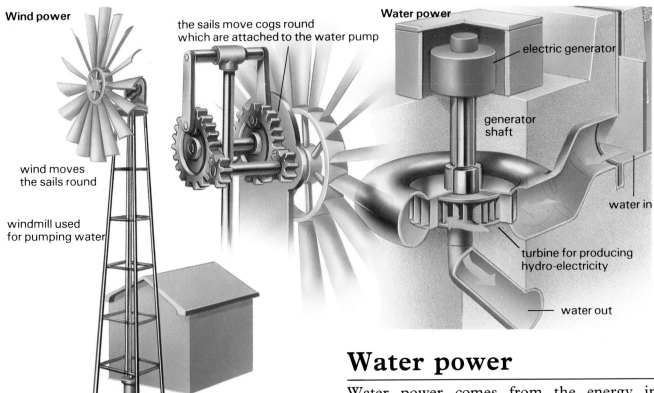

**Wind power**

wind moves the sails round

windmill used for pumping water

the sails move cogs round which are attached to the water pump

**Water power**

electric generator

generator shaft

water in

turbine for producing hydro-electricity

water out

Much of the energy used in the world comes from coal, electricity, petroleum, and changes in the atom (nuclear energy). (See page 142 to 149.) But there are also minor sources of energy. Some of them, such as wind power, have been used for thousands of years. Others, such as solar-energy collectors, are very new.

## Wind power

The energy in the wind is used by sailing boats and sand yachts. Before engines were invented, even large ships depended on wind power.

Windmills were used for hundreds of years for grinding wheat and other cereals. Today they are still often used by farmers for pumping water. Some of them operate generators for producing electric power. Usually, they can only produce small amounts of electricity, perhaps enough for a single farm.

## Water power

Water power comes from the energy in flowing or falling water. It was one of the first types of energy that people learnt to use. About 2000 years ago, somebody invented the *water wheel*, a wheel with paddles round its rim. When moving water strikes the paddles, it makes the wheel rotate (turn). The turning wheel is used to drive a machine. In this way, the energy of the water is changed into mechanical energy.

For hundreds of years, water wheels were used in water-mills to grind cereals. The wheels were turned by fast-flowing rivers.

Today, the most important use of water power is the production of electricity. Water is made to flow from a high level to a lower level. The water turns turbines, which operate electric generators. A turbine works in the same way as a water wheel. Electricity produced in this way is called *hydro-electricity*.

Usually, a hydro-electric power station is built beside a river. A dam is constructed to hold back the river water, and then feed it with great strength to the turbines.

# Tidal and wave power

The ocean tides hold great amounts of energy as they rise and fall. This energy can be used for various purposes. Tidal power stations, for example, are hydro-electric power stations that change the energy of moving tidal water into electricity.

The up-and-down movement of the sea's waves is also a source of energy. It can be used to produce electricity.

## Geothermal power

Geothermal power comes from heat inside the Earth. In New Zealand and Iceland, some houses are heated by hot water that bursts up through the ground in *geysers* (hot springs). Steam from inside the Earth can be used to turn turbines. The turbines drive generators to produce electricity.

*A geyser in Rotorua, New Zealand.*

# Solar-energy collectors

Most of the energy in the world comes originally from the Sun. But solar-energy collectors use energy from the Sun that would otherwise be wasted.

**Collecting the energy** There are two methods. In one method, parabolic (bowl-shaped) mirrors focus the Sun's rays on to a *collector*. The collector is usually a number of pipes containing air or water. The Sun's heat warms the air or turns the water into steam.

In the other method, a *flat-plate* collector traps the Sun's heat in much the same way as a garden greenhouse does. The heat can also be used to produce hot air or steam.

**Using the energy** Energy collected from the Sun can be used in many ways. One of the most important is for house heating. Hot water or hot air is circulated round a house, through pipes and radiators.

Steam can be used to turn a turbine that operates a machine or helps to make electricity. The Sun's rays can even be concentrated to heat furnaces and to cook food.

**How solar energy can be used to heat a house**

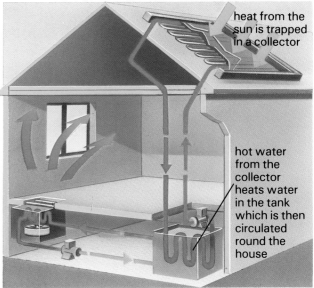

heat from the sun is trapped in a collector

hot water from the collector heats water in the tank which is then circulated round the house

# Farming and Fishing

Farming was the world's first industry, and is still the most important. Only a small part of the world's population would be able to live if there were no farmers to grow food crops and to keep animals for milk and meat.

The earliest people on Earth had to find food wherever they could. They hunted animals, and searched the forests for fruit, nuts, and other things to eat. Civilization began when people discovered that they could grow the plants they needed for food.

**A variety of crops**

wheat

rice

fruit and vegetables

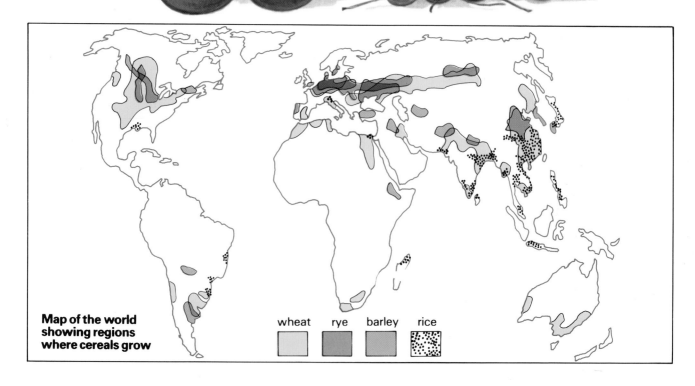

**Map of the world showing regions where cereals grow**

wheat    rye    barley    rice

# Types of farming

**Cultivating crops** Farmers *cultivate* (carefully grow) crops for food and for making other products. (See also page 76.)

*Cereals* are the most important of all crops because they provide the *staple* (main) food of most of the world's population. Cereals are grasses. They include rice, wheat, rye, barley, maize and oats.

Two out of three of all the people in the world eat rice as their main food. The next most important cereals are wheat and rye which are the chief cereals for making bread. (See page 156.) Wheat and rye grow best in cool climates. Rice grows best in hot, wet climates.

*Vegetables* are also important, especially the potato. As a food crop, it is nearly as valuable as rice and wheat. It produces more food per hectare than any cereal. Beans of various kinds are also very important as food. Other major vegetables include cassava, cabbage, peas, sweet potatoes and yams.

*Fruit and nuts* are included in the diet of people in most parts of the world. Some fruits, such as apples, plums, and strawberries, grow well in mild climates. Citrus fruits, such as oranges and lemons, and bananas need hot climates. Nuts grow in most regions.

*Sugar* is obtained from two crops: sugar cane and sugar beet. Sugar cane provides most of the world's sugar. It grows in hot climates. Sugar beet grows mainly in countries with mild climates.

*Tea, coffee and cocoa* are the crops that provide the world's most popular non-alcoholic drinks. Tea is made from the leaves of the tea plant, coffee from the beans of the coffee bush, and cocoa from the beans of the cacao tree. All of them grow in tropical countries.

*Fibre crops* are grown to provide materials for textiles and similar products. They include cotton, sisal, jute, and hemp.

*Other crops* of importance include rubber and tobacco. Tobacco is made from the leaves of the tobacco plant. Rubber comes from *latex*, a juice that oozes from a rubber tree when its bark is cut. Latex is not the tree's sap.

**Raising farm animals** Farmers raise animals not only for food but also for leather, wool and for domestic uses. (See also page 106.)

*Cattle* are kept for their milk or their meat. Dairy cattle provide milk, and such milk products as butter and cheese. Beef cattle are for meat.

*Sheep and goats* are raised for meat and milk. Meat from sheep is called *mutton*.

*Pigs* are kept principally for their meat. The various kinds of meat are known as *pork*, *bacon*, and *ham*.

*Poultry* includes all kinds of farmyard birds, such as chickens, ducks, and geese. They provide eggs as well as meat.

**Farm animals**

cows

sheep

*Above right: Wheatfields in Tanzania, Africa.*
*Above: An oil palm plantation in Ghana, Africa.*
*The men are spraying the crops by hand.*

# Using the land

**Single-crop farming** This is usually carried out on large farms called *plantations*. Only one crop is grown. Crops grown in this way include tea, coffee, bananas, cotton and tobacco, whichever is most suitable for the climate and the soil.

**Mixed farming** This sort of farming is common in countries where the weather changes often. Farmers grow several kinds of crops, and probably also keep cattle, sheep, or pigs. If one crop grows badly because of the weather, the farmer has other crops or animals to depend on.

**Intensive farming** As much as possible is grown on each piece of land. This sort of farming is important in countries where farmland is scarce, such as Japan and Israel.

# Farming round the world

Many countries are short of food. In some parts of the world, thousands of people die of starvation when crops fail because of bad weather or floods.

In North America, Australia, New Zealand, Europe, and South Africa, most farms are efficient and produce large crops. In much of Africa, Asia, and South America, however, farmers produce only small crops, though they work hard. They use out-of-date farming methods. Many of them are *subsistence farmers*, that is, they grow just enough food for themselves and their families to live on.

The United Nations, an international organization, works, among other things, to make farming more efficient in the poor countries of the world. Through the Food and Agriculture Organization, it helps farmers to buy farm machines, such as tractors. It also helps them to *irrigate* (water) their land, and to buy *fertilizers* (materials that make the soil more fertile).

# Fishing

Fish is valuable as food because it is one of the chief sources of protein. In some countries with large coastlines, such as Japan and Norway, it is a major part of people's diet. Most of the fish that people eat are salt-water fishes, caught in the sea. But people also eat fresh-water fishes, caught in rivers and lakes.

**Inshore fishermen** People who fish in coastal waters and waters not far from land, can usually bring their catches back to port every day. Often, they use *seine nets* or *drift nets*. Seine nets are long nets that are drawn in a loop around a *shoal* (group) of fish. Drift nets or gill nets hang like curtains in the water. When fishes try to swim through, their gills are caught in the nets, trapping them.

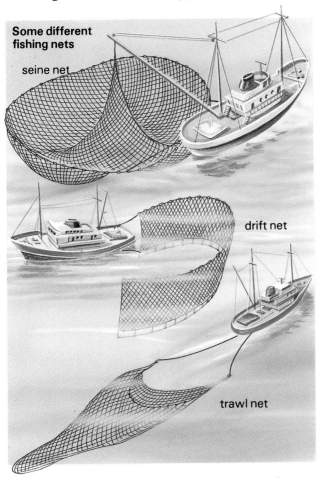

Some different fishing nets

seine net

drift net

trawl net

**Deep-sea fishermen** These fishermen sail across the oceans in *trawlers*, and may be away from port for several weeks. They catch, chiefly, fishes such as cod. Usually, they use *trawl nets*, nets like huge bags pulled behind the trawlers. The opening of the 'bag' can be as large as 30 metres across. The trawl scoops fishes out of the sea. Every few hours, the fishermen empty it into the ship. Because deep-sea fishermen are away from port for a long time, they have to preserve their catch on ice or load it into a refrigerator ship.

**Fishing grounds** Fishermen find the largest shoals of fish in the north-west and central Pacific Ocean, and in the north-east Atlantic Ocean. The countries that make the largest catches of fishes are Japan, Peru, and China. Many countries try to control the numbers of fishes that can be taken from the waters around their coasts. In some parts of the oceans, valuable fishes are becoming scarce.

*Below: Fishermen sorting their catch before taking it back to port.*

# Bread

One of the most delicious smells in the world is the smell of freshly-baked bread. Many people still bake their own bread or buy it from a local baker. But in many countries bread is now made in factories. Each factory sends its bread to hundreds of supermarkets and other shops to be sold.

Bread is a very good food, but most people eat it just because they like it. It is made by baking *dough*, a mixture of flour and water. Flour is a powder made by grinding the seeds of plants called *cereals*. Nearly all of these plants belong to the grass family. They include wheat, oats, and rye. The taste, colour, and texture of bread depend on the cereal that is used. (See also page 153.)

Bread is sometimes hard and heavy unless something is added to it to make it *rise*, that is, to make it lighter and more airy. Usually, a fungus called *yeast* is used for this purpose. When yeast is mixed with sugar and water, it fizzes up. The fizzing is caused by bubbles of carbon dioxide gas. When this fizzy mixture is added to dough, the bubbles spread through the dough and make it rise.

*Below: A small, local bakery in Germany.*

Some different loaves of bread

# From the field to the table

Farm machines called *combine harvesters* cut the ripe cereal at harvest time in the autumn. They cut, thresh and winnow at the same time, separating the grain (seeds) from the stalks and husks. The combine harvester funnels the grain into a suitable container, and leaves the stalks, called *straw*, behind in piles.

The grain is sent to a flour mill, where it is ground into powdery flour. If the whole of the grain is used, the flour is brown and is called *wholemeal flour*. If only the inside part of each seed is used, the flour is white. Sometimes, chemicals are added to bleach the flour, making it even whiter.

The flour goes to a *bakery*. There, the flour, the water, and the yeast mixture is made into dough, using big electric mixers. Sometimes, vitamins are added to increase the food value of the bread. A machine cuts the dough into loaf-sized pieces.

The loaves are placed in a large room to rise. Then they are put into huge ovens that can bake hundreds of loaves at a time.

When the loaves have been baked, they are allowed to cool. Then they are wrapped in waxed paper to keep them fresh. Some loaves are cut into slices before being wrapped. During the whole process, the bread has not been touched by a single person.

Lorries carry the loaves to shops, where they are stacked on the shelves for sale. They reach the customer as fresh as if they had been made locally.

# Preserving Food

Most people eat some preserved food every day. It may be vegetables from a can, frozen meat from a freezer, or fish that has been smoked. Preserving food means doing something to fresh food to make it last longer.

There are simple ways of making food last. Meat that has been cooked, smoked, or pickled (soaked in vinegar or salt water) remains good for longer than fresh meat. Food stored in cool, dry places stays fresh longer than food kept in warm, damp places. Many homes have refrigerators to keep food cool.

Food-processing factories use many methods of food preservation. Because food can be preserved, we can buy foods that were produced in countries thousands of kilometres away. We can also enjoy summer vegetables in the middle of winter.

## Why does food go bad?

Food that has not been preserved goes bad quickly. Tiny, living bacteria grow all over the food, making it rot. If the food is then eaten, the bacteria can cause food poisoning. Fungi also grow, and make the food mouldy. Chemical changes take place, too. The purpose of food preservation is to prevent bacteria and fungi growing, and also to prevent chemical changes.

*Below: Fruit that has been left to go mouldy.*

## Methods of preserving food

Food to be preserved should be of good quality. And it should not be bruised, or damaged in any other way.

**Canning** Food that has been properly preserved in cans or tins will last for a long time. Before being sealed in a can, it is heated to a high temperature. This destroys bacteria and other organisms that could make it bad. Machines remove all the air from the cans and seal them tightly.

Most cans can be kept safely for more than a year. Canned food is quick and easy to cook.

canning

**Freezing** Another way of preventing food going bad is to keep it at a very low temperature, much lower than freezing point.

Many kinds of food, including meat, fish, fruit, vegetables and dairy produce, can be preserved by freezing. Some cooked food, for example home-baked pies, can also be frozen.

Much food is frozen in factories, and then taken to shops, where it is stored in freezers. People can buy it, and keep it in freezers in their homes.

Most frozen foods can be cooked as soon as they are taken from the freezer. Some of them must be left to thaw (unfreeze). When frozen food has been thawed out, it must not be frozen again, as it could cause poisoning when it is eaten.

**Drying** Food that has had all of its moisture removed is safe from attack by bacteria and other organisms because they cannot live on dry food. In hot countries, some foods can be dried in the sun. Factories dry food in ovens called *kilns*.

Dried foods are very light. Some foods including eggs, milk and fruit are dried to make a fine powder. Water is mixed with the powder before it is eaten.

**Curing** Other methods of preserving food include curing – that is, salting, smoking, or pickling. The most suitable method depends on the food to be preserved. For example, meat and fish can be salted or smoked. Vegetables can be pickled in vinegar and spices. Fruit can be preserved by adding sugar to make it into jam. Sugar is also used to preserve the flavour of canned fruits.

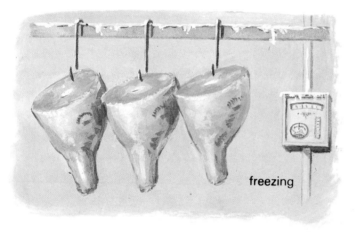

freezing

pickling

smoking

*Below: Salmon hanging up to dry in the sun.*

# Water

All animals and plants need water in order to live. If the Earth did not have water, it would be as empty of life as the Moon.

To stay alive and healthy, we must drink water every day. Our bodies need water to make use of food, and to get rid of waste and impurities.

Water is our most important drink, and we need it for cooking and for keeping clean. It is also used in most industries, in agriculture, in science, and in medicine.

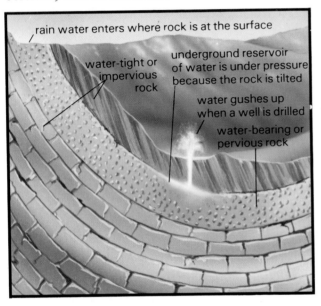

*Above: How an artesian well is formed.*
*Below: A dam creating an artificial lake.*

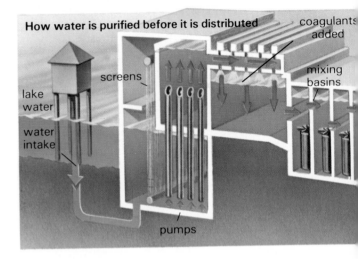

How water is purified before it is distributed

## Sources

We get water from many sources. Some of the purest water falls as rain or snow. We also use water from beneath the ground, and from lakes and rivers and the sea.

**Underground water** In the rocks and soil beneath the Earth's surface there is water. Most of it is rainwater that has seeped slowly downwards, where it collects in certain types of rocks. If a *well* (hole) is dug down to it, the water can be pumped to the surface. Sometimes, it gushes up under its own pressure. This type of well is called an *artesian well*.

**Lakes and rivers** These provide most of the water that we use. Lake water is generally cleaner than river water.

River water is often stored in artificial lakes called *reservoirs*. Engineers build a *dam* (barrier) across a narrow valley. River water flowing into the valley is trapped by the dam, and forms a lake. It is then carried away by pipes when it is needed.

**The sea** Sea water can be used for drinking and other purposes if the salt is removed. However, removing the salt is difficult and expensive.

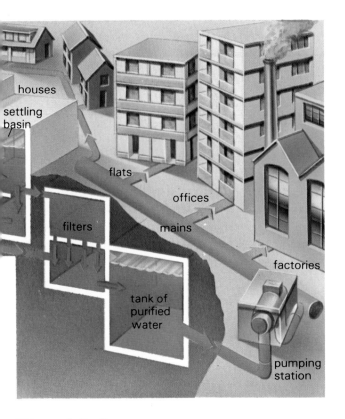

houses
settling basin
flats
offices
filters
mains
factories
tank of purified water
pumping station

# Purifying water

Before water is fit to drink, it must be purified. Otherwise, it may be dirty, may have a bad taste or smell, or may even contain chemicals or *bacteria* (tiny organisms) that cause disease.

The water from a lake, river, or reservoir is carried by pipe to a *waterworks*. There, the water is cleaned, filtered and sterilized.

**Coagulation** Chemicals called *coagulants* are added to the water to clean it. They gather together all the tiny pieces of dirt in the water, and carry them down to the bottom. The dirt is then removed.

**Filtration** The water then flows through layers of fine sand. The sand cleans it still further, and removes any bacteria.

**Sterilization** The water is also treated with chemicals to kill bacteria. The chemical commonly used for this purpose is *chlorine*.

# Distributing water

The purified water is pumped from the waterworks to towns and villages, through large pipes called *water mains*. A network of smaller pipes distribute the water to houses, hospitals, factories, and other buildings. Water is also pumped to large raised tanks, often called *water towers* where it is stored.

# Water shortage

Water covers seven tenths of the Earth, but many regions are short of water. Some deserts have hardly any water at all, and, as a result, few people live in them.

Some dry regions are *irrigated* (watered) by water carried in canals or in pipes. Inventors have suggested various ways of irrigating the deserts. One of the most unusual suggestions is that huge icebergs should be towed from the Arctic and Antarctic Oceans and the ice carried to hot desert regions.

*Irrigated land in Swaziland, Africa.*

# Clothes

Clothes are nearly as important to people as food and shelter. Nobody could live for long in very hot places or in very cold places without some sort of covering.

Thousands of years ago, people used animal skins to cover their bodies. Later they discovered how to spin thread and weave it into *cloth* (see page 164).

Today, most cloth is made by machines. Skilled workers use electric sewing machines to make useful and attractive clothes out of cloth.

## Why do people wear clothes?

People wear clothes for many reasons. Clothes give protection in bad weather, or when playing games or doing dangerous jobs. Often people choose clothes that they think are attractive, and that make them feel good.

**Clothes for protection** In cold countries, people wear thick, warm clothes. Woollen clothes are particularly warm because they trap and use the body's own heat. Thick boots and fur-lined hats and gloves help to keep the cold out.

In hot countries, people need protection from the burning rays of the Sun. In hot desert regions, men and women often wear long, loose robes made from cotton or linen. Air is able to circulate around their bodies to keep them cool. The robes are usually made from light-coloured materials that reflect the Sun's rays.

Most people in hot countries need some form of head protection. It may be a separate piece of cloth tied around the head, or a wide-brimmed hat.

In some countries, people can wear the same sort of clothes all year round. But in countries that have a hot summer and a cold winter, people need light clothes for summer, and heavy, warm clothes for winter.

animal skin worn by Stone Age man

turban

wide-brimmed hat

cool clothes worn in East Africa

clothes w for protec against s storms in Morocco

naked South American tribesman

Muslim woman has her face covered

warm ski-suit

protective clothes worn for American football

kimono from Japan

army uniform

grass skirt from Pacific Islands

sari from India

school uniform

warm clothes worn in Lapland

uniform of a Beefeater – Guard of the Tower of London

# Clothes around the world

In many countries, traditional clothes are still worn. People sometimes wear certain clothes because of their religious beliefs. For example, some Muslim women always keep their faces covered.

In Japan, many women wear beautiful, embroidered gowns called *kimonos*. The gowns have deep sleeves and are tied at the waist with a wide sash called an *obi*.

Indian women wear graceful *saris*. A sari is a length of cloth that is draped carefully around the body, and then drawn over the head or shoulder. Some Indian and Pakistani women wear trousers, often of silk, with a tunic on top. In many parts of India, men wear a simple garment called a *dhoti*.

In Lapland, where the temperature is usually below freezing, the people wear thick brightly-coloured clothes made from wool and reindeer skins. In hot regions of Africa and South America, tribal people wear practically no clothes at all. Some of them cover their bodies with jewellery made from coloured beads and animal hair. Some use vegetable dyes to paint their bodies.

**Clothes as identification** Some people's clothes tell us immediately what sort of job they do. Or, they may tell us that the wearer belongs to a particular organization. Clothes of this kind are called *uniforms*.

Soldiers, sailors, and airmen wear smart uniforms with badges that show their rank. School children often wear a uniform, and Scouts and Guides also wear special uniforms and badges.

# Textiles

Nearly all of the clothes that we wear are made from textiles. Many things around the house, including carpets, curtains, sheets, and towels, are also made from textiles.

Textiles consist of thousands of fine, thread-like *fibres*. The fibres are twisted together to make a strong thread, sometimes called *yarn*. The yarn is woven to make textiles. Thin textiles are called *cloth*.

## Where do fibres come from?

Textile fibres come from many different sources. Many come from plants and animals; others are made in chemical factories. Fibres that come from plants and animals are called *natural fibres*. Fibres that are produced by chemical processes are called *man-made* or *synthetic fibres*.

**Cotton fibres** These are fluffy, white fibres that cover the seed pod of the cotton plant. They are gathered by hand or by machine, when the seed pod is ripe. The fibres are separated from the seed pod by a machine called a *cotton gin*. After ginning, the fibres are pressed together to form *bales* (bundles).

*Cotton plants growing in Turkey.*

**Wool fibres** Animals that have thick, hairy coats give wool. Most woollen fabrics are made from the fibres of sheep's coats. Sheep's coats are called *fleeces*. They are cut every year by people using electric clippers. This is called *shearing*.

Woollen fabrics are used to make warm clothes and blankets. They do not crush easily.

**Silk fibres** Small caterpillars called *silkworms* make silk fibres. Young silkworms eat huge quantities of mulberry leaves. When they are about one month old, the silkworms start to spin long, silky threads that they wrap round their bodies. This silky covering is called a cocoon. It is produced by glands in the silkworm's head.

Silk fibres are collected by placing the silkworms' cocoons in hot water. The water loosens the sticky gum that keeps the threads in place. Skilled workers carefully unwind the thread using special machines. The thread from one silkworm can measure over 1000 metres.

*Above: Bales of cotton in a textile factory.*

**Man-made fibres** Some man-made fibres are made from natural materials, but chemicals are also added. For example, the fabric called *rayon* is made from wood-pulp. Chemicals are added to the pulp to make a liquid. The liquid is forced through tiny holes in a nozzle called a *spinneret*. The fine fibres formed by the spinneret are passed through an acid bath, where they become hard.

# Weaving

Most fabrics are made by weaving (interlacing) two sets of threads together. (See page 236.)

Many people still weave fabrics on small hand looms. In factories, enormous high-speed mechanized looms can make hundreds of metres of fabric in a very short time.

**Animals whose coats give fibres for textiles**

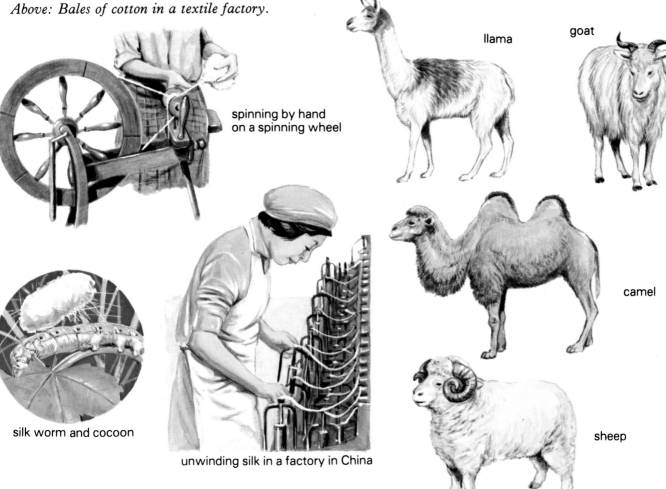

spinning by hand on a spinning wheel

llama

goat

camel

silk worm and cocoon

unwinding silk in a factory in China

sheep

# Everyday Materials

Some everyday objects

Human beings have two needs that are more important than any others. They need food and they need shelter.

In the richer countries, people take food and shelter for granted. They also take for granted all the things that are produced in factories and workshops to make life more comfortable, more interesting, and more amusing. Their homes contain hundreds of such articles: chairs, carpets, lamps, radios, refrigerators, cookers, cups, knives, bottles, tools and many more. City streets are crowded with cars and buses. Aeroplanes fly overhead, trains speed along the railway tracks, and ships carry passengers and freight (goods) across the oceans.

All these things are so familiar that people seldom think about them. Many of them are made of natural materials, such as wood and metals. Others are manufactured from man-made materials, such as glass and plastics, but even man-made materials come originally from materials found in nature.

All the time, more and more of the Earth's riches are being taken and used in factories. In time, some of the materials that we now depend on for our comfort may be used up. Petroleum, for example, may be hard to find in a hundred years' time. Petroleum is one of the world's most important fuels. It is also important in the making of plastics, and synthetic (artificial) rubber, the materials from which many common objects are manufactured.

## Wood

Wood has been important to human beings since early times. Over hundreds of years, people have used so much wood that they have destroyed vast areas of woodland. The great forests that once covered Europe have almost disappeared. In other parts of the world, too, many regions that were once covered by trees are now bare. People in many countries now understand the importance of saving the world's forests. New trees are planted to take the place of those that are cut down.

**From trees to timber** Workers called *fellers* or *lumberjacks* cut down the trees that have been marked for cutting. They use power saws, and can make a tree fall exactly where they want it to. The tree trunks and branches are then cut into logs.

The logs are carried to a *sawmill* by road or rail. Sometimes, they are floated down a river or across a lake to the mill. In the mill, they are cut up into boards.

**Uses of wood** Wood is one of the most important building materials. It is used for beams, floors, doors, windows and other building parts. Other industries also use it for making furniture, boxes, toys, boats, telegraph poles and hundreds of other products. Beautiful carvings can be made from wood. Wood is also pulped to make paper.

# Paper

Paper was invented in China nearly 2000 years ago. A man named Ts'ai Lun discovered that he could make a material to write on when he broke up the wood from a tree and flattened it out. The *cellulose* fibres (threads) in the wood matted together to form paper.

Cellulose is a substance found in all plants. It is also found in certain other materials, including cloth, so some high-quality paper is made from rags. Most paper is made from soft-wood trees such as fir, pine and spruce.

Paper has been important to civilization as a material to write on and print on. Without it, we would not have books, magazines or newspapers. It has many other uses, too. It is used for paper bags, cardboard boxes, lampshades, kites, plates and cups, clothes, building materials and many other things.

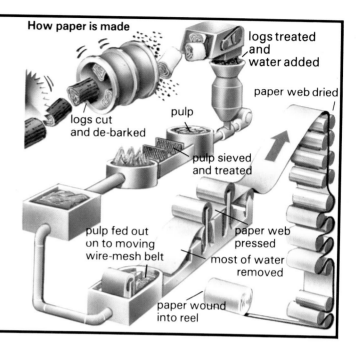

How paper is made

logs treated and water added

logs cut and de-barked

pulp

paper web dried

pulp sieved and treated

pulp fed out on to moving wire-mesh belt

paper web pressed

most of water removed

paper wound into reel

*Below: Logs being floated down the river to a mill in Canada.*

# Metals

We use metals for so many purposes that our way of life would be impossible without them. Thousands of different things in our world are made of metals, from pins to spacecraft.

People began using metals more than 5000 years ago. They discovered that they could hammer hard metals into tools and weapons. These metal implements did not break, and they remained sharp. Earlier people had possessed no tools except pieces of bone and stone that broke easily.

The discovery of metals was so important to the growth of civilization that we call two periods of history the Bronze Age and the Iron Age. These were the periods in which people learnt to use these metals.

**Bronze and Iron-Age tools**

**What are metals?** Metals make up a large part of the Earth. Chemically, they are *elements*, that is, they are among the basic materials of which the Earth is made.

Some metals exist in a form that we can easily recognize. *Gold*, for example, is found as gleaming pieces of yellow metal. But many metals are mixed with other substances to form *ores* that look like lumps of rock. The metal has to be *extracted* (removed) from the ore. Usually, this is done by crushing the ore and heating it. Some ores are found hundreds of metres under the ground. Deep *mines* have to be dug to reach them.

Some metals are more useful when they are mixed together to form *alloys*. For example, a strong metal may be mixed with a light metal to produce an alloy that is both strong and light. One of the first alloys to be made was *bronze*, a mixture of copper and tin.

**Metals in the modern world** *Steel* is one of the most important metals in the world. It is a very strong metal and cheap to make. It is an alloy of iron and carbon and sometimes other metals as well. Iron is therefore in great demand, but it is very common in the Earth's crust and mined as iron ore. Iron and steel give strength to large buildings, and they are used in cars, locomotives, and ships. If the steel industry did not exist, few other industries would be possible. Nearly all industries use machinery made of steel.

*Aluminium*, the most plentiful metal, is also extremely important in making machinery, and saucepans and other kitchen utensils are made of it. *Copper* and *brass* are used in electrical fittings and cables. Copper is also used in coins, together with such other metals as *zinc* and *nickel*. *Lead* is used on roofs, and also in printing type. *Mercury* is used in thermometers and other instruments. *Uranium* has growing importance as a source of atomic energy. (See page 142.)

*Above: White-hot molten steel at a steel works.*

**A variety of things made of metal**

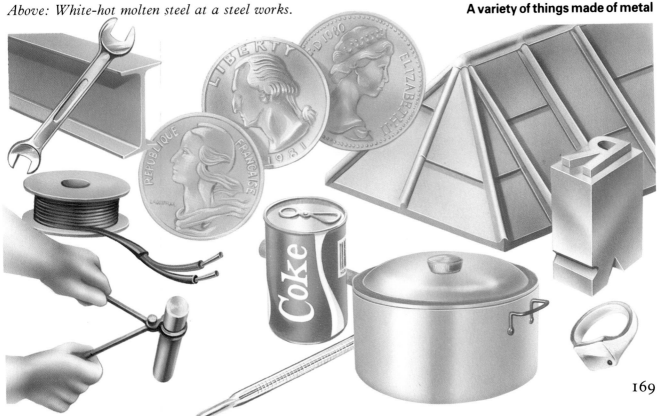

# Ceramics

Ceramics are objects made from various kinds of clay. Some of the most ordinary objects are ceramics, for example sewer pipes and electrical insulators as they do not conduct electricity. Some ceramics, though, are among the most beautiful things that people have ever made. They include brilliantly-coloured tiles, delicate porcelain, and statues and other figures that are works of art. The making of ceramics is often called *pottery*.

In making pottery, the soft wet clay is shaped on a *potter's wheel* or in a *mould*. Then it is *fired* (baked) in an oven to harden it. The oven is called a *kiln*. Often the clay is given a *glaze*, a shiny coating.

# Glass

Glass is made from the common materials sand, soda-ash, and lime. It has even more uses than ceramics. Special types of glass are used for various purposes. They include windows, mirrors, lenses for microscopes and for spectacles, light bulbs, ovenware, bottles and building blocks. Glass can be made in thin fibres (threads) that can be woven into cloth. It can be so flexible (easily bent) that it can be made into springs. It can also be so tough that a bullet will not break it.

To make glass, the sand, soda-ash and lime are heated together until they form a white-hot liquid. The liquid glass is then shaped by skilled workers.

# Plastics

Plastics are man-made materials that have thousands of uses. They can be flexible or hard and they do not rust or rot. They can be any colour, or can be transparent, like glass. The word plastics comes from a Greek word meaning *able to be moulded*. Plastics can be moulded into any shape.

*Above: A glass blower at work in the famous Waterford factory in Ireland.*

**What are plastics?** Plastics are made in factories from chemicals. These chemicals are obtained from petroleum, coal, salt, natural gas and other substances. There are two main kinds of plastics.

*Thermoplastic* plastics are shaped while they are hot, and harden as they cool. If they are heated again, they melt. As a result, they cannot be used near heat, but they are strong and most can be bent without breaking.

*Thermosetting* plastics are also heated while they are being shaped. But the heat makes them hard, and they cannot be melted again.

**Uses of plastics** One of the most important thermoplastic plastics is *nylon*. It is very strong, and is used to make gears and other parts of machinery. When it is drawn out into fine threads, it can also be used to make cloth. Other thermoplastic plastics include *acrylics*, which are strong and clear, and are not affected by

A variety of things made of plastic

*Left: A bath shaped in thermosetting plastic being checked at the factory.*

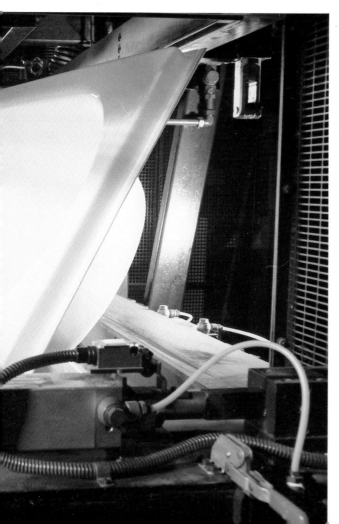

chemicals. They are used for lenses, lights, and false teeth. *Polyethylene* is used for plastic bags because it is light and bends easily. *Polyvinyl chloride (PVC)* makes water pipes, gramophone records, and waterproof coats.

The thermosetting plastics include *alkyds*, which are used for paints and electrical insulators, and *epoxies*, which make strong glues. *Polyesters* are shaped into bodies for cars and hulls for boats. *Phenolics* are not affected by heat. They are used for the nose cones of rockets, and for table tops. *Melamines* also withstand heat, and are used for cups, plates, and lampshades.

# Education

By means of education, we learn about the world. Education helps us to gain knowledge, to learn skills, and to make the best use of our talents which are the things we are naturally good at.

We can learn some things for ourselves. A baby slowly finds out, for example, how to pick objects up. This is the first step in education. All through life we continue educating ourselves in this way, by copying other people.

Some things are too difficult to learn on our own. We need somebody to teach us. Children's first teachers are their parents. Later, children go to school, and are taught by teachers who are specially trained for this work.

## Aims of education

Education helps each individual person to get more out of life. It helps the community (everybody, as a group,) by training skilled workers of all kinds, including scientists and artists.

**The individual** Every person learns basic skills such as reading, writing, and counting. Without such skills, life today would be very difficult. People may also develop other skills that will add to their enjoyment of life. They may, for example, discover that they can draw well, are good at sport, or can write poetry.

Education also helps people to think clearly, and to develop *moral values*, that is, to decide between right and wrong. It teaches them to enjoy the arts, such as music and painting. It helps them to understand the world, and to add all the time to the interesting things that they know.

**The community** People as a group gain from education because educated people can make a more useful contribution to community life. They provide the many different skills, and are better able to make the decisions, that are needed to run countries in the best way.

*Above: A baby learning while playing in the bath.*

**Stages of education**

play
school

secondary
school

# Stages of education

**Early education** Some children up to the age of about five years have *preschool education*. It aims to make them interested in learning, and to prepare them for school.

**Primary and secondary schools** Pupils enter these schools at the age of six or seven, and may remain up to the age of about 18. They are first taught to read, write, and count. They learn to use their hands and their voices, and they learn how to work with other people.

At a later stage, pupils study such subjects as history, geography, literature, mathematics, foreign languages, and science. These subjects add to their knowledge of the world, and give them new interests.

**Vocational schools** These train older students for careers. Some of them teach technical subjects, such as electronics, carpentry, cooking, or car repairs. Others provide training for such other careers as business, nursing, or hairdressing. There are also special colleges of medicine, law, architecture, and other professional subjects.

**Universities** These also have *faculties* (departments) that educate students for certain professions. They also provide higher education in science and the arts. An important part of university work is *research* (finding out things that add to the world's knowledge).

# Education around the world

Education is organized and paid for by the government in most countries. Some countries also have schools and colleges that are run privately. Some people believe that all education should be controlled by the government, to prevent a few children being given unfair advantages.

In most countries, children must, by law, attend school for a certain number of years. They can then decide whether to find a job, or to continue their education in a college or university. Each country has an educational system related to its history and its needs. In developing countries, including many countries of Africa and Asia, technical and industrial skills are more important than any others so that people can help with the development.

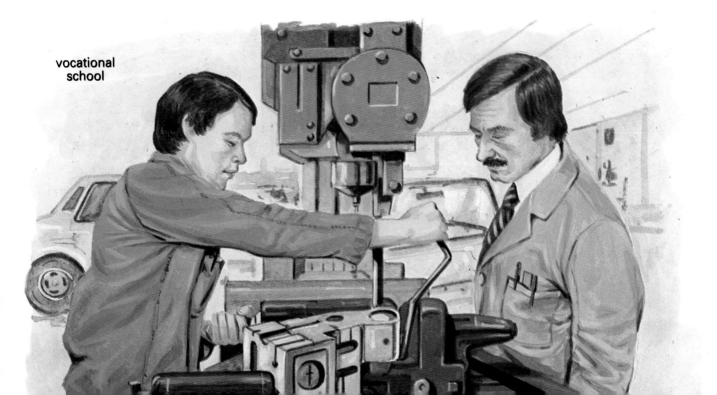

vocational school

# Health

*A variety of food which would make a balanced diet.*

Good health is a person's most valuable possession. Today, it is much easier to be healthy than it was in the past. Modern people know more about health, have better food, and live in cleaner surroundings. Also, scientists and doctors have learnt how to prevent or cure many diseases. Most people can quickly get help from a doctor or go to a hospital when they are ill.

As a result, people in the modern world generally live longer than people in the past. People who live in industrial countries can expect to live for twice as long as the people who lived a few hundred years ago. In some countries, the length of life has increased by 20 years since the beginning of this century.

There are still some countries where people's lives are short. They have not enough to eat, they live in dirty surroundings, and diseases are common. The World Health Organization and other organizations work to improve health all over the world.

## Healthy living

To keep fit and healthy, a person must eat good food, get proper exercise and rest, and keep clean.

**Food** Energy for work and play comes from food. The kinds of food that people eat vary from country to country. Good food everywhere contains certain things that are important to health, such as proteins, calcium, iron, and vitamins. Having water to drink is just as necessary as having food.

**Exercise and rest** Exercise helps the muscles to develop, and keeps the body working properly. However, sleep is even more important. It is as necessary to health as food and drink.

**Cleanliness** This is also important, because germs increase rapidly in dirt and grime, and cause disease. Frequent washing keeps the skin healthy. People keep their gums and teeth healthy by regular brushing.

# Public health

When people live together in cities, villages, and other communities, a disease can spread quickly from one person to another. This is called an *epidemic*. Governments have to make sure that epidemics do not happen.

**Sanitation** Proper sanitation is one of the most effective ways of preventing disease. Drains are built to carry away *sewage* (waste materials from kitchens, lavatories, and factories). Clean water is provided for people to drink and to use for washing. Arrangements are made to remove *refuse*, the rubbish that people throw away.

**Fighting disease** Governments, scientists and doctors have combined to fight certain diseases that once killed millions of people. Smallpox, which was one of the deadliest diseases, has been almost wiped out. People are *vaccinated* to prevent them catching it. Vaccination is a way of introducing weakened germs into the body of a healthy person. The vaccine causes the body to develop *antibodies* that act to prevent the disease. Vaccination has also helped to prevent other serious diseases, including diphtheria, tuberculosis, and poliomyelitis.

*Children having a medical check-up at school.*

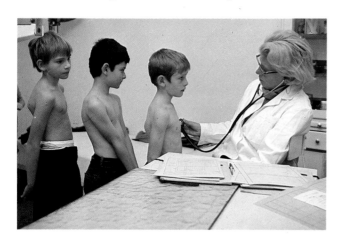

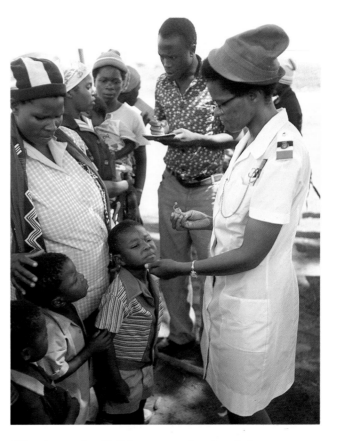

*The Save the Children organization helps to protect children against major diseases. Here, a doctor is working in Swaziland, Africa.*

Malaria, a common and deadly disease in hot countries, can be fought by destroying the mosquitoes that carry it. Swamps, where mosquitoes breed, are drained, ponds are sprayed with oil, and mosquitoes in houses are killed by *insecticides*.

# Health services

The health of communities has been improved by advances in the medical treatment of diseases. The discovery of *antibiotics* like penicillin, has saved the lives of countless people suffering from such illnesses as pneumonia and meningitis. New *antiseptics* fight infections. Surgeons can operate to replace damaged organs, including kidneys and even the heart.

# Hospitals

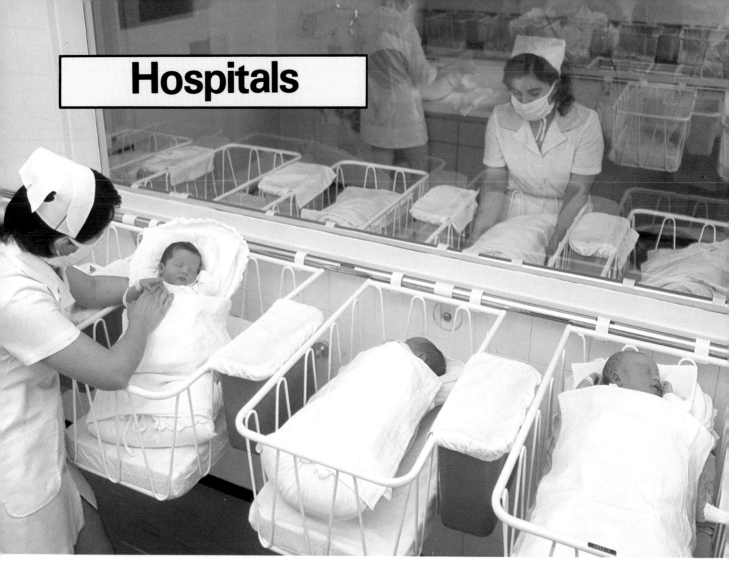

Modern hospitals are friendly, warm places where sick people are looked after and made to feel as though they are in their own homes. Many of the rooms have flowers, pictures, television sets, and radios. Children have toys to play with and books to read. But the most important thing is the care given by the highly-skilled doctors and nurses who work in hospitals. The doctors and nurses have medicines and up-to-date equipment to help them.

## Inside a hospital

Hospitals are a bit like small towns. They are built in such a way that it is quick and easy to get from one place to another. Covered passageways link buildings together. Hospitals have their own kitchens, laundries, store rooms, shops, and often their own power supply.

*Above: New born babies in a hospital.*

**Wards** The rooms where *patients* (sick people) stay while they are in hospital are called *wards*. There are often many beds in one ward. As a result, the patient has the company of other patients and of nurses all the time. Children are usually in a special children's ward. A nurse or doctor who wants to examine a patient can pull a curtain round the patient's bed.

**Operating theatre** Some patients go into hospital to have an operation. For example, they may have to have their tonsils or appendix removed. Operations are done by a *surgeon* (a doctor specially skilled in doing operations). The operating theatre must be completely free from any germs. All the special equipment that the surgeon needs is laid out on a trolley.

**Maternity ward** Most mothers go into hospital when their babies are about to be born. Both mothers and babies are looked after in the maternity ward. Sometimes new-born babies are so small that they have to be given special conditions in something called an *incubator*. The incubator helps them to breathe.

**Casualty department** Accidents happen all the time. When people are hurt in the home or in the street they are rushed by ambulance to the casualty department of a hospital. Doctors and nurses are there at all times of the day and night in case of emergencies.

When a patient arrives at the casualty department, he or she is examined immediately. The doctor decides which part of the hospital to send the patient to. An operation may be necessary, or the patient may go home as soon as the injury has been seen to.

*Below: A man having his chest x-rayed. A photograph of his bones or lungs, or heart will be made for the doctor to examine.*

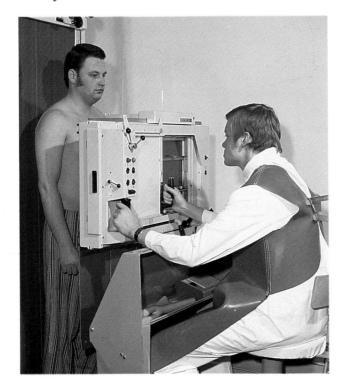

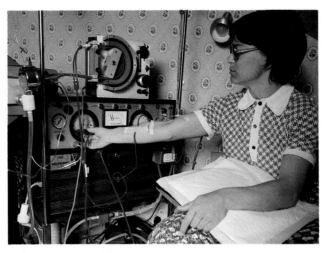

*This woman is using a kidney machine, as her own kidneys do not work as they should. The machine acts as an artificial kidney.*

# Medical machinery

Doctors use a wide range of modern equipment to cure illnesses and to make patients more comfortable. All the time, they are trying to find better ways of treating patients.

**Radiotherapy** A radiotherapy machine is often used to treat patients who have some form of cancer. Cancer is a disease that can destroy parts of the body. The machine sends out very powerful rays that can kill the harmful cancer cells. These rays can be dangerous to healthy people. The *radiotherapist* (person who controls the machine) watches the patient through a glass window.

**Respirator** A patient who has difficulty in breathing can be put into a respirator. The machine pumps air into the patient's lungs.

**Heart-lung machine** A heart-lung machine keeps a patient alive while surgeons perform a *transplant* operation to replace the heart. Transplant operations are extremely long and difficult. The machine takes the place of the heart while the transplant takes place.

# Money

Money is anything that people agree to use to pay for the things they want. If I sell shoes and you want a pair of shoes, you can pay me for them in money. I can use the money to pay for food or anything else that I need. The person who sells me the food can use the money to pay for something else, and so on.

Money is also a measure of the *value* of things. If you know how much money is needed to buy a pair of shoes, and how much money is needed to buy a transistor radio, you know how the shoes and radio compare with each other in value.

## Why do we have money?

The people who lived in forests and caves thousands of years ago had no need for money. They did not have to buy anything. They found their own food and made their own clothes.

Later, when people began to live in villages and towns, life was not so simple. Much more of everything was needed, and people wanted better things. Some people became expert at growing crops and keeping animals. Others became expert at making cloth, and some became expert at making bread. These people became farmers, weavers and bakers.

**The barter system** When the farmer needed bread, he could give the baker some eggs in exchange for it. When he needed clothes, he could exchange vegetables with the weaver for cloth. This way of paying for things is called *bartering*. In some parts of the world, people still barter things today.

As civilization developed, people realized that bartering was a clumsy way of obtaining the things they needed. When, for example, the baker did not want the farmer's vegetables or eggs, the farmer had no way of getting bread.

**The money system** Then somebody had the idea of using *tokens* that everybody would accept in exchange for goods. The baker accepted tokens from the farmer in exchange for bread, and could then spend the tokens on whatever he or she needed. The tokens were what we today call money.

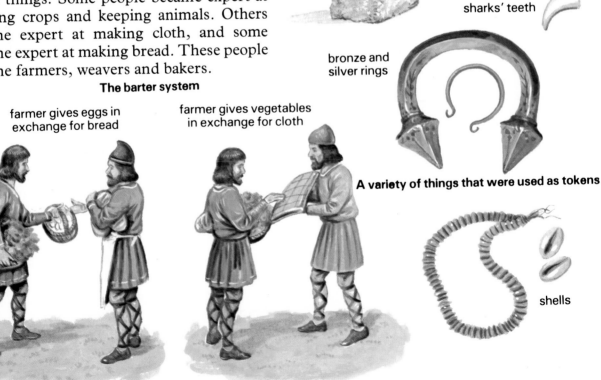

**The barter system**

farmer gives eggs in exchange for bread

farmer gives vegetables in exchange for cloth

salt

sharks' teeth

bronze and silver rings

**A variety of things that were used as tokens**

shells

electrum
(an alloy of gold and silver)
coin from Asia Minor 500BC

**Some early coins**

Chinese coin 600BC

Greek silver tetradrachm 400BC

tetradrachm of Tyne 100BC

Persian silver drachm AD591

Egyptian coin 300BC

English gold sovereign 1489

Spanish ducat 1634

# Modern money

**Coins** The metal in modern coins has little value, but each coin has its money value stamped on it. Every country *mints* (makes) its own coins. The coins of one country can be exchanged for the coins of another.

**Paper money** Coins are heavy, so they are chiefly for small payments. Large payments are usually made in paper money, specially printed by government banks to take the place of coins. Pieces of paper money are called *notes*.

**Gold and silver bars** These have value as money, and are sometimes used in trade between countries. Some countries store gold in banks and this has the real value represented by their paper money.

paper money

coins

gold bar

silver bar

# Early money

The first money tokens were things that people particularly valued. They were used because nobody could doubt their value. People in many places used cattle. Other people, who lived in regions where salt was scarce, used salt. Some people used shells that were rare and pretty.

Gradually, more and more people began to use pieces of precious metal as money, particularly pieces of gold and silver. They also used pieces of other metals, such as bronze. The value of each of these pieces, called *coins*, was the value of the metal it contained.

# Banks

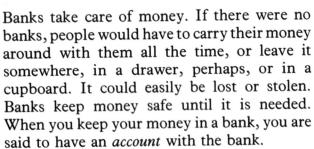

Banks take care of money. If there were no banks, people would have to carry their money around with them all the time, or leave it somewhere, in a drawer, perhaps, or in a cupboard. It could easily be lost or stolen. Banks keep money safe until it is needed. When you keep your money in a bank, you are said to have an *account* with the bank.

Banks also lend money. For example, a farmer needing a new tractor can ask a bank to lend the money to buy one. The bank will lend the money if it believes that the farmer will be able to repay the loan at an agreed rate. For every 100 units of money (such as dollars or pounds) that the bank lends, it will ask the farmer to pay an extra 10 or 15 units each year. This extra payment is called *interest*.

## Using a bank

When you keep your money in a bank account, the bank gives you a cheque book containing *cheques*. You can use the cheques to pay bills. If you want to, you can pay a bill by post, simply by sending a cheque.

If you buy a transistor radio costing 15 dollars (or pounds, rands, francs, or any other unit of money) from a shop called Super Radios, you fill in a cheque and give it to them.

Super Radios take your cheque to their own bank. The 15 dollars is added to their account in the bank.

Super Radios' bank tells your bank that you have made the payment. Your bank subtracts 15 dollars from the money you have in your account, and pays it to Super Radios' bank.

At regular intervals, your bank sends you a *statement* showing how much money is left in your account. You can pay more money into your account at any time.

**Using a bank**

| IN ACCOUNT WITH UNIVERSAL BANK TOWN BRANCH | | | |
|---|---|---|---|
| uper Radios COUNT No 79364392 | DEBITS | CREDITS | BALANCE |
| | | | 478·65 |
| PARTICULARS | | | 278·65 |
| E BALANCE FORWARD | 200·00 | | 293·65 |
| UG 83 3907602 | | 15·00 | |
| SEPT83 CASH/CHEQUES | | | |
| SEPT83 | | | |

**WORLD BANK Inc. STATEMENT**      RURAL BRANCH

| ccount Jane Smith | | No: 113976845 | |
|---|---|---|---|
| ATE PARTICULARS | DEBITS | CREDITS | BALANCE |
| UL 83 BALANCE FORWARD | | | 300·00 |
| UG 83 CASH/CHEQUES | | 180·00 | 480·00 |
| UG 83 71654469 | 8·70 | | 471·30 |
| PT83 71654470 | 15·00 | | 456·30 |

## Bank cards

Many people have credit cards. These are given to them by the bank and can be used to buy things without handling cash. The card is presented at the shop and the customer signs a bill. The shop then gets its money from the bank, and the customer can pay the bank later.
Most banks have also introduced machines which people can use to deposit or withdraw cash from their account, and to order statements and chequebooks. The customer has a card which they put into the machine, and their own code number so that no one else can use the card. They use a keyboard to give their number and to say what service they want. When the customer has finished any business, the machine gives back the card.

# Overdrafts

You must not use a cheque to pay out more money than you have in your account, unless the bank manager agrees to give you an overdraft. An overdraft is permission to use cheques even though you have no money in your account. It is a way of borrowing money. When you use your overdraft, you pay interest to the bank. When you can pay back the money, you put your account *in credit* again.

181

# Trade

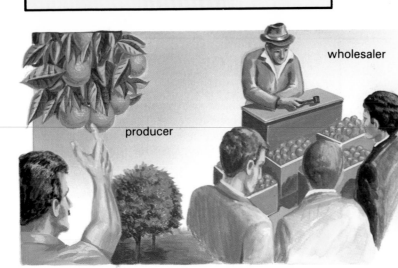

Trade is the transfer of goods from the people who make them (the *producers*) to the people who use them (the *consumers*). It consists mainly of selling and buying.

Because of trade, people can buy goods from almost anywhere in the world. A woman in France, for example, may be able to buy apples grown on a farm near her home. But her suit may be made of wool from Australia, she may drink coffee from Brazil, and she may listen to music on a radio made in Japan.

## From producer to consumer

Goods seldom pass directly from the people who produce them to the people who use them. Usually, there is a 'chain' of trade from the producer to the *wholesaler*, and then to the *retailer* and the consumer. The consumer is the person who uses the goods.

**Producers** These include *manufacturers* who make such goods as clothing, furniture, and machinery. They also include farmers who grow crops and raise animals, and mining companies that dig out coal, iron, and other valuable minerals from the Earth. Companies that sell electricity and other *services* are also producers.

*Above: The different people who deal with oranges as they pass from the producer in one country to the consumer in another country. On the way, they may have been changed into one of many things – such as marmalade.*

**Wholesalers** These are traders who buy large quantities of goods from the producers, and then sell them to the retailers. Wholesalers take the products of many manufacturers. As a result, they can distribute goods to retailers more cheaply and easily than the producers could do it themselves.

**Retailers** These are the shopkeepers who sell goods to the consumers. The retailer can go to a wholesaler's *warehouse* (store) and select the goods he or she needs, without having to go to many different producers.

# Exports and imports

When goods are produced in one country but used in another, there are even more stages in the chain of trade between the producer and the consumer. Companies that can arrange exports and imports have to take part in it. Exports are the goods and services that one country sells to another. Imports are the goods and services that a country buys from another.

Export and import companies arrange for goods to be transported between countries. They have to arrange ways of paying for the goods, and they make sure that government laws are not broken. These laws include rules about *customs duties* (taxes on imports).

*Below: The* Mairangi Bay, *a container ship, passing through the Panama Canal, fully loaded with containers.*

# Trade routes

Most of the world's trade is carried by ship. Thousands of ships sail across the oceans every day, loaded with products of every kind: wheat, coffee, meat, sugar, cotton, rubber, metals, and machinery. About one-third of all the ships at sea carry petroleum.

Most ships follow well-known routes across the oceans. In the past, sailors searched constantly for better sea routes from one continent to another. Christopher Columbus was looking for a trade route between Europe and Asia when he reached the Americas in 1492. Ferdinand Magellan was also searching for a trade route to Asia when he set out on his great expedition in 1519. This was the first expedition to sail round the Earth and prove that the Earth is round. Most people thought that it was flat.

The world's two greatest canals were built to provide easier sea routes. The Suez Canal shortened voyages between Europe and Asia. The Panama Canal linked the Atlantic and Pacific Oceans, which cut the need for sailing round South America.

# Ports and Harbours

Some of the world's busiest and most important cities are seaports. They are important because the thousands of ships that cross the oceans every day need places where they can load and unload passengers and *freight* (goods). Ports are built on *harbours* where ships can anchor safely. They have the equipment that ships need for loading and unloading.

## Types of harbours

Harbours must be sheltered, so that ships are protected against storms and strong winds. They must be large, so that ships are not in danger of colliding. They must have deep water so that large ships can safely enter them.

**Natural harbours** These are usually found in enclosed bays or in river *estuaries* (mouths). Ships can enter through a narrow opening between two arms of land. Some of the world's chief harbours are natural. They include the harbours of New York and San Francisco in the United States of America, Sydney in Australia, Rio de Janeiro in Brazil, and Singapore.

**Artificial harbours** These are made by building strong walls called *breakwaters* in the sea. They are built in places where harbours are needed, but where there are no suitable natural bays. They include the busy harbours of Dover in Britain, Los Angeles in the United States of America, and Europoort at Rotterdam in the Netherlands. Europoort is the largest port in Europe.

**Inland harbours** These are built on wide rivers, far from the sea. They include the harbours of London in Britain, Bordeaux in France, and New Orleans in the United States of America. Montreal in Canada is more than 1500 kilometres from the Atlantic Ocean, to which it is connected by the St Lawrence River.

## Loading and unloading

For loading and unloading, ships are tied up to platforms. *Quays* or *wharfs* are platforms along the shore of a harbour. *Piers* or *jetties* are platforms that stick out from the shore. The areas in which ships tie up are called *docks*.

Harbours must have the correct equipment for loading and unloading the many different kinds of ships that sail the oceans.

**Freighters** This name is given to ships that carry freight in their *holds* (huge storerooms below their decks). The goods are lifted out by large cranes, and transferred to warehouses on the dockside. The cranes can move along the dockside on rails.

Freighters can also use their own *derricks* (small cranes) to unload cargo from their holds into *barges* moored beside them. The goods are then taken on the barges to the quayside.

*Above: Grain carriers anchored in a harbour in Canada.*
*Right: Different types of unloading.*

**Container ships** Different equipment is needed for these ships. Their cargo is packed in huge boxes called *containers*. The containers are lifted off the ships by special cranes, and loaded on to trains or lorries.

**Grain ships** These carry wheat and other cereals. Pumps suck the cargo out of the ships' holds, and transfer it to storage tanks called *silos* on the dockside.

**Oil tankers** These carry petroleum. They include the world's largest ships. Some of them are too big to enter most docks. Often, they moor some distance from the dockside. Their cargo of petroleum is pumped by hose to tanks on the shore or, sometimes, it is pumped into smaller tankers moored nearby.

# Lake ports

Some important ports are built on lakes. They include Chicago in the United States of America and Toronto in Canada, both of which are situated on the Great Lakes. The large ports of Baku and Astrakhan in the CIS lie on the Caspian Sea, which is really a lake.

**Different ways of unloading**

goods lifted out by cranes and stored in a warehouse

containers lifted off and loaded on to lorries

oil pumped into tanks

# Cacao – A Typical Export

Cocoa is one of the world's most popular drinks. It is made from the seeds of the cacao tree, one of many products that are exported all over the world. For hundreds of years, only the people who lived in Central and South America enjoyed the chocolate-flavoured drink. But in the 1500s, the Spanish adventurer Hernando Cortés took some cacao seeds back to Spain. Soon people all over Europe were visiting 'chocolate houses' to meet their friends and to drink steaming hot mugs of cocoa. At this time cocoa was very expensive.

*Right: A graph showing the exports and imports of cacao beans, using the latest figures.*
*Below: Spraying cacao trees in Ghana. This protects the trees against disease and insects.*

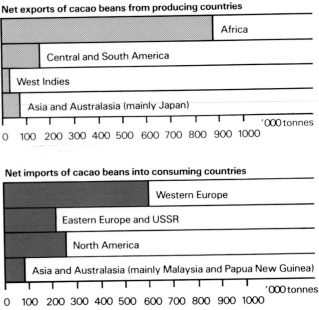

**Net exports of cacao beans from producing countries**

Africa

Central and South America

West Indies

Asia and Australasia (mainly Japan)

0  100  200  300  400  500  600  700  800  900  1000   '000 tonnes

**Net imports of cacao beans into consuming countries**

Western Europe

Eastern Europe and USSR

North America

Asia and Australasia (mainly Malaysia and Papua New Guinea)

0  100  200  300  400  500  600  700  800  900  1000   '000 tonnes

# From cacao to cocoa

Cacao trees grow in hot, wet places such as South America and western Africa. They grow to about 9 metres high and have few branches. Several years after planting, tiny pink flowers grow from the bark and branches of the tree. Some of them turn into oval-shaped fruits called *pods*. Each pod contains about 40 seeds, usually known as *beans*.

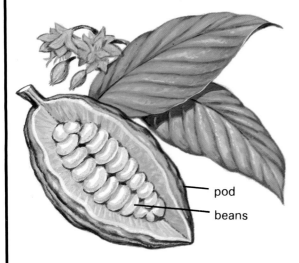

pod

beans

**Harvest** When the cacao pods are ripe, they turn red or orange. Workers cut them from the trees with sharp knives. They split the pods open to release the beans inside.

**Preparing the beans** First, the beans are left in the sun or placed in a heated tank to *ferment*. They swell and become moist (wet). They also turn brown.

The beans then dry out. Workers turn them over from time to time to make sure they dry evenly.

The dry beans are put into sacks and taken by road, sea, and air to factories all over the world to be made into cocoa and chocolate.

# Cocoa as a food

Cocoa and chocolate not only taste good, but are valuable foods. They contain carbohydrates, proteins, and fats. These give us energy and help us to grow. Mountaineers and soldiers often carry bars of chocolate to eat in cold, wet weather.

# Shopping

*Above: A vegetable stall at a market in France.*

Shopping has changed greatly during the last hundred years. In the past, people had to visit many different shops to buy such things as food, clothes, books, toys, and furniture. Today people in towns can buy most things they need in one or two large stores.

Many modern shops are *self-service*. Customers collect the items they want from the shelves, and put them into trolleys or baskets. When they have everything they need, they take their trolleys or baskets to a *checkout*, and pay the cashier.

Shopping at markets has always been popular. People often go to markets to buy goods at *bargain* prices which are lower than usual. In some countries, the marketplace is the only place where people can do their shopping.

Today people can also shop by post. They order goods from a *catalogue*. The goods are delivered to their house.

self-service at a supermarket

## Markets

The first markets were simply gatherings of people who wanted to exchange goods. Later, goods were sold in exchange for money.

Today, most towns and cities have a market at least one day a week. It may be held in a special outdoor marketplace, or in some large covered building. People with goods to sell set up a small *stall* or *stand* with the goods on it. Often, market stalls are simply set up along the side of a street.

Markets sell a wide range of goods. People visit food markets to buy fresh fruit and vegetables. In Bangkok, the capital city of Thailand, there is a famous 'floating market' where all the fruit and vegetables are sold from small boats.

Farmers go to special markets to buy and sell cattle, horses, pigs and sheep. Other markets sell furniture, jewellery or old clothes.

# Small shops

Many people prefer to do their shopping in small shops, where they know the shopkeeper. Small shops are often run by families. They sometimes stay open later than large shops, but their goods are nearly always more expensive than those in large shops. The reason is that large shops deal in huge amounts of goods, and can afford to sell them more cheaply.

Many small shops provide friendly and helpful services that large shops cannot offer. In small villages there may be only one or two small shops.

**The baker** Many baker's shops bake their own bread. You can buy bread and cakes that are fresh from the oven. (See page 156.)

**The butcher** Butchers will cut and trim pieces of fresh meat from any joint you want. They will often give advice about how you should cook the meat.

**The fishmonger** Fishmongers sell all sorts of different fish and will give advice about it.

**The greengrocer** In the greengrocer's shop you can see fresh fruit and vegetables on display, and choose what you want. The items are not already packaged, as they often are in large shops.

**The newsagent** Most newsagents will arrange for newspapers, magazines, or comics to be delivered to people's houses. Usually, they also sell sweets.

CLOUGH'S
WHOLESALE & RETAIL FISH MERCHANTS

fishmonger

shopping from a catalogue

## Shopping in the future

It may soon be possible for people in cities to do all their shopping at home. They will simply be able to turn on their television set and select goods from the items they see on the screen.

A special card will allow them to order directly, and the goods will be delivered to them quickly.

# Large shops

Large, modern shops are designed to make shopping as easy and as much fun as possible. Shops that sell a large number of different types of items, ranging from food to clothes and furniture, are called *department stores*.

*Supermarkets* are large shops that sell all sorts of food items and a few other household things. People use trolleys to collect their shopping from stacked shelves. *Shopping centres* have many small and large shops together in one place. They have large car parks, and shoppers do not have far to walk.

# Inside a department store

Department stores are usually large buildings with several floors. *Escalators* (moving staircases) and *lifts* carry customers between floors.

**Goods** Large signs tell customers where to find the goods they want. For example, kitchen utensils and electrical goods might be in the *basement* (the floor below the ground floor). Soaps and perfumes, small gifts, handbags, and jewellery might be on the ground floor. Other floors might have men's and women's clothes, furniture, toys, television sets, and radios. All the goods are displayed in a way that makes them look attractive and tempting.

Most large stores have a restaurant where customers have a cup of coffee or a meal. Many have a hairdressing salon. Other services include banks, and agencies for booking holidays or theatre tickets.

**Workers** Hundreds of people are needed to make a large department store run smoothly. The people who sell goods are called *sales assistants*. They must be able to advise customers on the items for sale. A *manager* is in charge of a number of assistants. Often, one manager supervises an entire floor of the store.

**Inside a department store**

Many of the people who work in a department store are seldom seen by the customers. *Accountants* and *clerks* deal with the finances of the store. They keep the accounts, and pay the staff. *Personnel workers* look after the staff. They are responsible for training new people.

*Window-dressers* are responsible for making the windows of the store look attractive and interesting. *Buyers* have a very important job. Usually, there is a buyer for each department. For example, there will be a buyer in charge of buying all the toys on sale in the store. The buyer must know what kinds of toys are likely to sell, and must be able to work out how many of each toy to have.

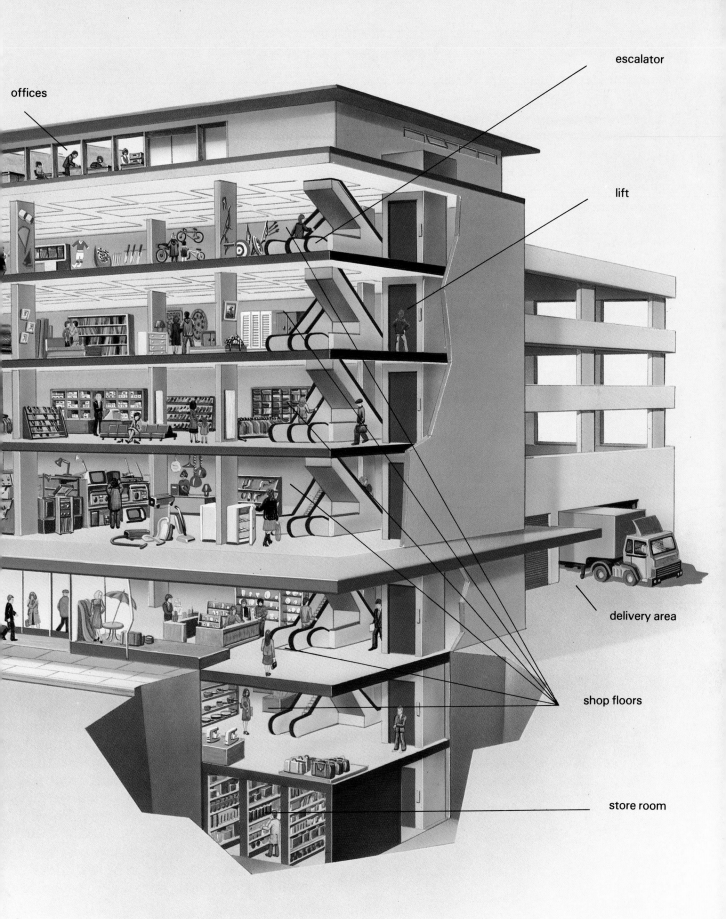

offices

escalator

lift

delivery area

shop floors

store room

# Advertising

Advertisements give us information and amusement. We are so used to them that it is hard to imagine life without them. We hear them on the radio, see them on television and at the cinema, and read them in newspapers and magazines. In the street, we are surrounded by posters and bright, coloured signs. There are even places in the world that are famous because of their advertisements. Part of Broadway, a street in New York City in America, is known as *the Great White Way* because of its thousands of advertisements in brilliant lights.

Good advertisements are interesting and amusing, and they tell us all sorts of things that we would not otherwise know. Through them, we learn what goods are for sale and where to buy them. Advertisements can be about clothes, food, furniture, medicines, and all the other things we use every day. Advertisements tell us about shows in the theatres and cinemas, and about concerts. They tempt us with pictures of exciting holidays. By means of advertisements, we hear about the latest cars and aeroplanes and the houses that people live in.

*Above: Some different ways of advertising.*
*Below left: An eye-catching way of advertising a dentist's office in India.*

Advertising is important to business because it provides a day-by-day link between *manufacturers* (the people who make things) and *consumers* (the people who buy and use things). Consumers must be able to rely on the truth of what an advertisement says. In many countries, the law forbids advertisers to say things that they know to be untrue or misleading. The law also stops advertisers using material that would offend people. Advertising is also controlled so that advertisers do not spoil beautiful views or buildings by putting up ugly posters or signs.

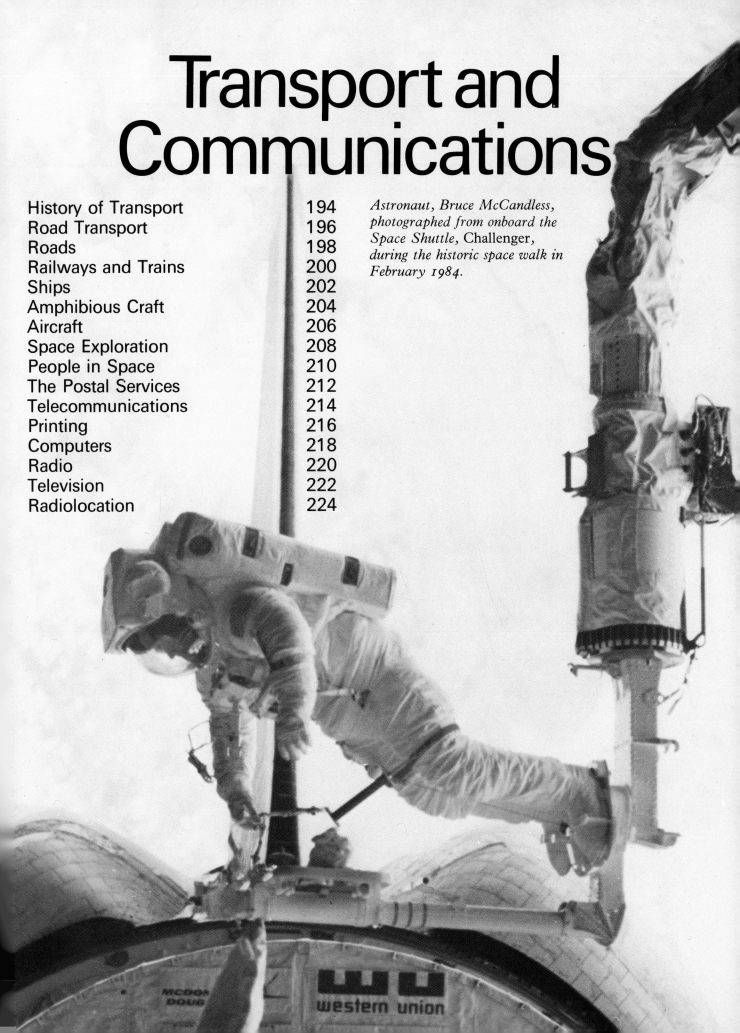

# Transport and Communications

*Astronaut, Bruce McCandless, photographed from onboard the Space Shuttle, Challenger, during the historic space walk in February 1984.*

# History of Transport

Until the 1800s, there were no motor cars, no aeroplanes, and no railway trains. Few people ever moved far from their homes. When they did, they walked, rode horses, or travelled in horse-drawn carts or carriages. Today, we take it for granted that we can travel quickly anywhere we want to. And some forms of transport travel at speeds of hundreds of kilometres an hour.

## The story of transport

Since earliest times, people have tried to find easier and faster ways of travelling.

**The wheel** The discovery of the wheel, about 5000 years ago, was the first big advance in land transport. Before wheels were invented people had to drag heavy loads on sledges. Sometimes they used animals to pull the sledges.

The first wheels were probably slices chopped from logs. In about 2000 BC, the Egyptians made wheels that looked very like the ones we use today.

The first vehicles with wheels were rough and uncomfortable, but during the 1800s horse-drawn coaches were more comfortable. However, travel was still very slow. A journey of 100 kilometres could take up to two days.

*Concorde, a supersonic airliner. It takes only four hours to cross the Atlantic. In 1927, it took Charles Lindbergh over 33 hours when he flew across in the* Spirit of St Louis.

**Sails** At about the same time as the wheel was discovered, people found a way to make their boats travel faster. They used *sails* (large pieces of cloth) to make the wind carry them along. Before this, they had to use oars to push their boats through the water.

**The Steam Age** During the 1700s an important invention made transport faster and more reliable. It was the *steam engine*. In 1769 a Frenchman named Nicholas Cugnot built a strange-looking tractor powered by a steam engine. It was heavy and clumsy, but could travel at a speed of 5 kilometres an hour.

Steam engines were best suited to railway locomotives. By the middle of the 1800s, people were travelling between cities on the first railway lines.

**The internal combustion engine** The biggest advance of all in the history of transport was probably the invention of the *internal combustion engine* in the late 1800s. It was much lighter than the steam engine and used petrol instead of steam.

The petrol engine soon changed the whole pattern of people's lives. It made the motor car possible, and, within 50 years, millions of people owned their own cars.

In 1903 the petrol engine was used to make an aeroplane fly. Before long, air travel became common.

# Future transport

We are still trying to find faster and better means of travelling.

Today, aeroplanes can fly at over 2000 kilometres an hour – faster than the speed of sound. Trains travel at over 200 kilometres an hour. Powerful rockets have taken men as far as the Moon.

Scientists and engineers are concerned with protecting us from the fumes made by the large number of cars on the road. One solution may be a car that runs on an electric battery. Such a car would solve another problem, too. The world's supply of petrol is quickly running out.

# Road Transport

estate car – Subaru estate

sports car –
MGB Roadster

Model T Ford

saloon – Ford Fiesta

*A model T, and some cars you might see on the road today.*

City streets all over the world bustle with traffic. There are cars, buses, lorries, motor-cycles, and bicycles. Many country roads are nearly as busy. All these vehicles help us to move around quickly and comfortably. Every year, millions of extra vehicles come on to the roads, and some people think that the cities are becoming too crowded. If all the people who own motor cars tried to drive to work, the traffic would not be able to move.

## Motor cars

The most popular cars are *saloons* or *sedans* that carry four or five people. People who live in the country and people with large families often have *estate cars*, or *station wagons*. These cars can carry up to ten people, or can be used to carry large loads. Other people prefer *sports cars*. These usually have room for only two people, but are small and fast.

**The first cars** In the 1880s two German engineers, Gottlieb Daimler and Karl Benz made the first cars that really worked. They were powered by petrol engines. Other early cars were made in France and Britain. One of the biggest advances in motor car manufacture took place in the United States of America. In 1901, Ransom E Olds began to *mass-produce* (make large quantities of) cars. Soon after-wards, Henry Ford began mass-producing his Model T, nicknamed the *Tin Lizzie*. Between 1908 and 1927, Ford sold just over 15 million Model Ts.

**Cars of today** These look very different from the *Tin Lizzie*. They have many extra com-forts and safety features. For example, they have clever *suspension* systems to give a smooth ride even on a rough road. They have heaters, and some are air-conditioned. They are fitted with safety belts to protect the driver and passengers in case of accident.

Some modern cars use diesel instead of petrol. *Diesel engines* are only slightly different from petrol engines. A few cars are powered by *turbine engines*. A turbine engine uses moving water, steam or gas to turn it.

# Bicycles

The first bicycles, built in the 1700s, did not have pedals. The rider 'walked' his bicycle along. In 1839, a Scottish blacksmith, Kirkpatrick Macmillan, made a pedal cycle. The rider slid pedals backwards and forwards to move it along.

Early bicycles were called 'bone shakers' because they were so uncomfortable. Modern bicycles are more comfortable, and are also much safer. Some of them can be folded up and carried.

# Motorcycles

Motorcycles were invented before motor cars. In 1869, two Frenchmen added a steam engine to a 'bone shaker' bicycle. Later, in 1885, Gottlieb Daimler built a better, petrol-engined motorcycle.

Today, there is a choice of many kinds of motorcycles. Some travel at speeds of over 300 kilometres an hour.

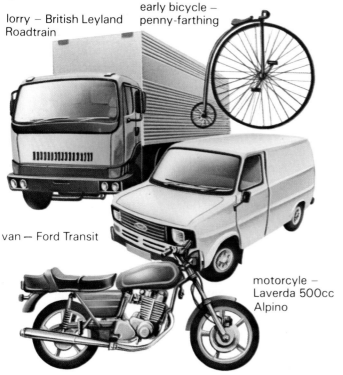

lorry – British Leyland Roadtrain

early bicycle – penny-farthing

van – Ford Transit

motorcyle – Laverda 500cc Alpino

# Trams and buses

The first reliable motor vehicle to be used for public transport was the electric *tram*. Trams run along rails in the road. They take their power from overhead electric cables or, sometimes, from an underground rail reached through a slot in the road.

Today, diesel-engined *buses* are more common because they do not need rails and can go anywhere. The *trolleybus* is a cross between a tram and a bus. It can be steered like a bus, but it has an electric motor and takes its power from overhead cables.

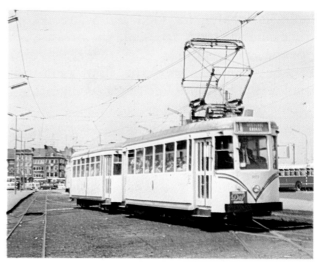

*Above: An electric tram in Belgium.*
*Left: A penny-farthing and some modern vehicles.*

# Lorries

Some of the most interesting vehicles on the road are the huge lorries sometimes called *juggernauts*. They carry heavy loads from country to country, often travelling 1000 kilometres on one journey. Trucks and vans carry smaller amounts of goods from town to town, and also deliver goods to our homes. Most large lorries and trucks have diesel engines. In most countries there are laws restricting length and weight of lorries.

# Roads

Roads connect up cities, towns, and villages. Without them, we would not be able to travel quickly from place to place in cars, lorries, or buses.

Narrow country roads are called *lanes*. Some bigger roads are called *main roads*. Wide roads, for faster traffic, stretching for hundreds of kilometres, connect important cities. They are known as *motorways* or *highways*. Roads in cities and towns are called *streets*.

## Early roads

The first roads were mud tracks made by animals looking for food and water. People thousands of years ago made their own tracks for the same reason.

The Romans were the first good road builders. They built fine roads 2000 years ago. Their roads were straight and long. They put down layers of gravel and chalk. On top of this, they put a layer of large flat paving stones. At the sides, they made ditches to carry rainwater away.

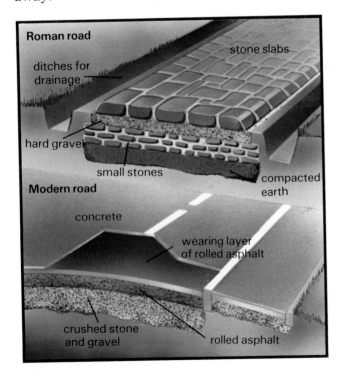

*Above: An earthmover being used in the building of a road.*
*Left: Diagrams to show the structure of a Roman and a modern road.*

## Modern roads

Modern roads are carefully planned and built. Their planners try to make them fit in with the countryside, so that it is not spoilt too much.

**Planning a road** Surveyors study maps of the area where the road is to be built. They decide on the best and easiest route. In some places, they may have to build a bridge over a river, or tunnel through a hill.

Engineers take samples of the soil. These tell them whether the ground is suitable for building on.

**Building a road** First the ground must be made level. Heavy machines called *bulldozers* clear away obstacles, such as trees. The rubble is carried away in huge *dumper trucks*. Giant *rollers* make the ground smooth.

The road is made in layers. First a layer of *hardcore* is put down. The hardcore consists of gravel, crushed stone, and other materials. Then a thick layer of *asphalt* mixed with crushed stone or gravel is put on top. Asphalt is rather like tar. It must be put down and rolled out while it is hot. A machine called a *roadmaker* spreads the asphalt. The road surface is then smoothed by a heavy roller. Some roads, especially motorways, have a top layer of concrete instead of asphalt.

All roads must be higher in the centre than at the sides, so that rainwater can drain off. The centre is called the *crown*.

# Safety on the road

White or yellow lines painted on roads help drivers to drive safely. Road signs warn drivers of dangers or give them instructions.

**Warning signs**

low flying aircraft or sudden aircraft noise    slippery road    accompanied horses or ponies crossing the road ahead     children going to or from school

traffic signals    pedestrian crossing    level crossing without barrier or gate ahead    road works

**Signs giving orders**

no cycling    no pedestrians    maximum speed    no right turn

no motor vehicles    no entry for vehicular traffic    turn left ahead (right if symbol reversed)    one-way traffic

© *Crown Copyright*

On motorways, fences called *crash barriers* separate traffic travelling in opposite directions. If a car skids, it hits the crash barrier and not a car travelling towards it.

The sides of motorways are often planted with trees and bushes. These make the road look better, and their roots help to stop the soil from moving.

# Railways and Trains

The first railways were not at all like those of today. Horses were used to pull a few trucks slowly along wooden rails. Modern trains travel at high speed and carry huge loads. One train can carry loads equal to those of hundreds of road vehicles.

Passenger trains carry people on business or on holiday. *Freight trains* (sometimes called *goods trains*) carry such things as coal, petrol (in tanks), and food.

Nearly all trains have a *locomotive* that pulls a string of *carriages* (for passengers) or *wagons* (for freight). Some local trains have no locomotive. Their coaches have their own electric motors.

## Locomotives

The locomotive provides the power that makes a train move. Sometimes, locomotives are called *railway engines*.

**Steam locomotives** The earliest locomotives got their power from steam. Making the steam was a hard, dirty job. A *fireman* or *stoker* travelled in the locomotive's cab with the driver. He spent the whole journey shovelling coal on to a fire. The fire heated water in the *boiler* and turned it into steam. The power of the steam was used to make the locomotive's wheels turn. Today, a few countries still use steam locomotives.

**Diesel locomotives** These are powered by diesel engines which are like the diesel engines used in buses and trucks, but bigger. Diesel locomotives need only one man to drive them, and they are always ready for use. A steam locomotive needs time 'to get steam up'.

Some diesel locomotives are diesel-electric. Their diesel engines drive *generators* that make electricity. The electricity powers electric *traction motors* that turn the wheels.

**Electric locomotives** These locomotives are the cleanest and most efficient. They get their electricity from overhead cables or from an extra rail on the ground.

**Three kinds of locomotives**

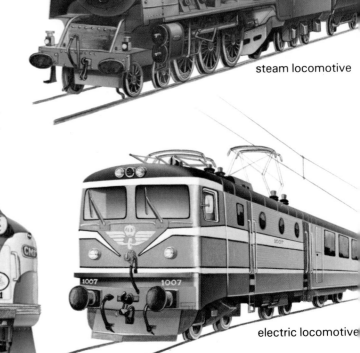

steam locomotive

diesel locomotive

electric locomotive

## Famous trains

One of the most famous trains is the *Orient Express*. It used to run across Europe, from Paris in France to Istanbul in Turkey. Recently reintroduced, today it only runs as far as Venice. Special trains today include the *Blue Train* between Cape Town and Witwatersrand in South Africa; the *California Zephyr* which crosses Colorado in the United States of America; and the *Indian Pacific Express*, between Perth and Sydney in Australia.

Steam locomotives used to have special names. one of the most famous was *The Flying Scotsman* which travelled between London and Edinburgh.

*The Orient Express.*

## The railway track

Trains run on steel rails. The rails are fixed to *sleepers*, made of wood, concrete, or steel. Stone chips are packed around the sleepers to stop them moving.

**Staying on the track** A train stays on the track because its wheels have special rims that stop them slipping off the rails. Part of the rim of each wheel sticks downwards inside the rail, and prevents the wheel moving sideways.

**Switching tracks** A driver cannot steer his train. The train has to follow the track. Sometimes it may have to be switched from one track to another to keep it on its correct route. This is done by means of *points*. The points are controlled by *signalmen* in a *signal box* or *signal cabin*.

## Signals

Safety on a railway is more important than speed. Signals beside the track tell train drivers when to go ahead, when to travel slowly, and when to stop. The signals are worked by the signalmen in signal boxes at various places along the track. The signalmen know when it is safe for a train to move.

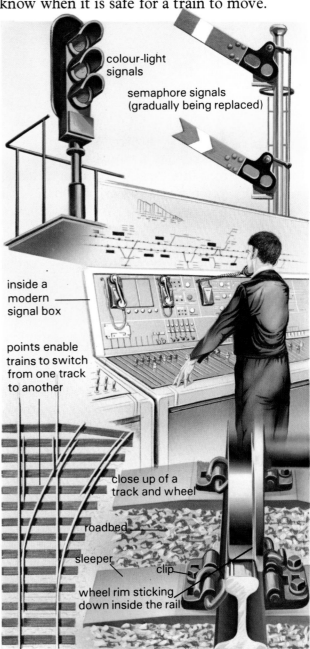

colour-light signals

semaphore signals (gradually being replaced)

inside a modern signal box

points enable trains to switch from one track to another

close up of a track and wheel

roadbed

sleeper

clip

wheel rim sticking down inside the rail

# Ships

*Above: A picture of the clipper* Sussex *from the National Maritime Museum, London.*
*Right: Some different passenger, cargo and warships.*

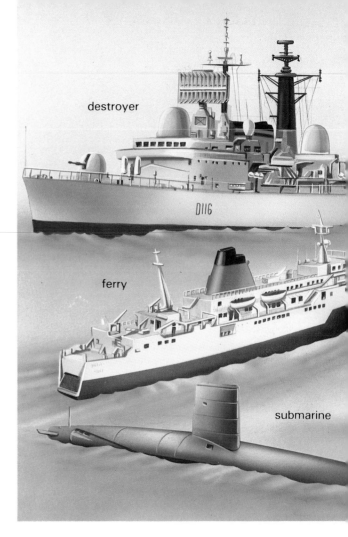

destroyer

D116

ferry

submarine

Nearly everybody finds ships exciting. We think of them sailing to strange, distant lands, or battling their way through storms at sea. Many people spend their lives working on ships, instead of having jobs on land.

Before the invention of the steam engine, three-masted wooden sailing ships called *clippers* were the fastest ships at sea. They had no engines, and relied on the wind to drive them along. But they could sail at 20 *knots* (20 nautical miles an hour). Many fast modern ships travel at less than twice that speed. (A nautical mile is longer than a *statute* or land mile. A nautical mile measures 6076.12 feet [1.852 kilometres]. A statute mile measures 5280 feet [1.611 kilometres].)

Today we have huge ships built of iron and powered by steam-turbines or diesel engines. There are even some nuclear-powered ships. A few big oil tankers are more than 370 metres long.

## Passenger and cargo ships

Some ships are like huge floating buildings. Others are smoky little 'tramp' steamers, seldom out of sight of land.

**Ocean liners** The most luxurious ships are like sea-going hotels. Their passengers have beautiful cabins, and there are restaurants, shops, cinemas, and swimming pools. Once, liners used to cross the ocean on regular services. Today, most of them are used for holiday cruises.

**Freighters** These ships carry heavy *cargoes* (loads) of food, coal, machinery, timber, and other goods across the oceans. Some have refrigerated sections where cargoes of food can be kept fresh.

Sometimes, cargo is just packed into a freighter's *holds* (storage space). Today a lot of cargo is shipped in *containers*. Containers are huge metal boxes. The cargo is brought to the ship by road or rail, already packed in containers. The containers are loaded into the ship by cranes. At the end of the voyage, they are lifted out of the ship, and go on their way again by road or rail.

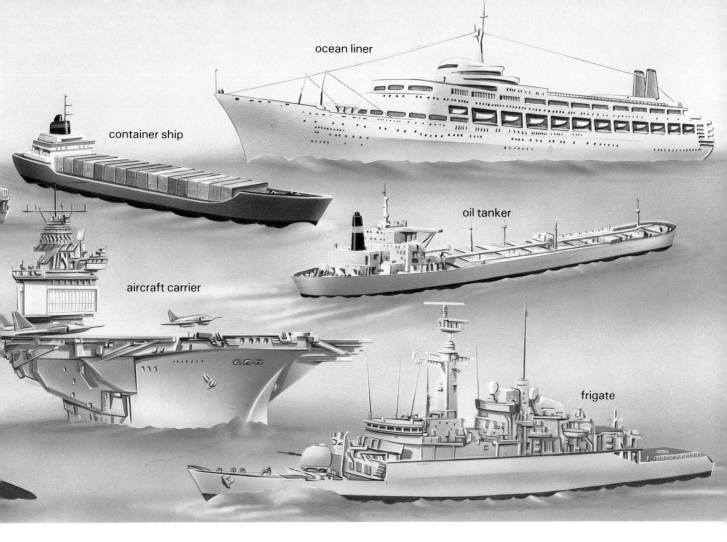

ocean liner

container ship

oil tanker

aircraft carrier

frigate

**Tankers** These are ships designed to carry liquids, chiefly petroleum. They are enormous floating tanks, and can easily be recognized by their long, low decks. They are the biggest ships at sea. They do not need large crews, because much of their equipment is controlled automatically.

**Ferries** Like small liners, these carry passengers, cargo, cars, and even railway trains. The journeys are only across lakes or short stretches of sea.

# Warships

Warships are fighting ships used by navies. Until after the Second World War (1939–45), giant *battleships* fought battles at sea. They were protected by armour plating, and their heavy guns could hit targets that were out of sight many kilometres away. *Cruisers* are not as well protected as battleships, but are faster.

**Destroyers and frigates** Today these ships carry modern missiles instead of guns. They are light, fast ships. Their electronic equipment can spot enemies from a great distance.

**Aircraft carriers** These ships can carry up to 100 fighting aircraft. Sometimes aircraft are launched into the air by a powerful *catapult*. When an aircraft lands on the deck of the ship, wires stretched across, called *arrester wires*, bring it quickly to a halt.

**Submarines** Boats that sail under the surface of the water have two *hulls* (skins). To make the submarine sink below the surface, the space between the hulls is filled with water. To make it rise, the water is pumped out. *Hydroplanes* (fins) on the sides help to control the boat as it sinks or rises. Nuclear-powered submarines can travel for thousands of kilometres without surfacing. Some carry deadly nuclear missiles.

# Amphibious Craft

Some of the boats that can be seen in harbours or on lakes or rivers are very different from ordinary boats and ships. They include various types of *amphibians*, vehicles that can travel on land or in the air as well as in water.

The *hovercraft* rides on a bubble of air and can come straight out of the water and up on to land. *Amphibious cars* and *trucks* can drive along roads, but become boats in the water. *Seaplanes* and *flying boats* are ordinary aeroplanes while they are flying, but take off from water, and 'land' on it again. Another interesting vessel is the *hydrofoil*. Although not really amphibious, it has wings which support it above the water when moving.

## Hovercraft

The hovercraft is also called an *air-cushion vehicle*. It is used mainly for short journeys across the sea or across lakes. It can travel on flat land as easily as on water, provided there are no high obstacles.

**How a hovercraft works** Fans, called *lifting fans*, suck air in through chimneys in the top of the hovercraft, and force it out beneath the vehicle. This creates a cushion of air that lifts the hovercraft off the ground. The cushion is held in by a curtain of air formed by strong jets blowing air downwards around the bottom edge of the hovercraft. Many hovercraft have a skirt called a *bag* around the edge. The skirt also helps to hold in the cushion of air. It may be several metres deep. With its aid, a hovercraft can ride over obstacles or high waves.

*Propellers*, like aeroplane propellers, drive the hovercraft forward. They can be swivelled to face in any direction. In this way, the craft can be steered. *Fins* also help to steer it. The propellers and the lifting fans are driven by gas-turbine engines, which are small, light, powerful and easy to repair.

*Above: A hovercraft. This one can carry over 100 passengers.*

**Diagram of a hovercraft**

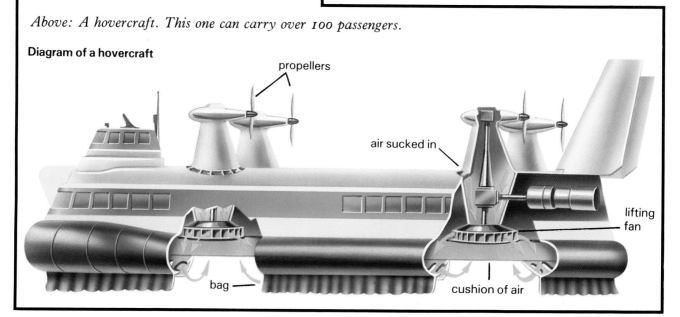

propellers

air sucked in

lifting fan

bag

cushion of air

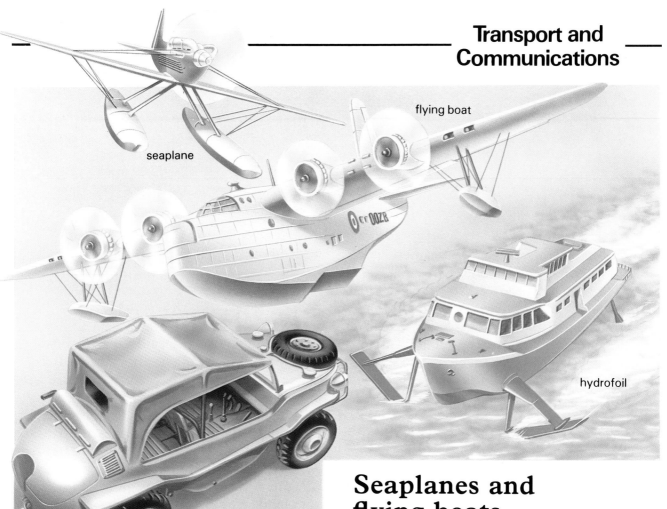

seaplane

flying boat

hydrofoil

amphibious car

**Uses of the hovercraft** Most hovercraft are used for carrying passengers, cars, and *freight* (goods) on short journeys over water. Some are used in industry for moving heavy loads. They are also used in the Arctic regions of Alaska, Canada and the USSR to cross ice in winter or boggy land in summer. Hovercraft have been used to carry explorers to very difficult places.

# Amphibious cars

Amphibious cars and trucks are like boats with wheels. When on land, they can be driven along the road, just like any other road vehicle. When they enter the water, they float and are driven along by propellers. Vehicles of this kind are used mainly by armies.

# Seaplanes and flying boats

Seaplanes and flying boats are used chiefly in places where the land is broken up by large stretches of water, for example, in northern Canada. They are also useful for flights between groups of islands. A seaplane, also called a *floatplane*, has floats in place of landing wheels. A flying boat rests on the water on its *fuselage* (body), which is shaped like a boat.

# Hydrofoils

A *hydrofoil* is a wing or fin used in the water, just as an *aerofoil* is a wing used in the air. Foils work in the same way as aircraft wings. The boats called *hydrofoil craft* have hydrofoils extending down into the water. When the boats travel fast, the hydrofoils lift them partly out of the water. The less of a boat there is in the water, the more easily it can move.

# Aircraft

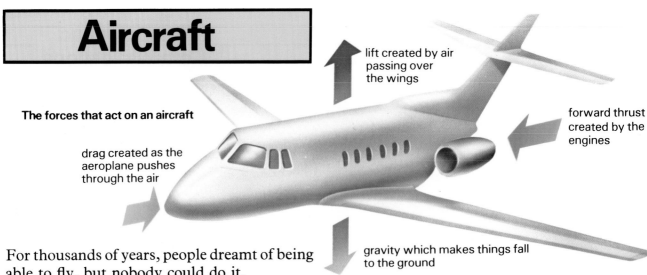

**The forces that act on an aircraft**

lift created by air passing over the wings

forward thrust created by the engines

drag created as the aeroplane pushes through the air

gravity which makes things fall to the ground

For thousands of years, people dreamt of being able to fly, but nobody could do it.

In the 1400s, the great Italian artist Leonardo da Vinci realized that people would only be able to fly by making a flying machine. He designed one on paper, but it probably would not have worked. In 1903, two American inventors made the first powered flying machine that could carry people.

## How an aeroplane flies

An aeroplane has to overcome the force of gravity. Gravity is the force that makes an object fall to the ground when it is dropped.

An aeroplane overcomes gravity by creating a different force, called *lift*. The aeroplane creates lift in the same way as a bird does, by the movement of air over its wings. The top surface of the wings is curved. Air passing over the curved top has further to go than the air passing underneath. It travels faster. This creates lift.

**How lift is created by air passing over the wings**

air flows faster over the top of the wing creating lift

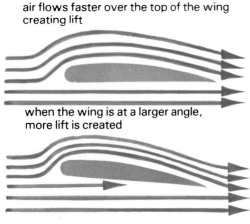

when the wing is at a larger angle, more lift is created

## The first aeroplane

In December 1903, Orville Wright made the first powered aeroplane flight ever. It lasted 12 seconds, and he flew for a distance of 37 metres.

The flight took place at Kitty Hawk, North Carolina, in the United States of America. The aeroplane was named *Flyer I*. Its wings were made of wood and cotton. Orville Wright and his brother Wilbur had designed and made it.

Wright brothers' *Flyer*

helicopter

# Aircraft today

*Flyer I* flew at about 11 kilometres an hour. It had a petrol engine that turned a propeller. Some aeroplanes today still have propellers, but most have jet engines. Some jet-engined planes can fly at more than 3500 kilometres an hour. A few special planes with rocket engines can fly much faster than that.

**Airliners** Millions of passengers are carried every year by airliners. They are the buses of the air, flying on *scheduled* (regular) services between airports.

The biggest airliners are often called *jumbo jets*. They can carry hundreds of passengers at a time. The most famous jumbo jet is the *Boeing 747*. It is a two-storey airliner, with a large passenger lounge downstairs, and a small one upstairs.

The fastest airliners are *Concorde* (made by Britain and France) and the *TU-144* made by the Soviet Union. Both fly at *supersonic* speeds. These are speeds faster than the speed of sound (1225 kilometres an hour at sea level).

*A Boeing 747.*

**Military aircraft** Many of the fastest and most cleverly-designed planes belong to air forces. They are designed to protect a country against attack from the air, to carry bombs or rockets, or to study what an enemy (or possible enemy) is doing.

Two interesting types of military aeroplanes are *swing-wing planes* and *jump jets*. Swing-wing or variable geometry planes can alter the shape of their wings in flight. Jump jets or VTOL (vertical take-off and landing) planes can rise straight up into the air from the ground. Then, they fly like ordinary fast planes.

# Helicopters and gliders

Aeroplanes are the commonest type of aircraft. But there are many other types. They include helicopters and gliders.

**Helicopters** An aeroplane has fixed wings and an engine to drive it forward. A helicopter has a *rotor* on top that spins round. The rotor acts as wings, and also drives the helicopter forward.

**Gliders** These are like ordinary aeroplanes, except that they have no engines. They fly by riding on currents of air.

jump jet

207

# Space Exploration

*Above: A Saturn V rocket lifts off carrying an Apollo spacecraft.*

Travel in space is one of the greatest adventures in history. For hundreds of years, people dreamt about travelling in space, just as they dreamt about flying. Space travel has been possible only since suitable rockets were developed in the 1950s.

## Getting into space

Space travel has many problems. In the past, two problems were more difficult than any others. The first was making an engine that was able to work in space, where there is no oxygen. The other was making an engine powerful enough. Both of these problems were solved by the development of the rocket.

## How a rocket works

If you blow up a balloon and tie its neck, the balloon does not move. If you untie the neck, the air rushes out and the balloon flies madly around the room.

When the neck is tied, the air inside the balloon pushes equally against the rubber skin in all directions. When you untie the neck, the air can escape on the neck side. However, it is still pushing against the skin on the side opposite to the neck. As a result, the balloon moves in this direction.

A rocket engine works in just the same way. Fuel is burnt inside the rocket and produces hot gases. The gases can escape from the back of the rocket, but their forward pressure drives the rocket forward.

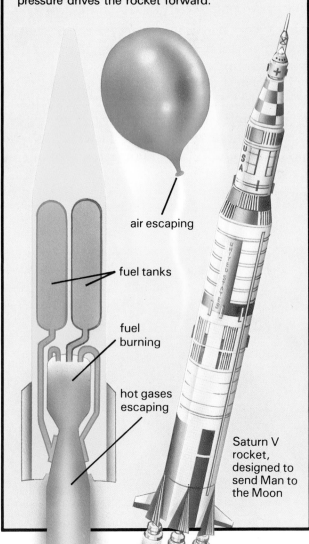

air escaping

fuel tanks

fuel burning

hot gases escaping

Saturn V rocket, designed to send Man to the Moon

**Space engines** No petrol-engined aircraft can fly in space. Its propeller can work only where there is air. Even an ordinary jet engine will not work in space because it needs oxygen from the air to burn its fuel. A rocket engine also needs oxygen to burn its fuel. So, it carries its own oxygen with it, either in its fuel or in a separate tank.

**Engine power** A rocket engine is more powerful than any other type of engine. It can move a spacecraft or other object fast enough to escape the Earth's *gravitational pull*. The gravitational pull or force of gravity is the force that makes objects fall to the ground when they are dropped. It pulls them towards the centre of the Earth. The minimum speed required to escape from gravitational pull is 40 000 kilometres an hour or 11 kilometres a second. This speed is called *escape velocity*.

At speeds lower than escape velocity, a spacecraft moving away from Earth would gradually slow down then fall back to Earth.

*Below: Two space probes. Pioneer 10 flew by Jupiter in 1973. Mariner 10 visited Venus and Mercury in 1974.*

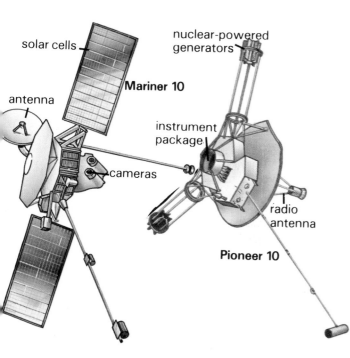

solar cells

nuclear-powered generators

**Mariner 10**

antenna

instrument package

cameras

radio antenna

**Pioneer 10**

*Above: Tiros 11, an American weather satellite launched from Cape Canaveral in November 1960.*

# Satellites and probes

The first objects carried into space by rockets were artificial satellites and probes. Later, human beings travelled into space in spacecraft.

**Artificial satellites** Rockets carried these into space. Now they *orbit* (travel round and round) the Earth like artificial moons. They send valuable information back to Earth by radio. They help meteorologists (scientists concerned with the weather) to forecast future weather conditions. They make studies that help other scientists, engineers, farmers, and military planners. They also carry radio and television broadcasts to every country in the world.

**Probes** Unmanned spacecraft are sent to the Moon and the planets to find out more about them. These probes carry many kinds of measuring instruments. Radio transmitters in the probes send photographs and information back to Earth.

# People in Space

Putting satellites and probes into space was a technical triumph. But even more exciting was space travel for human beings.

The first person to travel in space was a Russian air force officer, Yuri Gagarin. On April 12 1961, he circled the Earth once, in a spacecraft sent up by rocket. Since then, many Russian *cosmonauts* and American *astronauts* have journeyed into space, and some have landed on the Moon.

## Travel in space

Conditions in space are very different to those on Earth. There is no gravity so the astronauts are *weightless*. They can float effortlessly in all directions. There is also no atmosphere to provide air for the astronauts to breathe, or to protect them from extreme temperatures and harmful radiation.

**Training** Astronauts undergo very special and hard training before they are launched into space. It gives them as much experience as possible of the conditions and problems they might encounter in space flight. They spend an enormous amount of time inside a dummy of the spacecraft they will be flying in. The dummy is identical to the real thing and is coupled to a machine called a *flight simulator* which makes it react as though it were actually flying in various conditions. The astronauts experience temporary weightlessness inside an aircraft flying up and over in a tight arc.

**Life in space** When the astronauts are in space they are supplied with air from the *life support system*. The air is changed regularly, and the temperature is kept even. Because of the weightlessness, astronauts have to squeeze drink straight into their mouths. It is impossible to pour liquid in space. It just stays where it is. Space food is now much better than the food earlier astronauts had to endure, which came in toothpaste-type tubes. Meals on

*An Apollo astronaut about to step on to the Moon's surface.*

the Space Shuttle consist of pre-cooked or fresh food kept frozen until needed. Some food is freeze-dried. It is contained in plastic bags, and cold or hot water is squirted in to rehydrate (put the water back in) it. Some foods are ready to eat. Bite-sized sandwiches are rehydrated by

*Apollo 11 astronauts, the first men on the Moon, transferred to a dinghy after splashdown.*

the saliva in the mouth as they are chewed.

Astronauts usually sleep in sleeping bags hooked to the wall. They have to be zipped in carefully to stop them floating away!

# Man on the Moon

The first journey to the Moon was made in 1966. An *unmanned* (crew-less) Russian spacecraft landed on the Moon. It sent television pictures of the Moon's surface back to Earth.

To carry astronauts to the Moon and back again, the Americans built a *lunar module*. A large spacecraft was designed to carry the module close to the Moon. The module was able to fly down to the Moon's surface, land, and then fly back again to the spacecraft.

On July 20 1969, the lunar module *Eagle* landed on the Moon with two astronauts on board. Neil A Armstrong became the first person to step on to the Moon's surface. During later Moon landings, astronauts drove electric Moon 'buggies' around.

# Space laboratories

An important new development in recent years has been the placing of laboratories in orbit around the Earth. Conditions in space provide an opportunity for much important scientific research.

The Russians launched the first laboratory in April 1971. They launched several others, and in 1984 a crew spent eight months in space. The American Skylab was launched in May 1973. Three teams of astronauts visited it, the last spending 84 days in orbit.

Spacelab was built by the European Space Agency. It is equipped with all kinds of instruments and apparatus for scientific and engineering experiments. Like the shuttle, it is re-usable. Since it was taken into space in 1986, the Russians and Americans have followed suit with their own re-usable shuttles, and great progress has been made in this field.

## The Space Shuttle

The Space Shuttle is a re-usable space vehicle, part plane, part rocket. It can carry spacecraft, such as satellites, into orbit, and in the future may be used to ferry parts to build a space station. Spacelab, a space laboratory designed to be carried by Space Shuttle, was launched on 28 November 1983. Scientists were carried into Space to do experiments in the laboratory. The Shuttle can also bring satellites back to Earth for disposal or repair.

On the launch pad, the *orbiter* sits on top of a huge tank which has two rocket boosters attached to it. The tank and boosters fall back to Earth after take-off, but the boosters can be used again. The orbiter returns to Earth after its mission is completed and lands on an ordinary runway.

# The Postal Services

*The Romans carried messages on horseback.*

Postal services carry thousands of millions of letters and parcels all over the world every year. Some letters and parcels have to travel thousands of kilometres to reach the people they are addressed to. A single letter may be carried by car, train, and ship or aircraft before it reaches its destination. Yet very few items are lost. Letters and parcels carried in the post are called *mail*.

## How the mail travels

Most letters reach their destination in a few days. Their journeys may be long and difficult.

**Posting and collection** When you send a letter to somebody, you write his or her name and address on the envelope. Then you stick a stamp on the envelope, and put it into a *letter-box*, sometimes called a *mail-box*. The stamp shows that you have paid to have the letter sent on its journey.

The letters are collected form the letter-box and taken to the local *sorting office*.

**Sorting** In the sorting office, letters are separated from parcels. Then the letters are stacked face up with their stamps in the same corner. A machine *cancels* (marks) the stamps so that they cannot be used again, and prints a *postmark* that shows the name of the sorting office, the date, and, sometimes, the time.

The letters are then sorted. In some countries, machines check the stamps to see whether the correct *postage* (the cost of sending a letter) has been paid. The letters are sorted into groups, depending on the country, region, or city to which they are being sent. Machines or workers called *sorters* put them into *sorting frames* that have a separate box for each place.

In some countries, each city, street and village has a *postal code* or *zip code*. The operator of the sorting machine types the postal code on the machine's keyboard as each letter passes him, and the machine does the rest.

### A letter's journey

stamp cancelling

posting and collecting

**Transport** The mail is carried to its destination as quickly as possible. Much mail travels by train. Some trains have wagons called *travelling post offices*, where mail can be sorted as the train travels at speed. Usually, these trains can pick up mail at various points without stopping.

Overseas mail goes by ship. Or, if it is *air mail*, it travels by aircraft. A letter sent by air mail costs more than a letter sent by ordinary mail, but it gets there much more quickly.

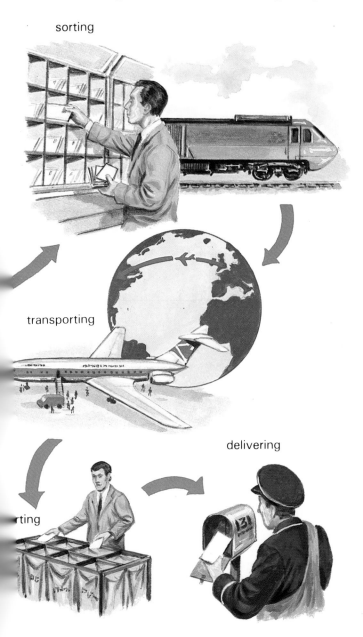

sorting

transporting

delivering

rting

*Above: A letter will be delivered wherever you live. This postman has to wait until the tide goes out to deliver letters to St Michael's Mount in Cornwall, England.*

**Delivery** Many letters have to be sorted at several points along their route. They are sorted when they reach a different country, or a region, or a city. In time, every letter arrives at the *post office* nearest to the address on the envelope.

In the post office, postmen and women take the letters for their own route. They sort them into the order to be delivered.

When a letter is delivered to your house, you are probably not surprised to recieve it. However, it has had many adventures and been handled by many people on its way to you. The postal services help you to contact people all over the world.

# Telecommunications

The first important invention in long-distance communication was the *telegraph*. People many kilometres apart could communicate with each other by using bursts of electricity called *impulses* sent along a wire. Later, the *telephone* was invented. It also used electricity and wires.

## Telegraph

The first telegraphs were invented by Samuel Morse in the United States of America and William Cooke and Charles Wheatstone in Britain, in 1837.

**How the telegraph works** When an *electric current* is passed through a coil of wire, the coil acts as a *magnet*. It can be used to move something that makes a sound or a mark. The *magnetic field* lasts only as long as the current is flowing. By switching the current on and off, a message can be sent.

**Modern developments** At first, all telegraph messages were sent by hand. But today, operators use machines called *teleprinters*. The operator spells out the message on a machine that looks like a typewriter.

*This girl is sending a message by telex.*

## Morse code

Samuel Morse's telegraph used a code in which short impulses of electricity called *dots* and long impulses called *dashes* were used for letters and numbers. The letter B, for example, was one dash and three dots (– . . .). This way of communicating became known as the morse code. Given below is the code for letters and numbers. Other signals include one for 'received' and 'understood'.

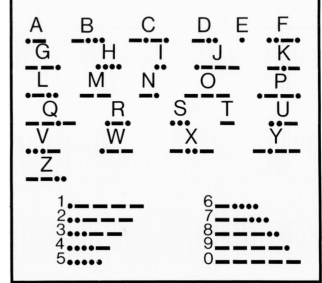

## Teleprinters and Telex

A teleprinter works in the same way as the telegraph. It has a keyboard just like that of a typewriter. When a letter key, such as the letter B, is pressed, electric impulses are sent along a wire to the teleprinter at the other end. This teleprinter prints the letter B on a piece of paper.

The teleprinter sends the electric impulses directly, or it punches holes in a paper tape. The tape is then passed through another part of the machine, which sends the message.

Teleprinters in business offices are linked to an international network called *Telex*. Any teleprinter can be connected to any other teleprinter by dialling its number on a dial. The dial is the same as the dial on a telephone.

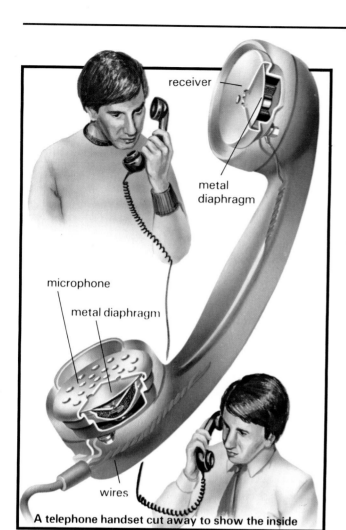

A telephone handset cut away to show the inside

**Making a connection** Before you can speak to another person on the telephone, the two telephones must be connected together. This can be done manually by a *telephone operator* at a *switchboard*. Or it can be done automatically when you *dial* the number of the other telephone.

# Cables and satellites

The wires that carry telegraph, telephone, and Telex messages stretch all over the world. They are usually called *cables*. Some of them stretch for thousands of kilometres under the oceans. Many messages can be sent at the same time on one cable.

Today, messages are also sent in other ways. Sometimes, for example, telephone calls from one continent to another are sent part of the way by radio. Communications satellites (see page 209) are also used to transmit some messages.

*Below: A cable-laying ship. The cable is fed out over the bows of the ship to lie at the bottom of the ocean.*

# Telephone

The telephone, like the telegraph, sends messages over long distances by means of electric impulses along a wire.

**How the telephone works** To use a telephone you pick up the *handset*. The handset has a *microphone* to send your words, and a *receiver* to receive the words of the person at the other end.

When you speak into the microphone, your voice makes a metal disc *vibrate* (tremble). The disc is called a *diaphragm*. The trembling causes electric impulses to pass along wires to the telephone of the person at the other end. There, the receiver changes the impulses back into the sound of your voice.

# Printing

Before printing was invented, books were among the rarest things in the world. They were written and illustrated by hand, and each book took many months to make. Today, nearly everything we read has been printed by machines that can produce thousands of copies quickly.

Millions of newspapers are printed in a matter of hours. We can read in our morning newspapers about events that took place on the other side of the world only yesterday.

## Methods of printing

The ancient Chinese printed by carving words and pictures on blocks of wood. The greatest advance in printing was the development of *moveable type* by Johannes Gutenberg, a German printer, in about 1440. He used a separate piece of metal *type* for each letter of the alphabet.

**Letterpress printing** In letterpress printing, each letter of the alphabet is a separate piece of metal type. The letter itself stands up above the body of the type, and presses ink on the paper.

The first printers had to arrange the letters by hand. They put the letters into a metal tool called a *composing stick*. The job of arranging letters to make words is called *typesetting*. Today, machines make type-setting faster.

*Below: Stages in printing a four-colour picture.*

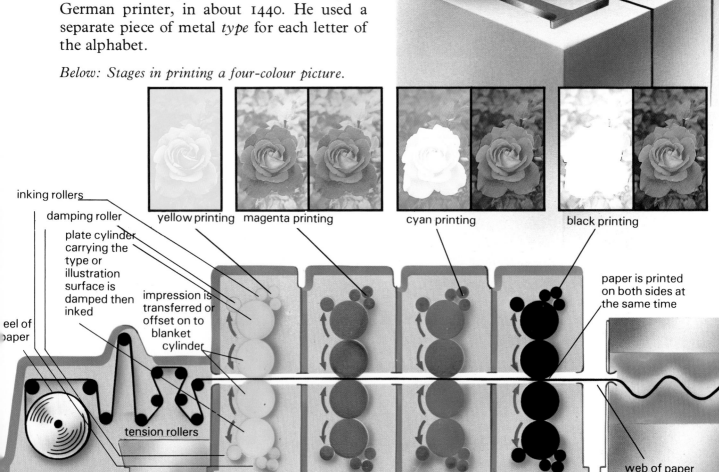

letterpress printing

yellow printing    magenta printing    cyan printing    black printing

inking rollers
damping roller
plate cylinder carrying the type or illustration surface is damped then inked
impression is transferred or offset on to blanket cylinder
eel of aper
tension rollers
paper is printed on both sides at the same time
web of paper

*Linotype* and *Monotype* machines look like giant typewriters. They can typeset words and *cast* (make) pieces of type automatically. This is quicker than a person selecting the individual pieces of type from a box. Machines can also space words to make all the lines *justified* (all the same length). Monotype machines cast one letter at a time. Linotype machines cast a whole line.

lithography

gravure printing

*Above: Three different printing processes.*
*Below: Diagram to show how paper is printed on a web-offset press.*

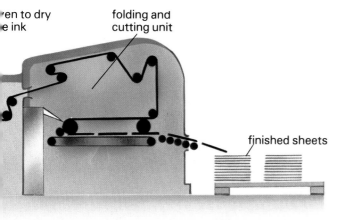

en to dry
e ink

folding and
cutting unit

finished sheets

**Lithography** A flat surface is used to print from. A photographic process is used to transfer the picture of the type on to a flat aluminium *plate*. The plate is treated with chemicals so that only the part to be printed will accept the printer's ink.

**Gravure printing** This works in the opposite way to letterpress. The printing surface is hollowed out and the ink is pressed into the hollows. This method is often used for very high-quality work.

# Printing pictures

Before a black and white photograph can be printed, it must itself be photographed through a screen. The screen, called a *half-tone screen*, breaks the photograph up into thousands of tiny dots. In the white areas of the original photograph, the dots are small and far apart. In the dark areas, they are large and close together.

If you look at a printed black and white picture through a magnifying glass you can see the dots clearly.

Colour pictures are usually printed using only four different colours of ink. They are magenta (red), cyan (blue), yellow, and black.

A special camera separates the original picture into these four colours. Separate printing plates are made for each colour. In the *printing press* (the printing machine), the paper passes over each printing plate in turn and picks up one colour at a time.

# The printing press

Modern printing machines, called presses, can print, fold, and trim sheets of paper automatically.

The type surface is inked by huge *rollers*, and large rolls of paper are fed into the press. The fastest presses, *rotary presses*, can print on both sides of the paper at the same time.

# Computers

Computers are electronic machines that make accurate mathematical calculations (sums) at great speed. They can complete in seconds calculations that would take people days to work out.

A skilled person can make a computer do many tasks by feeding the right information and instructions into it. This is called *programming* it. Computers can, for example, work out pay slips, file letters, keep a spacecraft on its correct course, help to diagnose diseases, and run an automated factory.

Computers cannot think for themselves. They can only do what they are programmed to do. Compared with the human brain, they can only do a few simple things. However, they can do those things millions of times faster than a person can and, if properly programmed, they do not make mistakes.

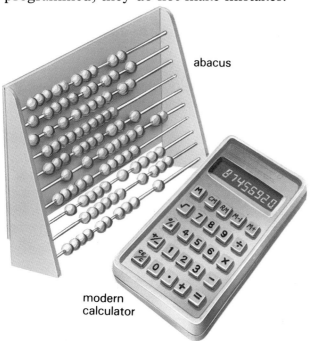

abacus

modern calculator

*An abacus, a simple type of digital computer, and a modern calculator.*

## Types of computers

All computers belong to one of two basic types: digital or analogue.

**Digital computers** These are the more common. They are the type used by people in business, scientists, and other people who want to do fast calculations. Digital computers relate all problems to numbers, and produce their answers by counting numbers.

The simplest example of using a digital computer is counting on your fingers. Cash registers and adding machines are simple digital computers. Pocket calculators are small computers. They can do extremely difficult calculations at lightning speed.

**Analogue computers** These work by changing one *quantity* into another. A clock is a simple example. It changes *time* into *movement*. The clock tells you how much time has passed by showing you a corresponding amount of movement by the clock's hands. A thermometer tells you the temperature by showing you the height of mercury in a tube. Large analogue computers are often designed for research or for use in industry.

## Operating computers

Computer operators use a special 'language' to put information into a computer and to get information from it.

**Computer language** Digital computers work in numbers. They do not use the numbers 1 to 9 as we usually do when making a calculation. Computers use only the numbers 1 and 0.

A computer has thousands of electronic 'nerve cells' to do its work. They are all exactly alike. They are rather like tiny electric switches. They are always either on or off. One position represents the number 1, the other represents 0. The computer works on a simple on-or-off system, and builds up any number it wants by using 1 or 0. So, 0 is 0, 1 is 1, but 3 is 11 in computer language, 4 is 100, and 5 is 101.

**Computer parts** A computer can be given many different programs to carry out a wide range of tasks. The program can use the on-off electric signals not just to represent numbers, but words, pictures and even sounds. In this way, you could get a home microcomputer to play games and music, teach you a subject of your choice, work out how much money you will need for projects, keep a diary, print out letters and bills and so on.

The program is fed into the computer's *memory* where it is stored in the form of electric signals. To use the computer, an *input unit* like a keyboard is operated. This sends information, to the computer's *central processing unit*. This unit obeys the instructions and uses the information to get a certain result. This result goes to the computer's *output unit*, which is often a video screen or printer.

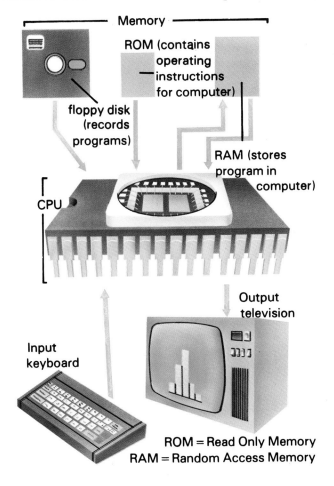

*Above: A modern computer being operated.*
*Left: The four main units of a computer are the input unit, the memory, the central processing unit (CPU) and the output unit.*

# Computers and automation

One of the most important uses of computers is *automation*. Automatic machines are used in factories and other industrial plants. Automation is common in the petroleum and chemical industries.

Machines in fully-automated factories are controlled by computers. The computers are programmed to keep the machines working efficiently. Information about what the machines are doing is fed back to the computer. The computer compares it with what efficient machines should be doing. If there is something wrong, the computer corrects it.

# Radio

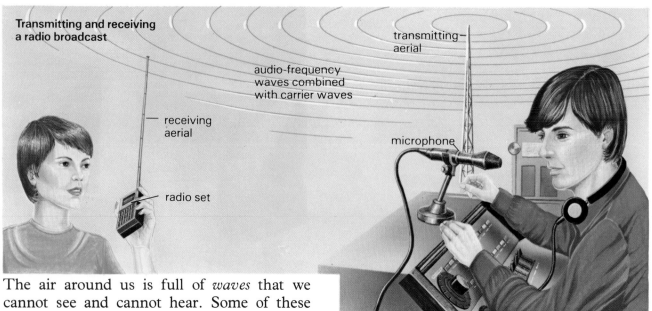

Transmitting and receiving a radio broadcast

transmitting aerial

audio-frequency waves combined with carrier waves

receiving aerial

radio set

microphone

The air around us is full of *waves* that we cannot see and cannot hear. Some of these waves are *radio signals* that make it possible for us to communicate with people in all parts of the world.

Radio is less than 100 years old. But it is hard for us to imagine what life would be like without it. It has become one of our most important sources of information and brings us entertainment from all over the world.

## Uses of radio

**Information** News broadcasts on the radio tell us about world events as soon as they happen. Weather forecasts tell us what weather to expect. Educational broadcasts and talks increase our knowledge.

**Entertainment** Radio brings plays and music into our homes. Sports commentaries are often as real as though we were present. Radio games and quizzes amuse millions of listeners.

**Keeping contact** Radio keeps aircraft and ships in contact with the land. Ships and boats can radio for help in case of trouble. Radio beams keep aircraft on course and help to prevent collisions.

## How radio works

Radio is the fastest means of communication that has ever been invented. It reaches out to listeners in every part of the world.

**Making a broadcast** When a broadcast is made, sound (a play, perhaps, or music) is turned into radio waves. The waves are *transmitted* (sent) into space. They spread out rather like the ripples that extend across the surface of a pond if you throw a stone into the water. Radio waves travel at the speed of light, about 300 000 kilometres a second. They pass through the air, and through solid objects.

Radio waves only travel in straight lines. They cannot follow the curve of the Earth's surface, but some waves can travel round the world in a series of bounces. They bounce off the upper layers of the Earth's atmosphere and off the surface of the Earth.

**Listening to a broadcast** The listener's radio set 'catches' the waves. It turns them into an exact copy of the sound that was broadcast.

# Transmitting and receiving

**In the studio** A microphone changes the sound waves of voices or music into electro-magnetic waves. These waves are called *audio-frequency waves*, meaning that they vibrate at the same *frequency* (beat) as sound waves.

**In the control room** An engineer may mix the waves from several microphones. An *amplifier* is operated to increase their strength. The waves are fed to the transmitter by wire.

**At the transmitter** The audio-frequency waves are combined with extremely powerful *carrier waves*, capable of travelling long distances. The waves are sent out into space by a transmitting *aerial*.

**The receiving aerial** In a radio set, a receiving aerial picks up the waves. They are by now very feeble. Waves from many other transmitters are picked up at the same time. All the waves are fed into the radio set.

**In the radio set** A *tuner* unit is used by the listener to select the broadcast (that is, the set of waves) that he or she wants. The waves are made stronger by an amplifier. Then a *detector* unit separates the audio-frequency waves from the carrier waves. A *loudspeaker* changes the audio-frequency waves back into sound waves.

*A disc jockey in a studio of a radio station. When he plays a record, the sound travels on waves. Radio waves travel at nearly 300 000 kilometres per second.*

# Television

Television allows us to see and hear events as they happen, even though they may be taking place far away. When you turn on your television set, you can watch a play as though you were sitting in a theatre, you can see a game of football that is being played in another country, or you can travel with an explorer through the jungle.

Television works in much the same way as radio. A television camera takes a picture of a news event, a tennis match, or something else, and changes the picture into a series of electric currents. The currents are transmitted as radio waves from an aerial. They are picked up by the aerial of a *television set* or television receiver. In the television set, the currents are changed back to build up the picture seen by the camera. At the same time, the sound of the event that is being televised is transmitted just as though it was ordinary radio. (See page 220.)

**A television camera**

## Transmitting pictures

When early experimenters were trying to think of a way of sending moving pictures by radio, they realized that there was no easy way of transmitting whole pictures. Instead, they worked out a way of breaking a picture up into thousands of dots, some of them dark, some bright. According to its brightness or darkness, each dot is transmitted as a strong or weak electric current.

**The television camera** This forms a picture of whatever it is pointed at. An *electron gun* in the camera shoots a beam of *electrons* at the picture. The camera now *scans* the picture. It divides the picture up into a large number of horizontal lines, that is, lines running across it. The beam runs across the picture line by line, from left to right, top to bottom, just as you read the lines on a page. The beam completes a scan of the picture about 30 times every second.

At each spot along each line, a tiny electric current is produced. Its strength depends on how bright that particular tiny spot is. These currents are transmitted, and are picked up by the aerial of the television set.

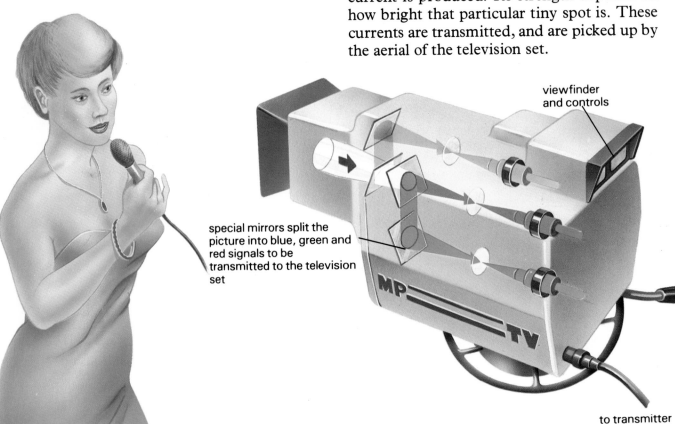

viewfinder and controls

special mirrors split the picture into blue, green and red signals to be transmitted to the television set

MP          TV

to transmitter

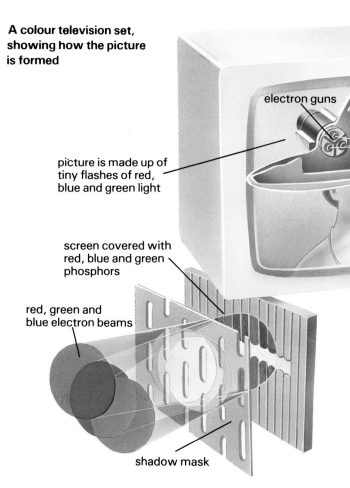

**A colour television set, showing how the picture is formed**

electron guns

picture is made up of tiny flashes of red, blue and green light

screen covered with red, blue and green phosphors

red, green and blue electron beams

shadow mask

*Below: A television programme being filmed outside. Many pieces of equipment are needed.*

**The television set** The heart of the television set is a *cathode ray tube*. The tube has an electron gun like the one in the television camera. It shoots a beam of electrons on to a screen on the front of the tube. The screen has a coating of *phosphors* that glow white. The beam scans the screen, line by line, in the same way as the camera scans the picture. It builds up the picture on the screen, just as the camera saw it.

# Colour television

Colour television depends on the fact that any colour can be produced by mixing the three *primary colours* of light: red, blue, and green. A colour television camera divides each picture up into the three primary colours. It transmits waves representing all three colours.

The colour television set that picks up the transmission has three electron guns, one for each colour. Instead of a coating of white phosphors, the screen is covered with tiny dots or stripes of red, blue, and green phosphors. A *shadow mask* (a thin metal sheet with a pattern of holes in it) guides the beams from the electron gun to phosphors of the correct colour. We see three images at once (red, green and blue) which the eye puts together to form one full-colour picture.

# Radiolocation

## Radar

Radar is rather like a radio searchlight that can point out distant objects. It uses radio waves to locate things, even hundreds of kilometres away. It can do this even in darkness or in fog. The name *radar* comes from the words *RA*dio *D*etection *A*nd *R*anging.

**How radar works** Radio waves are transmitted in short bursts from the aerial of a radar set. When they 'hit' an object, they are reflected back to the radar set. A radio receiver picks up the reflected waves, the *echo*, and special equipment measures how long it took them to reach the object and return. The distance of the object can then easily be worked out, because radio waves travel at about 300 000 kilometres a second.

The direction of the object can also be worked out. The transmitting aerial or *antenna* focuses the radio waves into a beam and sends them out in only one direction at a time. The aerial can be rotated (turned round) until an echo is picked up. The object lies in the direction the aerial is then pointing.

**Uses of radar** Ships use radar to 'see' other ships, harbour entrances, and dangerous objects such as icebergs. Aircraft use it in a similar way. Airports use radar to prevent collisions between aircraft. Weathermen can detect storms with it. Police check the speed of vehicles on highways by radar. Radar also tracks space satellites and other spacecraft.

## Sonar

Sonar is used by ships for locating underwater objects and for measuring the depth of the water in which a ship is sailing. The name *sonar* comes from the words *SO*und *N*avigation *A*nd *R*anging.

Sonar works in a similar way to radar, but it uses sound waves instead of radio waves. Sound waves are sent into the water. When they meet an object they are reflected back. The time they take to travel to the object and back is measured, and shows how far away the object is.

*Below: Some uses for sonar and radar.*

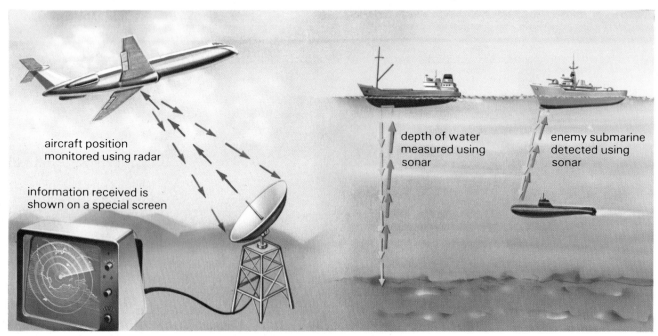

aircraft position monitored using radar

information received is shown on a special screen

depth of water measured using sonar

enemy submarine detected using sonar

# Arts and Entertainment

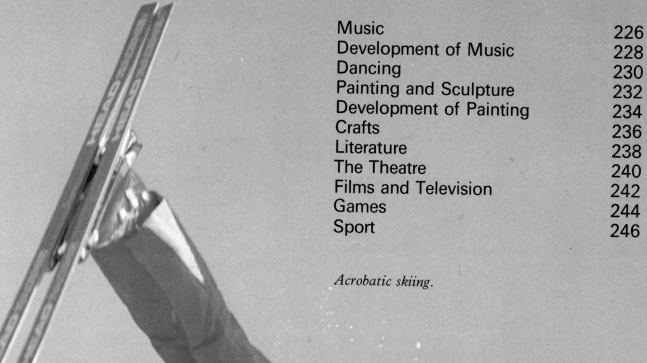

*Acrobatic skiing.*

# Music

Music is one of the most natural of the arts. People all over the world express their feelings in music – by singing, by playing musical instruments, and by dancing to music.

Music is all around us. We hear it on the radio, on records, and at concerts. In the country, and in parks and gardens everywhere, there is a special kind of natural music – the song of the birds.

## What is music?

Music is made up of sounds arranged in a way that people enjoy listening to. Sounds in music are called *notes*. Some are high and some are low. Some are short sounds, and others are long sounds. Most pieces of music have rhythm and melody.

**Rhythm** The regular *beat* of a piece of music is called the rhythm. The simplest music consists only of rhythms beaten out on something that makes a sound, such as a hollow piece of wood or a drum.

**Melody** A melody is a *tune*. It is an arrangement of high notes and low notes that pleases people and stays in their minds. Most pieces of music have melodies. Some are easy to follow, such as the melodies of 'pop' songs. Others are more difficult. A symphony by Beethoven or Tchaikovsky, for example, contains many different melodies.

## Musical instruments

Musicians (people who make music) around the world use hundreds of instruments for making music. Each instrument has its own sound, which is different from the sound of any other instrument.

There are four main types of *musical instruments*: percussion instruments, wind instruments, stringed instruments and keyboard instruments.

**Instruments of the four main types**

string
keyboard
percussion
wind

**Percussion instruments** These make musical sounds when they are struck, either by the player's hand or by something else. They are the simplest instruments. They include drums, bells, and tambourines.

**Wind instruments** These are tubes made of wood, metal, or some other material. They make sounds when the player blows into or across a mouthpiece. In some instruments, the player changes the notes by opening or closing holes with his or her fingers. Wind instruments include recorders, flutes, clarinets, oboes, horns and trumpets.

**Stringed instruments** These make musical notes when their strings are rubbed, plucked or struck. The player plucks with his or her fingers or with a *plectrum* (a piece of plastic or tortoiseshell). Stringed instruments include violins, cellos, harps, guitars and sitars.

**Keyboard instruments** These have rows of *keys*, which the player strikes. There is one key for each note. The player can play several notes at a time. The best-known keyboard instruments are pianos (or pianofortes), organs, and accordions.

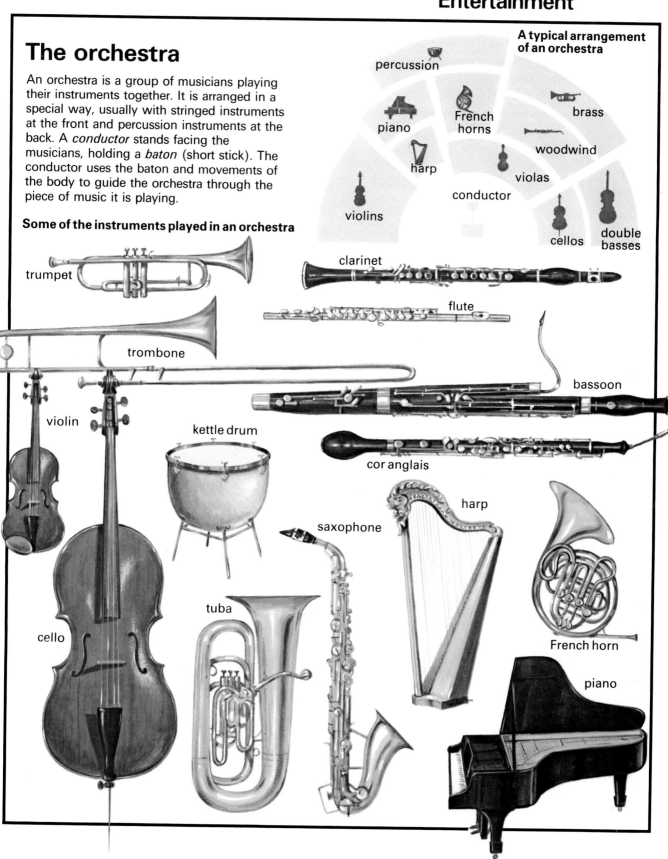

# The orchestra

An orchestra is a group of musicians playing their instruments together. It is arranged in a special way, usually with stringed instruments at the front and percussion instruments at the back. A *conductor* stands facing the musicians, holding a *baton* (short stick). The conductor uses the baton and movements of the body to guide the orchestra through the piece of music it is playing.

**A typical arrangement of an orchestra**

percussion

piano

French horns

brass

harp

woodwind

violins

violas

conductor

cellos

double basses

**Some of the instruments played in an orchestra**

trumpet

clarinet

flute

trombone

bassoon

violin

kettle drum

cor anglais

cello

saxophone

harp

tuba

French horn

piano

227

# Development of Music

The people who lived thousands of years ago sang songs and played music just as people do today. We are not sure what their music was like, because they had no way of writing it down. But we know what kinds of instruments they played. A few ancient instruments still exist, and we have pictures of many others.

## Religious to orchestral music

Until the 1300s and 1400s, most music in Europe was sung or played in churches as part of religious services. Other types of music included the folksongs of people in villages, and the songs of the minstrels who travelled from castle to castle.

**Musicians of the Middle Ages**

shawm
lute

**Counterpoint** Much early music was in counterpoint. Several melodies (tunes) were sung or played together, weaving in and out of one another. Two of the last and greatest composers of counterpoint music were Johann Sebastian Bach and George Frederick Handel, who worked in the early 1700s.

**Four famous composers**

Igor Stravinsky
Ludwig van Beethoven
Wolfgang Amadeus Mozart
Richard Wagner

**Orchestra and instrument** Many later composers abandoned counterpoint and wrote music that had strong, clear melodies. They intended their music to be played by an orchestra. Among the great composers of the late 1700s were Joseph Haydn and Wolfgang Amadeus Mozart, whose music is often gay and sparkling. The music of Ludwig van Beethoven is more serious and full of feeling. In the late 1800s Piotr Tchaikovsky wrote melodious and deeply expressive music.

Some other composers wrote mainly for just one instrument. In the 1800s, Frédéric Chopin composed some of the world's best-loved pieces of piano music.

## Opera

An important advance in music took place at the end of the 1500s with the beginning of opera. An opera is a play in which the words are sung. The music is the most important part of the play.

The first great composer of opera was Claudio Monteverdi, who lived in the 1600s. Many of the most popular operas were written later, in the 1800s. They include works by Giuseppe Verdi, Gioacchino Rossini, and Georges Bizet. Richard Wagner wrote long musical dramas based on German legends.

# Modern music

**Classical** In the late 1800s, some composers began to experiment with new ways of treating rhythm and melody. One of these composers was Claude Debussy, who took some of his ideas from Asian music.

Debussy wrote music that is dreamy and that shows much feeling. He influenced many other composers, including Igor Stravinsky, Bela Bartok, and Dmitri Shostakovich.

**Pop** Today, most people, particularly young people, listen to pop music. It uses tunes and rhythms from many different kinds of music. Pop music is often very loud, with a strong beat. It is written to be enjoyed for a short time, and then forgotten when something new takes its place.

*Culture Club, a modern pop group.*

**Jazz** This began in the United States of America when the Negro slaves were freed in 1865. They used whatever instruments they could find, and their music, jazz, became popular throughout the country. By the early 1900s, it was known all over the world.

Much jazz is made up as the musician goes along. This is called *improvisation*. The musician begins with a simple tune, and then explores all the different ways of playing it.

# Asian music

Asian music uses sounds and rhythms that are different from those in the music of Western countries. Asian musical instruments are different, too. Indian music is based on song, and flows and changes like the human voice. The music of China has been influenced by the music of several other countries, including India and Persia, now called Iran.

# Dancing

Dancing is closely connected with music. People dance for the same reason that they make music – to express their feelings. Most people dance simply for the fun of it. Others are *professional* dancers. They dance to entertain audiences in theatres and similar places. In some countries, dancing can have a religious meaning.

## Dancing for fun

Nearly everybody has danced at some time or other just because they felt like dancing.

**Folk dancing** Folk dances are dances that have been handed down from person to person for hundreds of years. Each country has its own folk dances.

Some dances are very simple. People may just link arms and move in time to music. Many dances in Greece are like this. Other folk dances are more difficult. The dancers change partners, and weave in and out between other dancers. This happens in Scottish dancing and many American square dances.

*Below: People dancing at a discotheque.*

Greek dancing

Scottish dancing

American folk dancing

English morris dancing

modern ballroom dancing

**Ballroom dancing** This developed from folk dancing. Usually, a man and a woman dance together. The *waltz* is a graceful ballroom dance that first became famous in Vienna, in Austria, in the 1700s. It is still danced today. The *quickstep* is a fast and lively dance. Several popular ballroom dances are based on folk dances from South America and Central America. They include the *rumba* and the *tango*.

**Disco dancing** Many young people like dancing to recorded pop music at a *discotheque*. Coloured, flashing lights are often used to give a feeling of excitement. The dancing is lively and full of energy. It is easy to learn.

ballet dancing

some ballet positions and steps

# Ballet

In many countries, people go to theatres to watch ballets being danced. Most ballets tell a story in music and dance. Others just create a *mood* or feeling, such as joy or sadness, in which the audience can share.

Ballets have no words. The music and the movements of the dancers tell what is happening. Without saying anything, the dancers have to make the audience understand what they are doing and feeling.

One of the most important people in ballet is the *choreographer*. The choreographer plans the ballet, and works out all the steps and movements of the dancers.

The people who design the *scenery* and *costumes* are also important. The scenery carries the audience into the make-believe world of the ballet. It is used to make the stage look like the place where the dancers are supposed to be. This might be a forest or perhaps a palace. The shape and colour of the costumes that the dancers wear tell the audience what sort of person each dancer is supposed to be.

# Religious dancing

Religious dances are common in Asia and Africa. Some are danced by one person. Others are danced by a group, or even by all the people of a village.

India has some of the most beautiful religious dances. They tell stories of Hindu gods and heroes. The dances are very difficult. Dancers spend their lives studying and performing them.

In Africa, dancing is an important part of village life. Villagers dance to ask their gods to help them; to give them good crops, rain, or other things.

231

# Painting and Sculpture

The earliest paintings that we know about were made 20 000 or more years ago by Stone Age people who lived in caves in France, Spain, and Africa. These early artists painted scenes of animals and people on the walls of their caves. The paintings can still be seen today.

As Man became civilized, painting and sculpture became great arts, together with music and literature. The painter or sculptor now tries to show not just what he sees but also what he feels.

## Painting

Early paintings, including paintings from great civilizations such as those of ancient Egypt and early Greece, have a flat look. Artists did not know how to use *perspective*, how to make things look real and as though they could be walked round. In time, artists became very skilled in using perspective, and in showing the effects of light and shade.

**The painter at work** The painter's materials are fairly simple: paint, brushes, and a surface to paint on.

*Paint* is made of a colouring material called a *pigment*. Usually, the pigment is a powder. It is mixed with a liquid so that it can be spread over a surface. The liquid may be water, oil, *tempera*, or some other material. Tempera is made of the whites and yolks of eggs. Usually, the painter mixes the paints on a *palette* which is a thin board. The painter can hold it easily while working.

*Brushes* may be made of stiff or soft hairs, and may be flat or pointed. A painter may use several different kinds of brushes while working on a painting.

*The surface* may be paper (with water paints) or canvas stretched on a wooden frame (with oil paints). *Fresco* paintings are made on a plaster wall. Some paintings are made on wood.

*Stone Age men painting on the wall of their cave.*

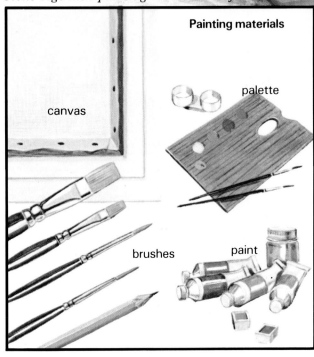
**Painting materials**
canvas
palette
brushes
paint

**Types of paintings** Most painters paint things that they can see. But painters also work from imagination. *Landscapes* are paintings of scenes, usually country scenes. *Portraits* are paintings of people. *Still lifes* show groups of objects arranged in a way that pleases the painter because of the shapes and the colours. The objects may be, for example, fruit in a bowl, or a collection of bottles. Other subjects for paintings include animals, people at work or play, religious scenes, and scenes from history.

**Carving** The sculptor takes a piece of stone, wood, or other material, and makes a figure by cutting or chipping away a little piece at a time.

**Modelling** A figure is shaped from wet clay, wax, or some other material. The figure is then left to dry and harden.

**Modelling and casting** The sculptor makes a mould around the clay or wax figure. The mould is filled with hot metal. When the metal cools, it is an exact copy of the clay figure.

# Sculpture

Sculpture is the art of making figures from clay, stone, wood, metal, or other materials. Usually, the figures are of people or animals. Sculpture is one of the oldest arts.

A sculptor can make a figure in three ways: by carving, modelling, or modelling and casting.

*Below:* Recumbant Figure, *a sculpture by Henry Moore in the Tate Gallery, London.*

## Casting a figure

The sculptor first makes a clay or wax figure. Then, small pieces of tin called *shims* are pushed into the figure (**1**) to make the mould easy to remove. The figure is covered with plaster. This is made by mixing a powder called *plaster of Paris* with water. The plaster hardens around the figure (**2**). Then the sculptor removes it and a hollow mould, in two parts, is left (**3**). The sculptor then pours hot metal into the mould, carefully held together (**4**). When the metal has cooled and hardened, the mould is taken away, leaving a metal figure (**5**).

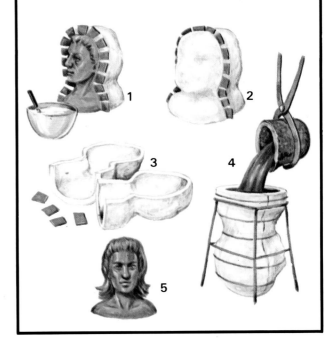

# Development of Painting

The Raising of Lazarus, *a fresco painted by Giotto in the Arena Chapel in Padua, Italy.*

By studying a painting, we can usually tell when it was painted, because artists at different periods of history have used different styles. For example, in the 1200s, most painters in Europe made simple, colourful paintings of scenes from the Bible. These paintings are beautiful, but do not look like real life. In the period called the *Renaissance*, from the 1400s onwards, painters tried to make their pictures more lifelike. Later, in the 1800s and 1900s, the Impressionists and other artists considered lifelike paintings too stiff. They tried to paint what they felt rather than what they saw.

## Painting in the Middle Ages

Many pictures that were painted in Europe 600 or 700 years ago still look as bright and fresh as the day they were made. Artists of this period, the Middle Ages, used rich, jewel-like colours – bright blues, reds, greens, and gold. They nearly always painted scenes from the Bible. Because they did not know about perspective, the people and places in their pictures often look flat and unreal. One of the greatest painters of this period was Giotto, who lived in Florence, in Italy.

## The Renaissance and later

The Renaissance was one of the most exciting periods in the history of painting. Artists began to paint the people and things they saw around them, as well as painting scenes from legends. Their pictures were much more lifelike than those of earlier painters because they understood perspective. They studied the way the human body is made. They also studied the effects of light and shade, and ways of making new colours.

The greatest painters of the Renaissance include Leonardo da Vinci and Michelangelo in Italy. Both were also famous as sculptors and architects.

In the 1700s, the English artist William Hogarth shocked people by the way he painted unpleasant things in the life he saw around him. At about the same time, Sir Joshua Reynolds and Thomas Gainsborough became known for their beautiful portraits. In France, the paintings of Antoine Watteau and Jean Honoré Fragonard showed what life was like for the rich before the French Revolution.

The Fall of Man and the Expulsion from Eden *by Michelangelo, a detail of the Sistine Chapel ceiling in the Vatican, Rome, Italy.*

*Above:* Still Life with Soup Tureen *by Cézanne in the Louvre, Paris, France.*
*Right:* Woman with a Fan *by Picasso in the Hermitage, Leningrad, USSR.*

# Modern painting

Towards the end of the 1800s, many artists began experimenting with new ways of painting. They thought that painters had been following too many rules.

**The Impressionists** These were a group of French artists who put their paintings on show in Paris in 1874. They were specially interested in the use of light and colour. Famous Impressionist painters include Paul Cézanne, Claude Monet, Edouard Manet, and Edgar Degas.

**The Cubists** These developed a style of painting that showed a subject from several points of view at the same time. They were trying to create sculpture on a flat piece of paper. Pablo Picasso was one of the first Cubists. He became famous in the early 1900s. Georges Braque worked with him for a while.

**The Surrealists** These explored and painted the world of dreams and imagination. They developed their style during the 1920s. Many of their paintings are rather frightening to look at. A leading Surrealist painter was Salvador Dali from Spain.

**Abstract artists** These used one of the most unusual of all the modern styles. They tried to show how they really felt about whatever they were looking at by abstracting (taking out) and painting only the parts they found most interesting. As a result, it is not always easy to tell what an abstract painting is about.

# Crafts

Most of the things that we use every day are made in factories by workers operating machines. Before machines were invented, everything had to be made by hand. Towns and villages had their own local craftsmen, each of whom made a particular thing. The *shoemaker* made shoes, the *tinker* made pots and pans, the *weaver* made cloth, the *tailor* or *dressmaker* made clothes. There were many different craftsmen.

Today, some people still make things by hand, either to sell or just for fun. Such activities are called *handicrafts* or *crafts*.

## Types of handicrafts

Many different tools and materials are used in handicrafts. Most of the materials are easy to find in the ground or from plants and animals.

**Pottery** This is a popular handicraft. All pottery objects are made from *clay*. Clay is a sticky, wet type of earth. When it is *fired* (baked) in an oven it becomes hard. A special oven called a *kiln* is used.

The potter makes a pot by pinching or coiling the clay into shape with the fingers. Sometimes a piece of clay is placed on a flat, round disc called a *potter's wheel*. The wheel is spun round. As the wheel spins, the potter pulls the clay upwards into shape. The wheel helps to give the pot an even shape.

The potter often gives the pot a shiny coating called *glaze*. The glaze colours the pot, and makes it smooth and waterproof.

**Weaving** Cloth is made by using two sets of threads. One set, called the *warp*, runs up and down the length of the cloth. The other set, called the *weft*, goes across the cloth.

The weaver stretches the warp threads on to a frame called a *loom*. The weft thread is passed in and out between the warp threads. At the end of each row, the weft is pushed down with a *beater* to make the cloth firm.

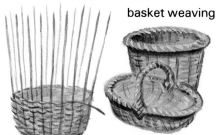

basket weaving

*Below: A potter shaping a pot on a wheel.*

**Villagers making things by hand**

*Above: Woven material on a loom.*

leatherwork

carving

knitting

**Some popular handicrafts done today**

**Basket weaving** Baskets are made in a similar way to cloth. Upright warp canes are set into a base. Weft canes are threaded in and out, row by row, until they reach the top.

**Carving** Few tools are needed for carving which is one of the oldest handicrafts. The tools are a hammer, a chisel, and a carving knife. The carver cuts shapes from such materials as wood, stone and marble.

Some carvings, such as totem poles, are huge. Other carvings are tiny. They may, for example, be detailed pieces of jewellery or ornaments.

**Other handicrafts** There are many more types of handicrafts. In *leatherwork*, bags, belts, and other objects are made from leather. Designs are punched into the leather with special tools. Beads are used in *beadwork* to make colourful belts and jewellery. In *macramé*, lengths of string are knotted into patterns. One of the commonest crafts is *knitting*. By using knitting needles, wool can be made into sweaters, scarves, or other garments.

237

# Literature

Literature is an art, just as music and painting are arts. It consists of the best things that people have written including the best stories, the best plays, and the best poems. Literature is important because it helps us learn about the world and people in it, from different places and times in history. Many authors use literature to tell people about their political beliefs or criticisms of society.

## Fiction

Fiction is any piece of writing that is purely imaginary. The *author* (writer) invents imaginary people and happenings. Sometimes, he or she uses real people and real events, but mixes them with imaginary people and imaginary events.

**Myths and legends** These are stories about gods and heroes, handed down from person to person for hundreds or even thousands of years. To begin with, storytellers learnt them by heart. Later, they were written down.

**Novels** Long stories telling of events in the lives of a number of *characters* (people) are called novels. Sometimes they may cover a few days or weeks of someone's life. Other times they may tell a story that spans someone's whole lifetime.

**Short stories** Shorter and simpler than novels, these have fewer characters. They often deal with just one event or one person.

**Plays or dramas** These are stories written to be performed by actors, usually in a theatre. The actors dress up as the characters, and speak and behave as the characters would in real life.

The two main types of plays are *comedies* and *tragedies*. A comedy is funny and usually has a happy ending. A tragedy is serious and usually has an unhappy ending.

**Poems** Some of the greatest works of literature are written as poems. *Poetry* is a special kind of writing. It forms patterns of sounds and thoughts. It is written to stir the reader's imagination.

Poems are written in lines of definite length. Many of them have *metre* and *rhyme*. Metre means that the words are arranged with a definite rhythm, almost like a piece of music. Rhyme means that certain sounds are repeated, usually at the ends of lines. Here is an example taken from a poem by Eugene Field.

> Wynken, Blynken, and Nod one *night*
> Sailed off in a wooden shoe, –
> Sailed on a river of crystal *light*
> Into a sea of dew.

## Non-fiction

There are many types of non-fiction. Non-fiction tells about real people, real happenings, or the ideas that people have.

*History* tells what life was like in the past. A *biography* is the story of a person's life. If it is written by the person himself it is called an *autobiography*. An *essay* is a short piece of writing on a particular topic. *Diaries* and *letters* are sometimes so interesting and well-written that they become literature.

## Children's literature

Some authors write stories and poems specially for children. In the past, many children's books were written to teach children how to behave and what to think. Often, they were rather dull and uninteresting. But today there are thousands of beautiful and amusing children's books. Some of the best-loved children's stories were not originally written for children at all. They include *Grimm's Fairy Tales* and *Robinson Crusoe* by Daniel Defoe. Now, there are classic stories for children in the same way as there are for adults.

# A selection of Children's 'Classics' and 'Modern Greats'.

*Alice's Adventures in Wonderland* and *Through the Looking Glass* Lewis Carroll
*Ballet Shoes* Noel Streatfeild
*Black Beauty* Anna Sewell
*Borrowers, The* Mary Norton
*Charlie and the Chocolate Factory* Roald Dahl
*Charlotte's Web* E B White
*Children of Green Knowe* Lucy M Boston
*Christmas Carol, A* Charles Dickens
*Dream Time, The* Henry Treece
*Earthsea Trilogy* Ursula Le Guin
*Eighteenth Emergency, The* Betsy Byars
*Ghost of Thomas Kempe, The* Penelope Lively
*Heidi* Joanna Spyri
*Hobbit, The* J R R Tolkien
*Hundred and One Dalmatians, The* Dodie Smith
*Iron Man, The* Ted Hughes
*John Diamond* Leon Garfield
*Jungle Book, The* Rudyard Kipling
*Just So Stories* Rudyard Kipling
*Just William* Richard Crompton
*Kidnapped* Robert Louis Stevenson
*Lion, the Witch and the Wardrobe, The* C S Lewis

*Little House on the Prairie* Laura Ingalls Wilder
*Little Prince, The* Antoine de Saint-Exupéry
*Moonfleet* J Meade Falkner
*Mrs Frisby and the Rats of NIMH* Robert C O'Brien
*'Paddington' Books* Michael Bond
*Peter Pan* J M Barrie
*Playing Beatie Bow* Ruth Park
*Princess and the Goblin, The* George MacDonald
*Railway Children, The* E Nesbit
*'Ramona' Books* Beverly Cleary
*Secret Garden, The* Frances Hodgson Burnett
*Stig of the Dump* Clive King
*Story of Doctor Dolittle, The* Hugh Lofting
*Swallows and Amazons* Arthur Ransome
*Tom's Midnight Garden* Philippa Pearce
*Treasure Island* Robert Louis Stevenson
*Turbulent Term of Tyke Tyler, The* Gene Kemp
*Water Babies, The* Charles Kingsley
*Watership Down* Richard Adams
*What Katy Did* Susan Coolidge
*Wind in the Willows, The* Kenneth Grahame
*'Winnie the Pooh' Books* A A Milne
*Wizard of Oz, The* L Frank Baum

*Below: An illustration by Kate Greenaway of* The Pied Piper of Hamelin, *a poem originally written by Robert Browning.*

*Below: An illustration by Heath Robinson for* A Christmas Carol *by Charles Dickens.*

# The Theatre

The theatre is a world of make-believe. People go to the theatre to watch actors and actresses performing *plays* as though they were real life. Sometimes, everything seems so real that we almost forget that it is just a story.

Plays that make us feel sad are called *tragedies*. Those that are funny are called *comedies*. Some of the world's greatest writers have written both tragedies and comedies for the theatre. One of the most famous of them was William Shakespeare, who died in 1616.

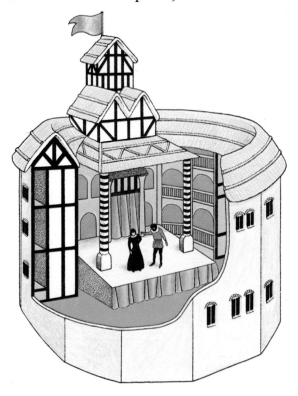

## Inside a theatre

A theatre has two main parts: the *auditorium*, where the audience sits, and the *stage*, where the actors perform.

**The stage** This is usually a raised platform in front of the audience. It is framed by the *proscenium arch*. In some very modern theatres, the stage is on the same level as the audience who sit in a circle round it. This is called *theatre-in-the-round*.

**Stage lighting** During the play, the stage is lit by powerful lights and the auditorium is left in darkness. Many kinds of lights are used. Often, a single light called a *spotlight* follows an actor as he moves around. Exciting light effects are made by using coloured lights.

*Above: A scene from a Noh play, a form of Japanese theatre.*
*Left: The Globe Theatre, London, where Shakespeare acted.*

**Scenery** This is used to make the stage look lifelike. Different scenery may be needed for each *scene* (part) of a play. One scene, for example, may take part in a room, the next may be in a forest. The stage must be made to look like a room for the first scene, and like a forest for the next.

Sometimes some canvas called a *backcloth* hangs at the back of the stage. It is painted to look like the wall of a room, a clearing in a forest, or whatever else is needed. A different backcloth may be required for each scene.

To make the stage like a real room, painted *flats* would be positioned at the sides as though they were the room's other walls. Tables and chairs would be arranged on the stage, as though they were in a real room.

# People in the theatre

Many people are involved in preparing a play. Most of them are not actors, but they all play an important part.

**The director** This person has the biggest job. First, he or she chooses the actors for the play. The director is in charge of all the *rehearsals* (practice sessions). The director works closely with all the other people involved in the play.

**The stage designer** He or she is responsible for all the scenery and backdrops. A model of the stage is usually made first, so that the final effect can be seen.

**The costume designer** The person who has this job decides what *costumes* (clothes) the actors will wear, and designs them. Sometimes, an actor may have to change several times during a performance. The designer first makes rough sketches of ideas to show to the director.

**The lighting technician** Operation of the stage lights is done from a switchboard. The lighting technician makes sure that the right parts of the stage are lit. The stage designer gives instructions.

# Films and Television

In many countries films are called moving pictures or movies. They really are moving pictures of plays and of real-life happenings, such as sports events, concerts, animal life, battles, and almost anything else you can think of. All these things can be photographed on film, and people can look at them over and over again.

Some films are made specially to be shown in *cinemas*. A cinema is just like a theatre, except that the audience watches a film instead of actors on a stage. The film appears on a huge screen at the front of the cinema.

Films and television are closely connected, because everything we see on a television screen is really a film. It has been photographed by a camera and then *transmitted* (sent) by radio waves to television receivers in our homes. (See also page 222.)

## Films

Films are one of the most popular forms of entertainment. People go to the cinema to watch films, just as they go to the theatre to watch plays on a stage.

**Film makers** The people who make films have hundreds of different jobs. The important jobs are very like those in the theatre.

*The producer* is in charge of making the film. This person chooses all the other people involved in making the film. He or she also decides where the film is going to be made, and when work is to begin. *Writers* work out the *screenplay* (story). They prepare *scripts*, which contain the actors' words and also give general directions for each scene of the screenplay.

*The director* is in charge of the performance of the play, telling the actors how each scene should be performed, and telling the *camera crews* how it should be *shot* (photographed). The *actors and actresses* who take part in screenplays often perform on the stage in theatres, too. Some of them become world-famous. The most famous actors and actresses are called *stars*.

How a film is shown at the cinema

screen

projector

feed spool

rotary shutter lets light through to the film

lens

film, consisting of many separate pictures, moves very quickly from one spool to the other

take-up spool

film guide

light shines through the film, projecting separate pictures on to the screen very quickly so that they appear as one moving picture

An animated cartoon is a series of drawings, each slightly different from the last. When they are projected, the figures seem to move. In the early days, each drawing was done by hand, but now a system is used where only small parts of one background picture are made 'mobile'.

## Making a film

**Making a film** Some parts of a film are shot *on location*. That is, they are photographed in a real-life setting. For example, if part of the story is supposed to take place on a Pacific island, the film makers may go to a Pacific island to photograph it. Many scenes however, will be shot in a *studio*.

The studio contains *sets* which are make-believe rooms, streets, castles, or whatever else the film needs. The sets are made of wood, plaster, cardboard, and other materials, painted to look like real life. When they are produced and photographed well, they look, in the film, as though they are real.

# Television

Filming a television show is very like making a film for the cinema, but the actors and actresses have less space in which to move. A greater number of special effects may be needed.

While a show is taking place, several cameras are photographing it. The director can see the picture from each camera. He or she decides which picture should be sent out to the viewers and switches from camera to camera. Time is important because a programme must run for an exact length of time. Someone times each part of the programme for the director with a stopwatch.

## Special effects

Many clever pieces of photography are used in most films. A scene in a film that shows a traveller facing a pack of wolves may have been partly photographed in the studio. A film of wolves is shown on a transparent screen behind the actor who takes the part of the traveller. In another scene, a man may be shown hanging by his hands from a bridge, high above a river. In fact, the actor is only a metre above the studio floor.

# Games

There is no end to the games that people play. Adults and children play games. Some of them are very simple, some are quite difficult. Some are outdoor games, some are quiet games that are played indoors. Many games are played at parties, and are always great fun.

Children today play the same sort of games as children played hundreds of years ago. Children in ancient Rome, 2000 years ago, played catching games and hop-skip-and-jump games that are still popular. And the same types of games are played in countries all round the world.

## Simple games

Some games are very simple. Often, the players have just one thing to do, but they cause a lot of laughs.

**Follow my leader** One player is chosen as leader, and the others line up behind her. They have to follow the leader wherever she goes, and must do everything that she does.

*A game of follow my leader.*

**Leap-frog** One player 'makes a back' by bending over with his hands on his knees. Another player touches his back with her hands while jumping over him. Then she bends down and 'makes a back' in front of him. The third player jumps over each of them in turn, and so on to the last player, who has to jump over all the others.

## Chasing games

Chasing games are also simple, but they can be exciting. They often require a lot of energy.

**Tag** or **Touch** or **It** One player is made 'it' and runs around trying to touch one of the other players. The other players have to dodge him. A player who is touched then becomes 'it'. In some games, the new 'it' has to keep her hand on the spot where she was touched until she can touch another player. Much of the fun lies in trying to touch a player on his or her ankle or back or some other awkward spot.

*Above: Children playing together.*

**Cat and mouse** One player is picked as cat and another as mouse. The rest of the players join hands and form a ring. The cat stands outside the ring and has to catch the mouse, who is inside. Both cat and mouse can run in and out of the circle, under the other players' arms. The other players can help the cat or the mouse by raising or lowering their arms.

# Party games

Party games are best when there are a lot of players. Some go on for a long time.

**Blind man's buff** This is one of the oldest party games. One player is 'it' and is blindfolded with a scarf or handkerchief. The others stand in various parts of the room, and remain very still. The blindfolded player tries to find one of them. When he succeeds, he has to guess whom he has caught. If he is right, that player becomes 'it'.

*A game of blind man's buff.*

**Sardines** This game is played in the dark, all over the house. One of the players hides, and the others have to look for her. Any player who finds her, joins her in her hiding place, until, at last, they are all packed in like sardines.

**Hot and cold** One of the players leaves the room, and the others hide an object somewhere. When he comes back, he has to find it. As he searches, the others tell him he is 'hot' (when he gets near it), or 'warm', or 'cool', or 'cold' (when he is far away from it).

# Sport

Sports require physical fitness as well as skill, enthusiasm, and a quick mind. Some of them also require teamwork, the ability to work with other people. Sometimes people taking part in sports show bad temper when they lose, but nobody likes a player who is a bad loser. Everybody admires a person who shows *sportsmanship*. That is, a player who can win without boasting, and who can lose without being angry or miserable.

Not everybody has a chance to take part in sport. But millions of people enjoy watching others playing football or tennis, swimming, or running. They crowd into sports grounds, stadiums and clubs to watch their favourite players taking part in matches and events of various kinds, and to hope that they are going to win. Sports programmes are among the most popular broadcasts on television and radio.

*Above: An athlete competing in a triple-jump competition.*
*Left: Cyclists in a road race.*

## Types of sports

**Individual sports** In these sports a player takes part as an individual, not as a member of a team and not playing against an opponent. They include many forms of *athletics*, such as running, walking, hurdling, jumping, and weight-lifting. In *gymnastics*, competitors perform exercises and show their skill on special apparatus. Competitors in the *pentathlon* have to show their skill in five different sports. *Cycling* is also popular. There are road races and races in a stadium.

**Team sports** In these sports one team plays another team. The world's most popular team game is *soccer* (association football) which is an 11-a-side game. Other forms of football include: *American football, Canadian football, Australian rules, Gaelic football, rugby union,* and *rugby league.*

*Baseball* is played mainly in the United States of America, where it is the summer sport. *Cricket* is played mainly in countries of the Commonwealth. *Lacrosse* and *hockey* are also popular team games. *Ice hockey* is one of the fastest sports.

**Combat sports** These date back to the Olympics in ancient Greece, where some events involved *unarmed combat. Wrestling* and *boxing* are probably the most popular combat sports today. *Judo, karate,* and *kung-fu* developed in Asia. They have become increasingly popular in the West.

Some combat sports allow the use of weapons. They include *fencing* and *kendo.*

**Equestrian sports** Sports for horses and riders include *show-jumping.* Riders have to take their horses over a series of specially-prepared fences and jumps. In *eventing,* show-jumping is combined with a long cross-country course. Eventing also includes *dressage,* in which riders and horses have to show their skill and control in performing difficult movements. *Polo,* a team game played on horseback, is fast and skilful.

Horses are also ridden in races. There are *flat races, steeplechases* (over fences) and also races over *hurdles.*

**Water sports** These include *sailing, rowing, powerboat racing, water skiing,* and *wind surfing.* They also include *swimming* and *diving.* A team game, *water polo,* is played 7-a-side.

*Above: A cricket match.*
*Above right: A rider in a show-jumping competition.*
*Right: Wind surfing, a popular water sport.*

# Amateurs and professionals

Most people that play in sports are *amateurs*. That is, they take part just for enjoyment. They do not receive any payment, but they may win prizes such as medals and trophies.

Some sports are played by *professionals* for money. Professional teams are really run as businesses. They include teams in many of the more popular sports, such as football, baseball, and ice hockey. Large sums of money change hands when a player transfers from one team to another.

*Right: Three athletes with medals at the Olympic Games, an international competition for amateurs. Below: Professional footballers.*

# Index

# Index